THE SECOND
GREAT DEPRESSION

Booklocker.com, Inc.
2005

THE SECOND GREAT DEPRESSION

Warren Brussee

DEDICATION

Two people spent much time reading and giving feedback on this book. Christopher Welker and Jeffery Kolt not only gave constructive input, but they also gave me the encouragement any author needs to complete a book.

My wife Lois, my greatest supporter, found the book frightening, even though she was aware of the subject matter beforehand. After she read it, I had to convince her that we were financially prepared for the depression that this book had just convinced her was coming.

DISCLAIMER

CONTENTS

ABOUT THE AUTHOR

Warren Brussee spent 33 years at GE as an engineer, plant manager, and engineering manager. His responsibilities included manufacturing plants in the USA, Hungary, and China. Mr. Brussee has multiple patents related to both products and processes.

Warren Brussee earned his engineering degree at Cleveland State University and attended Kent State towards his EMBA.

The author's earlier books, *Statistics for SIX SIGMA Made Easy* and *All About Six Sigma,* were written to make Six Sigma user-friendly, such that a more diverse group of people could use this powerful data-based methodology. This book, *The Second Great Depression*, is geared for intelligent people who also want to use data, but in this case to help them navigate their own financial future.

AUTHOR'S NOTES

In the late nineties, two other people and I developed a real-time computerized stock investment program to identify insider trading that had caused a stock's price to go up. The program used statistical tests to identify signs that employees had seen a new product, or other positive development, that they felt would positively affect their company, triggering the purchase of an unusual amount of stock.

This computer program was successful in the positive nineties' stock market. Over a period of two years, several millions of dollars were successfully invested. However, the market changed in 2000, and the algorithms were no longer finding investment opportunities. The good thing was that the computer program took us out of the market. However, we wanted to invest in *all* markets, so I began to look for algorithms that worked in this "new market". It was when reviewing the current market that I became aware of some dire problems in the economy. Those insights triggered the eventual writing of this book.

I had written two earlier books, *Statistics for Six Sigma Made Easy* and *All about Six Sigma*, published by McGraw-Hill, so I felt comfortable in my ability to select and analyze data. The essence of Six Sigma is getting good data and letting this data drive decision making. The economy and the stock market have reams of data which were used for the tapestry of this book, and from which the premise of the coming depression emerged.

In this book I also tell a story. There are many supporting graphs and charts that show how we are currently on the edge of a depression, but the events leading up to the present, starting with the nineties, are just as important as the graphs. Just as someone can't understand the first Great Depression without understanding the years preceding it, current graphs on the economy make little sense without understanding the mindset of the people that caused the economy and the stock market to be where they are. This understanding also assists in making some determination on what is going to happen in the near future.

PART I

The Essence of Why We Will Have a Depression

CHAPTER 1: The Crazy Nineties
Craziness in the nineties' stock market prices is the precursor for the coming depression. People stopped saving and became irrationally exuberant on building debt.

CHAPTER 2: The Debt Bubble
The American economy has been fueled by consumers who reduced their savings and began spending more than what they could afford. This created debt and housing bubbles.

CHAPTER 3: So, why will the Good Times End?
The growth of stock buyers aged 30 through 54 has leveled off, and the number of households owning mutual funds has peaked. There is no longer a growing demand for stocks.

CHAPTER 4: What will the Coming Depression be Like?
Starting in 2007, the depression will affect many. Unemployment and inflation will be high, except houses will deflate in value. The market will drop 70%, and the economy will go to its knees.

CHAPTER 5: What Else may Trigger the Depression?
The wars in Iraq and Afghanistan, terrorists, energy prices, a drop in the dollar's value, the deficit, the balance of payments, inflation, and interest rates will all contribute to the depression; but debt is the likely depression trigger.

CHAPTER 6: Could this Book be Completely Wrong?
Looking at the supporting data on debt and consumer spending, it is difficult to believe that the premise put forward in this book is completely wrong.

CHAPTER 7: Can't the Fed Stop the Coming Depression?
No! In fact, the Fed's past decisions have just delayed the inevitable, trading several short recessions in the past for the coming big depression.

CHAPTER 1
The Crazy Nineties

I had two neighbors in the late nineteen nineties, one a retired doctor and the other a retired small business owner, who were never seen in the daytime when the stock market was trading. But in the evenings, they would have smiles on their faces akin to those of teenage boys who, the evening before, had talked their girlfriends into the backseat of their cars. These neighbors had both become day traders, and each of them felt that they had discovered the secret to wealth. Neither of them ever shared with me their "methods" of playing the market, but their wives worried that they were buying stocks based on hunches, rumors, recent headlines, etc. Apparently no in-depth analysis of stocks was being done, nor did they make any effort to see if they were doing any better than the market in general. All they cared about was that, on an almost daily basis, their on-paper worth was increasing. They believed that they had discovered the secret to making a lot of money without working!

They weren't alone in their craziness. Something strange was happening to most of country during the nineties. Computer nerds, who were never thought to be giants in the practical world of business, were given almost unlimited funds to pursue their latest business ideas related to the net or other software ventures. These newly ordained entrepreneurs told everyone that their dot-com businesses did not have to make a profit; that the idea was to develop a customer base using information technology, and the profits would come later. They used esoteric measures, like "eyeballs," to determine how many people were visiting their websites, which they felt was a measure of their business success. Or they counted how many other worthless web sites were sending visitors to *their* worthless site. They didn't even bother estimating when they would make a profit, nor was there any analysis of what those future profits would be. They said that the important criterion in these new-era businesses was generating customers; profits would just naturally come later. Some of their projections of customer base growth took them quickly to exceed the population of the world, but no matter. Venture capitalists and investors believed them. So did my neighbors. We *all* believed!

Not only were investors like my neighbors sucked in; grizzled CEOs of large companies, who should have known better, gazed at these dot-com companies in awe. These were the same executives that, just a few years before, were trying to look, act, and dress like the Japanese, who were the previous rock stars of industry. These techie-wannabe executives tried to do high-fives and make their companies look and perform like the dot-coms. These experienced executives took crash courses on using the net. Of course, this was only after one of their in-house techies bought them computers and taught them how to boot up. GE's CEO Jack Welch even bragged that investors looked at GE as being equivalent to a dot-com company. He made all GE executives take courses on surfing the net, and each individual business within GE had to set up their own web site where customers could peruse that business's management and product lines. Any project having interaction with the net got priority corporate funding. Jack Welch and many other corporate heads also did what was necessary to make their stock prices act like dot-com stocks. No matter that most of the perceived financial gains during this era came from accounting creativity that made bland corporate performance look stellar by pushing costs into future years and doing other financial wizardry.

Baby boomers, who were wondering if they were going to be able to keep up with the gains realized by their parents' generation, suddenly saw their salvation. Like my day-trader neighbors, the baby boomers would buy stocks in this new era stock market and watch their riches grow. As more and more of them bought stocks, the demand drove prices up to ridiculous levels. The feeding frenzy had begun. As a result of all this buying pressure, in the later years of the last century the stock market performed brilliantly.

It wasn't just naïve investors who got overconfident in their abilities related to the market. In 1994, Bill Krasker and John Meriwether, two winners of the Nobel Prize in Economics, started a company called Long Term Capital Management (LTCM). These two "geniuses" had done massive data analysis on the "spreads" between various financial instruments, like corporate bonds and Treasury bonds. When these spreads got wider than what was statistically expected (based on their computer program), LTCM would buy the financial instrument likely to gain from the correction that was expected to occur shortly.

Using this methodology, LTCM was unbelievably successful for four years. By leveraging their money, they had gained as much as 40% per year for their investors, and Bill Krasker and John Meriwether got very wealthy.

They were so successful that, by 1998, LTCM had $1 trillion in leveraged exposure in various financial market positions. Then, LTCM became victim of the "fat tail" phenomena, which is where a normally balanced distribution of data now has a lot of data far out to one end of the distribution tail. The reason this happened is that everyone who played in similar financial markets all decided to get out at once, and LTCM was seeing results that their computer models had predicted would *not statistically happen in more than a billion years*! Unbeknownst to them, because of the sudden exit of the others playing this financial game, the relationships of the "spreads" between various financial instruments had changed, which made the earlier computer-generated probability predictions invalid.

The risks that LTCM had taken were so dangerous that LTCM was close to upsetting the whole world's financial institutions. Fed Chairman Alan Greenspan and several of the world's major banks got together to offer additional credit to LTCM to successfully avert this potential global financial disaster.

The two "geniuses" still lost over $4 billion, and the relaxed credit that was established by the banks to save LTCM later enabled companies like Enron to do their thing. This story is indicative of the overconfidence shown throughout the nineties. If LTCM had not been leveraged to such an extreme level, they probably would have survived this event. But they had gotten overconfident and greedy. Everyone in the nineties thought they could get something for nothing by playing financial games, which in this case included being leveraged to the hilt.

Anyone who was able to capitalize on the market gains of the nineties was fortunate indeed. In fact, if you bought the S&P 500 stocks in 1994 and sold them in 1999, your investment tripled in value. Figure 1-1 is a graph of the real gains (discounting the effect of inflation) of the S&P 500 stocks since 1900 showing how unusual and dramatic those 1994-1999 gains were, as evidenced by the huge upward spike on the right-hand-side of the graph.

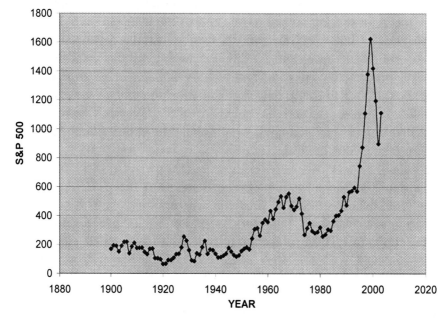

Real (without inflation) S&P500 Value History (2003 $)

Figure 1-1

However, buying stocks in 1994 and selling in 1999 is not the normal way people invest, nor were many people fortunate enough to time the market that well. The general way of saving is to invest on a consistent basis and then hold the stocks. This is also the savings method advised by most market "experts." If someone saved a fixed amount every year, starting in 1994, the same beginning year as above, and was still investing this fixed amount through 2003, he or she would only be ahead 33% (including inflation). This assumes a 1.5% annual mutual fund management cost, which is typical of what most 401(k) pension savings programs charge. This 33% gain is almost identical to what someone would have gotten with a basically zero risk Treasury Inflation Protected Security (TIPS) paying 3%, which we will discuss in a later chapter. So even for those who started to invest in the dramatic market of the nineties, without some fortunate market timing, the gains realized by most investors were not all that phenomenal.

Others have come to similar conclusions on the stock market. John Bogle, founder of the very successful Vanguard Group, estimates that the average return for equity funds from 1984 through 2001, a time period which includes the great stock market bubble of the nineties, was just slightly more than inflation! Contributing to this disappointing performance were the fees charged by mutual funds and the "churning" of stocks – constant stock turnover, which not only adds trade costs, but also causes any gain to be taxed as regular income, rather than at the reduced tax rate of capital gains.

However, in most people's memories, the nineties were a time of great gains made in the stock market. They can't get out of their minds the 200% gain that could have been realized by buying in 1994 and selling in 1999.

Let's try to identify what made the stock market grow like it did at the end of the last century. When we look for the most likely cause, let's keep in mind Occam's razor, a logical principle attributed to the mediaeval philosopher William of Occam, which emphasizes that the simplest explanation is usually the best.

Between the years 1990 and 2000, due to the baby boomer surge, the number of people in the age group 30 through 54 increased almost 25%. These are the primary stock buying ages. Below the age of 30, people are involved with getting an education or starting their careers. Once people become 55, some of them begin to move investments into more conservative areas, getting ready for retirement. Figure 1-2 is a chart showing this 25% increase in the age 30 through 54 potential stock purchasers.

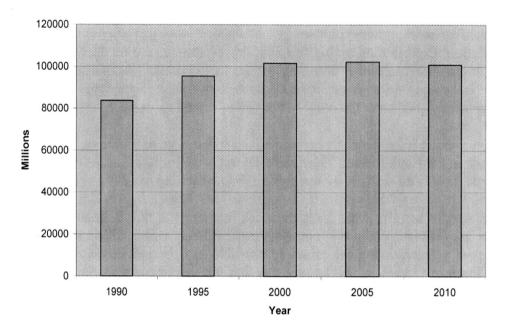

Figure 1-2

At the same time of this surge of potential stock buyers, there was an increase in awareness of and participation in the stock market. Stock ownership by families went from 23% to over 56% in the period of 1990 to 2001, largely due to the growing number of 401(k) pension plans whose regular savings from income were designated for mutual funds. This is shown below in Figure 1-3.

Percentage of Households Owning Mutual Funds

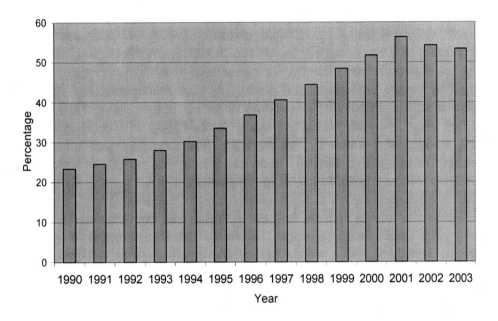

Figure 1-3

This increased stock market interest, coupled with the previously noted increase of people aged 30 to 54, meant that there were approximately three times as many potential stock buyers at the end of last century than at the beginning of 1990. This put an unusual pressure on the demand side of the traditional demand-versus-supply relationship. This is not a difficult concept, and its importance has been known for hundreds of years. There are other more esoteric explanations given for the nineties stock price rise, but this is the simplest and therefore most likely cause.

We must emphasize the importance of this increased demand. A relatively small percentage of stocks are in play on any given day. When one of these stocks becomes available for sale, if there are a large number of people interested in buying that stock, the stock will trade at a higher price than normal due to the demand. Simply put, that is what happened in the nineties. People weren't analyzing whether a stock was priced correctly or doing any in-depth analysis of a company's potential. There were just a lot of people who wanted to buy stocks at any price because they believed that the price would go even higher in the future.

This was not only true of individual investors, but it was also true of the professionals picking stocks for the mutual funds. Every week, the increasing number of automatic investment dollars generated by 401(k) savings plans was dumped on mutual fund managers' desks. The fund managers could delay the investment of this money for a few days or weeks if they thought the market would go lower. But they would eventually have to jump into the stock market, driving up demand. No mutual fund manager could keep large portions of their investment money out of the stock market for extended periods of time. After all, their customers wanted to invest in the market.

Media coverage of the market became intense, and many people began to actively trade stocks on the internet. The almost instant investment information on the web enabled many people to become day traders or self-proclaimed investment experts. The trade costs of playing the market dropped dramatically with the advent of discount brokers and on-line trading. The almost continuous rise of the market just fed the self aggrandizing of these investors.

Many people began to extrapolate their paper gains for the next 20 years and could see themselves as millionaires with little more effort than the few minutes it took at a computer keyboard to enter their current stock picks. This was how they were going to get their proverbial pot of gold. There was no point in trying to save outside of the stock market. Even if the market took a temporary drop, the stock market gurus assured them that it would always come back and go even higher.

At no point did these people stop to wonder if the stocks they were buying were over-priced, or whether the companies really had growth potential. Nor did they ever stop to think that there was not enough money in the world for every investor to become truly wealthy. They couldn't conceive that, when they finally decided to sell their stock, there could be no one to buy the stock - that everybody would already be fully invested with no additional money to put into the market. Sure, if their timing was right, they could be one of the lucky early sellers and do very well. But the following sellers would do worse, and the next sellers even worse, until perceived stock gains miraculously turned into losses. The demand-versus-supply relationship would be turned on its head, with more stocks available than there would be buyers for those stocks.

In the nineties, there was no reason for investors to question the wisdom of what they were doing. The Motley Crew was on the radio on weekly broadcasts explaining how *they* were doing it. Investment groups were rampant, including a group of grandmothers who got national attention based on their claim of beating the market experts. People regularly monitored the on-going media competition between the dartboard stock picks and the market experts. Chat lines gave "inside information" on stocks. Anyone *not* playing the market was obviously naïve or stupid.

TV business news guests were explaining how the information age was enabling companies to realize efficiencies-through-knowledge with little capital investment, thereby justifying the unusually high stock prices. Instant information enabled companies to have minimum inventory and to adjust product mix quickly if consumer tastes changed. This was predicted to eliminate the normal up-and-down cycles in the economy. The market would just consistently go up!

Industrial processes could be fine-tuned using information system feedback, and methodologies like Six Sigma promised only three defects-per-million-parts-produced if data were used to drive decision making. There was no need to invest in new production equipment because the old-era equipment would run so much better with this new-era information knowledge.

There were books that touted the Dow at 36,000 or even 100,000. No matter that the rationale for the high Dow values was based on fantasy future earnings that would never come to be. Also, these books stated that there was no more risk in investing in the stock market than in other more traditionally conservative investments, such as bonds. All the stock investor had to do was wait out the downturns in the market – the market always came back and went to even higher levels. Of course, the books didn't mention that, when the effect of inflation was included, it may take well over twenty years before the investment recovered, and most people's investment window couldn't tolerate that. All the misleading information on the market's potential would have been humorous, if it weren't for the fact that many people were risking their lifetime savings on the unrealistic dream of getting rich with no effort!

Then, in 2000, the Motley Crew began to lose money. It was starting to become obvious that information technology in most cases just enabled more junk mail and junk information. People already had more information than they could handle *before* the information era started. The additional information just caused people to spend more time sorting.

Someone discovered the accounting error in the Grandmas' claimed gains in the market. The Grandmas forgot that they were regularly infusing additional funds into their investment club, which was not factored in when they calculated their supposed gains. Efficiency gains touted in government statistics on productivity were found to be largely due to changes in the government's accounting system baseline; like counting productivity gains based on the increased speeds of computer processing, rather than any real gains truly affecting productivity. The hyped image of the new era market strength was beginning to get blurry.

We started to see our neighbors out walking during the day, no longer day trading in the stock market. They grumbled that the market was *no longer acting rationally*! Again, they did not choose to share their results with me, but their wives indicated that all their paper gains had been lost, along with a bundle more. The market fooled many people in the nineties because it seemed so logical, and it just kept going up; investors began to feel invincible in their stock-purchase decision making.

This nineties stock market price bubble is obvious in retrospect when we look back at the Gross Domestic Product (GDP) for this period and see that it was literally unaffected by all the fuss. The Gross Domestic Product is the total market value of all final goods and services produced in the United States in a given year, equal to total consumer, investment and government spending, plus the value of exports, minus the value of imports. If companies had really gotten superb performance during the late nineties, it would have been evidenced in some measurable effect in the GDP and would certainly have been seen by now. After all, at some point the value of these new era companies should have increased the output of the country in a very measurable manner. Instead, the GDP just marched on pretty much as it had in the past. Figure 1-4 is a graph in logarithmic scale showing this lack of a GDP spike. The graph is shown in logarithmic format because a constant improvement will show itself as a straight line when plotted logarithmically. (For anyone wanting an explanation on how a logarithmic chart makes a constant improvement appear as a straight line, see the end of the Appendix. But it is not necessary to understand this to be able to read this chart or understand the information.)

Real GDP (1996 dollars)

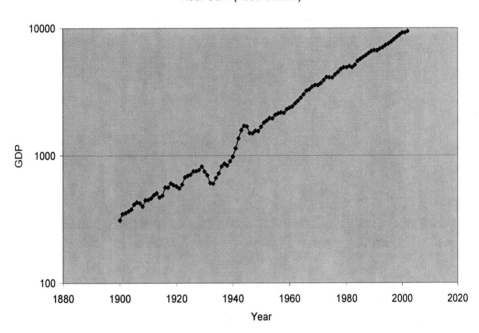

Figure 1-4

Figure 1-4 shows that in the nineties there was no sudden change in the on-going quantitative gain in the GDP. The line showing the GDP just continued upward at the same rate it had been the forty five years before the nineties. The new-era information driven society had absolutely no effect on the GDP.

Besides being invisible to the GDP, the stock dividends did not justify the high prices of stocks. Figure 1-5 is a chart showing that in the nineties the stock price versus dividend *ratio* just took off and still remains high at the end of 2003, compared to price/dividend ratios before the nineties. The increase in the price/dividend ratio means that people are paying far more for the same amount of dividend that they were previously getting at a much lower stock price.

Year-end Price/Dividend Ratio

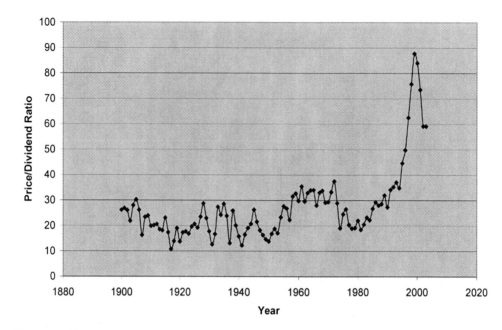

Figure 1-5

So dividends didn't seem to justify the high stock prices. Some investors felt that the high prices were justified because *future* dividends would jump dramatically as the expected gains realized by the new era technology took hold. Below is Figure 1-6, plotted logarithmically, that shows that dividends have grown consistently since the early 1960's, and there has been no spike related to the nineties' stock price increases.

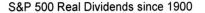

S&P 500 Real Dividends since 1900

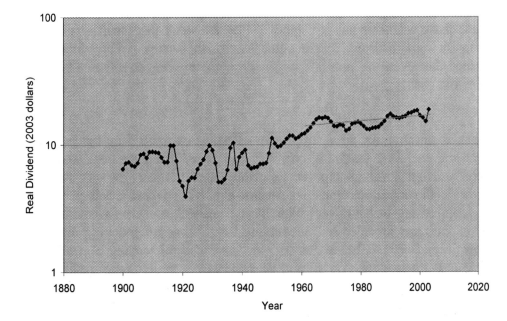

Figure 1-6

Note that the above graph includes nine years after the stock price spurt starting in 1994, and the dividends have shown no corresponding jump. The straight line superimposed over the last forty years is there to emphasize that the average dividend has been growing at a reasonably uniform rate during that period.

Dividends are the criteria we must use to measure long term company performance, because they are the profits that the owners actually get out of their investments. If you bought a pizza restaurant, you may choose to use initial earnings to expand or improve the restaurant, but at some point you will want to take some money out of the company for personal use, because that is the whole purpose of investing. Dividend payout can be delayed while growing a business; but if the earnings *never* generate dividends, then real earnings were either never there, were wasted on bad investments, or were used to enrich others' pocketbooks rather than the owners of the business. Just as with the pizza restaurant example, someone may choose to buy stock in a company that is temporarily investing in growing the business rather than paying dividends. But if this were to go on for too many years, prospective stock purchasers will begin to turn away because they will begin to doubt whether the company will *ever* pay dividends. Then the stock price will level off and eventually start to drop. The fact that Microsoft is now paying dividends is evidence that even the ultimate high tech company had to eventually turn to paying out cash.

Published earnings are so easily manipulated, as evidenced by the failures of Enron and the like, that it is now difficult to evaluate the real worth of a company using earnings reports, especially if a company is very large and diverse. In the nineties, companies became expert at making earnings appear to be whatever they wanted. Real spending on research and development (R&D) was reduced and replaced by "accounting R&D" that labeled any project with even minimal risk as being R&D. This gave the misleading appearance of continuing investment for future growth while getting the resultant tax benefits. Individual pieces of equipment, which were previously depreciated separately, were now "bundled" together, then amortized over a larger number of years. This reduced current expenses and made profits appear larger. No matter that this action would make it far more difficult to replace individual pieces of equipment in the future as new technology made them outmoded, because to replace one piece the whole bundled assembly had to justify recapitalization. Items that previously had been expensed were now classified as investments, making current earnings appear more robust by delaying current costs into the future while showing high investment numbers. Outsourcing generated instant gains, but sacrificed the manpower skills needed to grow future businesses. The list goes on. Note that all these changes were legal and separate from the more obvious shenanigans of the likes of Enron.

Since the price/earnings ratio is by far the most popular measure to determine if stocks are overpriced, I am including the below graph, Figure 1-7, for the edification for those who want to see it for a reference. In the graph, the vertical axis of earnings is proportioned to optimize the fit with the S&P 500 price or value. This chart shows that the earnings and price grew somewhat in concert until 1995, when the price just took off. As is true for the price/dividend ratio, this chart shows that the stock market is overpriced versus the historical relationship between price and earnings. However, this book will *not* be using this graph or earnings in any analysis, because of the aforementioned reasons that the earnings are too easily manipulated.

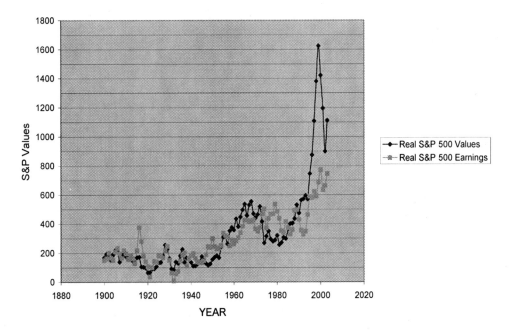

Figure 1-7

So we have seen by looking at the GDP and dividends that there was no real performance improvement that justified the dramatic rise in stock prices in the nineties. *The most logical reason for the rise in stock values in the nineties is that the price increase was due to the unusually high demand for stocks, driven by the increase of the buyer base overwhelming the supply of available stocks.* Sure, there were some new dot-com companies that were added to the milieu of stocks (of which many eventually rewarded their investors by going belly-up), but the pressure on almost all the stocks to be bid up due to the high demand was intense. This is what caused the stock market price jump in the nineties.

This craziness in stock market prices started a series of events which are the precursors for the coming depression. Along with the "irrational exuberance" of stock prices, people stopped saving because they thought that the stock market gains would guarantee their future. They also became irrationally exuberant on going into debt, with no concern on how they were going to pay it all back. After all, they were going to become rich through their stock market investments!

CHAPTER 2
The Debt Bubble

In this chapter, we will see that, while stocks were being bid-up in the nineties for no real reason other than demand, the continuing growth of the American economy was fueled by consumers who reduced their savings and began spending more than what they could afford. This created a debt bubble. People often used the extra money they got by reducing their rate of savings and by going into debt to buy SUV's that got terrible gas mileage, or to purchase large homes with little or no down payment. These purchases not only increased current debt, but also put in place higher energy and maintenance costs for future years. In just one generation, we had converted from an economy based on savings and hard work, to a debt-driven economy, where people spent whatever was needed to support what was perceived as a "deserved" life-style, whether they could afford it or not. *This chapter will show that, at some point, living beyond one's income will come to an unhappy end, and this will trigger the coming depression.*

During the nineties, perhaps in celebration of their perceived success in making loads of money in stocks, consumers went on a spending spree. In order to support this spending spree, consumers reduced their savings rate as a means of getting additional ready cash. Why bother saving additional money when their current investments, and their 401(k) contributions, were obviously going to make them wealthy. By 2004, the savings rate, as a percent of disposable income, was down to 1%, having dropped from 8% in 1990. Figure 2-1 illustrates this reduction in personal savings.

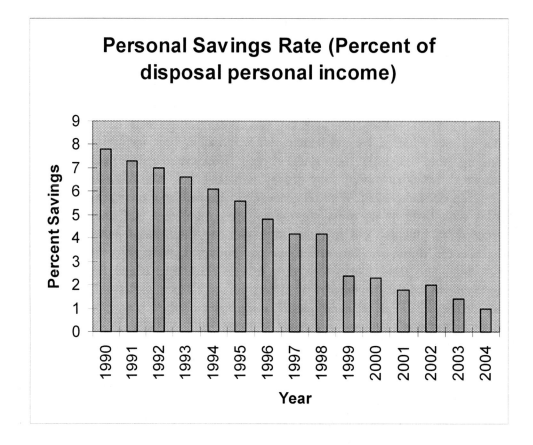

Figure 2-1

The Personal Savings Rate, as defined by the Bureau of Economic Analysis of the U.S. Department of Commerce, is what is *left over* from personal income after subtracting personal taxes, Social Security, Medicare, and personal outlays for food, housing, clothing, etc. Personal income, in this definition, includes wages, dividends, interest, and rental income. Note that the above graph does not include any capital gains or losses due to stock market evaluation.

This chart needs some further discussion because many people wonder how you can have savings rates approaching zero, when they know so many people who are still saving through their 401(k) plans where they work. The explanation is that Figure 2-1 is the *average* savings rate. So if five people are saving $5,000 per year through their 401(k) plans, but one person takes

$25,000 out of *their* savings to pay for their child's education, the average savings rate for those six people is zero. On the average, people are not getting ahead on their savings, which does not bode well for baby boomers. Given the large number of people approaching retirement age, the savings rate should be increasing, not decreasing. The reason that the reduction in savings rate did not reduce the demand for stocks is that the huge influx of the people buying stocks, due the prior mentioned increase of potential stock buyers, easily exceeded any effect of the reduced savings rates.

Besides the extra funds that were now available to consumers because they had reduced their savings rate, a debt bubble was growing because consumers were spending more than they earned. Figure 2-2 shows the growth of the average financial obligation ratio, which is the ratio of total debt obligation versus after-tax income. This debt obligation includes credit card debt, auto payments, and rent or house payments

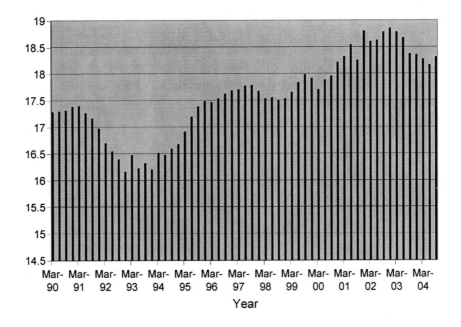

Quarterly Financial Obligations Ratio March 1990 through September 2004

Figure 2-2

This Financial Obligations ratio has been at record highs in recent years. The slight reduction in the financial obligation ratio in 2003, which has now reversed, was due to the lowering of interest rates by the Fed and reduced average yields on U.S. Treasury securities, which caused the interest rate on home mortgages to be dramatically reduced. This enabled people to refinance their homes and at the same time take out some of their equity to reduce their credit card debt. The total debt payments were therefore reduced, due to the greater proportion of debt involved in mortgage payments, which have a much lower interest rate than credit card interest. Also, there were lower interest rates on the credit cards themselves.

These temporary lower debt payments are now beginning to reverse, however, since people have *not* stopped spending, and interest rates are beginning to increase. The increased interest rates will increase credit card payments and affect adjustable rate mortgage loans, which have recently been popular with people refinancing homes or just entering the housing market.

Financial obligations are not the only things eating at the disposable income. Increased energy prices, affecting gasoline and heating costs, and rising medical costs are reducing the *available* disposable income.

Although current loan *payments* were lowered temporarily, as we saw in Figure 2-2, overall debt did not go down. Below, in Figure 2-3, you can see that consumer debt continues to rise unabated. People have not stopped spending more than they earn.

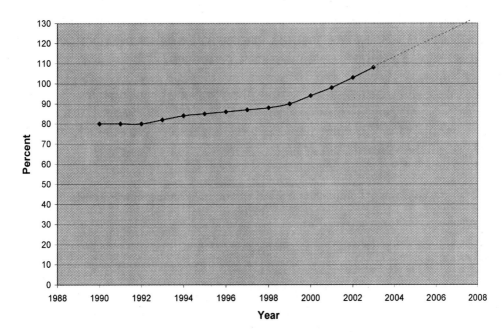

Figure 2-3

Although we know that consumer debt cannot just keep rising, we would like to make some estimate on how much longer the upward trend can continue. This will give us some idea on when the next stock market drop will occur, since a severe drop in consumer spending will follow the consumer debt hitting maximum. Although the following date-estimates may have some error because of their reliance on forecasting based on current trends, they give us some sense that the maximum consumer debt is close at hand.

The dotted extrapolated line in Figure 2-3 shows that, at the current rate of growth, consumer debt will be 130% of disposable income by 2007. This is a milestone of note because Japanese consumers, who had a similar jump in consumer debt in the 1980's, had 130% of disposable income debt just before entering their long and continuing recession. Since at that point the Japanese were still saving at an 11% rate, their personal debt did not have the degree of severity it does in the United States, where current savings rates are already approaching zero. Note that we projected the debt going up at the same rate it has in the last several years. As was previously noted, the growth rate of debt is likely to *increase* due to the current actions of the Fed to raise interest rates and the inability to lower savings rate much more, since it is trending to be zero by 2006. So 2007 is the *latest* that the market will take its next big downward move, at least as indicated by the Japanese precedent.

As this debt continues to grow, so does the number of bankruptcies. Below, in Figure 2-4, you can see how bankruptcy filings in 2003 were 420% of what they were in 1985. This chart shows that the bankruptcy growth rate, compared to the population growth rate, is huge.

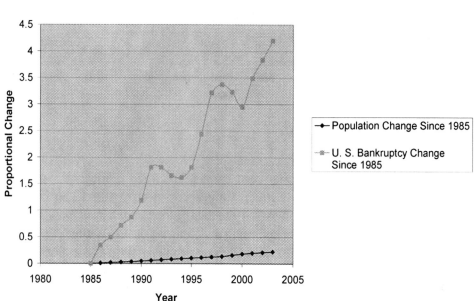

Figure 2-4

There have been temporary downward blips in this curve, and early data in 2004 indicates another slight downward dip due to the reduction in the financial obligation ratio. But the long term trend is definitely upward. 2,144,000 people filed for bankruptcy in 2003. The number of personal bankruptcies is growing at 10% per year. So if the current rate of growth of bankruptcies continues, by 2006 there will be an additional 700,000 people who will have joined the bankrupt ranks. Note that the annual increase of bankruptcies is likely to jump dramatically as the average debt approaches the level at which bankruptcy is declared, since there is a distribution (some people with higher debt, some lower) around the average debt. As the edge of this distribution approaches the bankruptcy level, the rate of bankruptcy growth will start rising even faster than the current 10% per year.

The recent legal attempt to make it more difficult to declare bankruptcy may help credit card companies, but this will do little to help the economy. The people who are over their debt limits will just be kept in an extended state of poverty, with dramatically reduced spending ability and with a resultant slowing of the economy. In fact, by reducing the accountability of the credit card companies for their cavalier attitude in mailing out millions of credit cards, the credit card companies will just be encouraged to continue their practice of extending credit to everyone, with a growing number of people getting into financial problems.

As we have mentioned, the stock market was going crazy in the nineties, and the great jump in stock prices was one of the causes of consumers having the confidence to spend wildly. Fed Chairman Alan Greenspan was certainly aware of the influence of the stock market prices on the rest of the economy. In fact, in December of 1996, at a speech to the American Enterprise Institute, he made his now famous "irrational exuberance" comment regards the high stock market prices. He stated that "we should not underestimate or become complacent about the complexity of the interactions of the asset markets and the economy." This is Greenspanese for *an overpriced market could eventually cause problems in the rest of the economy.* Yet, while he was making this statement, the Fed was allowing the M3 money supply (Figure 2-5 below), which had been reasonably stable for five years, to start rising dramatically. The M3 money supply includes cash, checking and savings accounts, money market accounts, CD's, Euro deposits, and repurchase agreements. This represents the quantity of money (in the generic sense) that can be used to purchase goods, services, and securities. So this increase in the money supply just exacerbated the already irrational exuberance in both the stock market and in consumer spending, because it put an unexpected and unneeded shot of extra money into the economy.

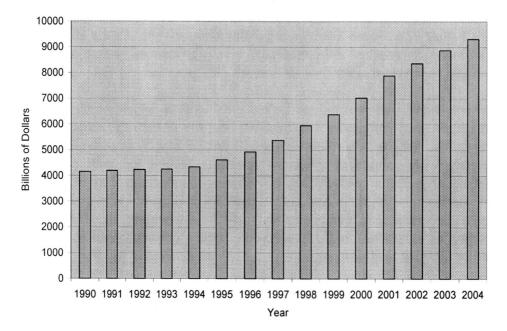

M3 Money Supply Since 1990

Figure 2-5

Then, in 2001, when the stock market took its sudden drop, to make sure consumers *kept* spending at a rate they could not afford, the Fed lowered its federal funds rate, the interest rate banks charge each other for overnight loans, from 5.5% all the way down to 1%. Since the lowering of interest rates, the value of the dollar against other currencies has been dropping dramatically, especially against the Euro.

At the time I am writing this book, the Euro costs almost 50% more than it did three years ago. This makes imports more expensive, so theoretically consumers should have switched to lower cost domestic goods, helping the United States economy grow. However, this didn't happen! Consumers kept buying their European cars, even though they cost more with the lower value of the dollar. The trade deficit has gone from $400 billion in 2001 to $600 billion in 2004. Consumers in the United States continue to buy what they want, from wherever they want, with no regard for price or for what additional debt is required.

This buying overseas causes another problem. The foreign countries, which have been the beneficiary of the trade deficit, now "own" half of the U. S. national debt, because these foreign countries use the extra funds they accumulate because of our trade deficit to buy U. S. stocks and bonds. Now, if these countries get tired of the current decline in the dollar, which makes their investments net losers, they will instead use their deficit funds to buy investment instruments elsewhere, for example in Europe. However, the U. S. *needs* these countries to buy our bonds because that is how we fund our deficit spending. So if the foreign investors start to hesitate to buy our treasury bonds, the interest on the bonds will have to be raised high enough that the foreign investors won't want to go elsewhere. This scenario is exactly what Fed chief Greenspan was warning everyone in a speech he made at a banking conference in Germany in November 2004. He warned that such an event would increase the interest charges on our deficit and render it "increasingly less tenable." That was Greenspanese for *we won't be able to afford it.*

Let's try to put everything all together and see why we think it is inevitable that consumer debt will soon trigger the coming depression.

The Fed has already been raising short term interest rates, which are quickly reflected in the prime rate. The prime rate affects most credit cards and home equity loans. The Fed has already increased its overnight interest rate from 1% to 2.5%, as you can see below in Figure 2-6.

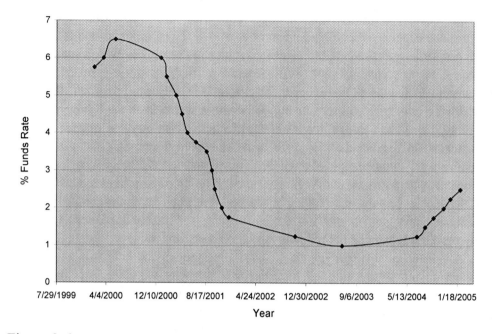

Figure 2-6

The Fed has made it known that they will continue to raise the overnight funds rate until it gets to a more historically "neutral" level, which most people guess will be 4%. This will be a total increase of 3%. Looking at Figure 2-6, you can see that half of this increase has already occurred.

In 2003, 28% of people opted for adjustable rate mortgages (ARMs), and the interest rate they got was close to 4%. The interest rates on about half of these ARMs are tied to the 1-year Constant Maturity Treasury (CMT) index, which is related to the average yield on U.S. Treasury securities (which, based on Greenspan's above warning, is likely to rise dramatically). The interest rates on these adjustable rate mortgages are adjusted annually as the CMT changes. The remaining adjustable rate mortgages are mostly tied to the 3-year or 5-year Constant Maturity Treasury (CMT) indexes, and their rates are adjusted every three or five years accordingly.

It is a reasonable guess that the 1-year Constant Maturity Treasury (CMT) index, which affects adjustable rate mortgages, will also increase by 3% (which will take it back to the level it was early in year 2001), given Greenspan's warning that the foreign purchasers of our Treasury bonds are going to start demanding higher interest on these bonds. In Figure 2-7 below, you can see that over half of this projected increase has already occurred.

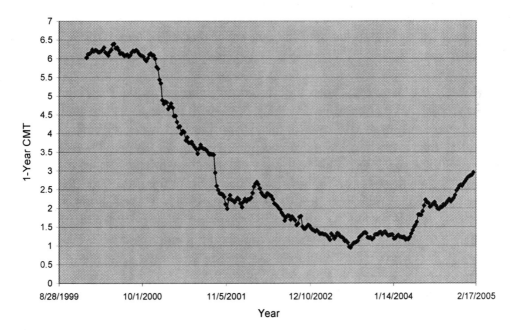

Figure 2-7

You can see in Figure 2-7 that the CMT started increasing after 3/12/2004. The odds of this upward swing of 1-year CMT rates being due to random cause is less than one-in-a-thousand. This increase is *not* a temporary perturbation.

Let's look at a typical couple who have an adjustable mortgage rate (ARM) of $150,000 and an after tax income of $50,000 per year. The current interest payment on their mortgage is $6,000 per year. If their mortgage rate is adjusted up 3%, per the above estimate, their payment will increase by $4,500 per year. Also, if they have $10,000 in credit card debt, the payment on that debt will go up $300 per year.

Looking back at Figure 2-2, you can see that the debt obligation was growing at approximately 1% every two years, before the temporary reprieve that came through home refinancing. Since Figure 2-3 showed that the consumer has not stopped building debt, this increased debt will add another 1%, or $500, to the debt obligation between 2004 and 2006. The total of these increases is $5,300 per year, which is over 10% of the couple's after tax income of $50,000 per year. If you look back at the Financial Obligations Chart in Figure 2-2, it shows that in 2004 the percent of disposable income (in this case, $50,000 per year) was 18%. The above data indicates that this will jump 10% by 2006, to 28% per year.

But wait! We have only been looking at the increase in their debt payments. Energy costs have risen approximately 30% within the last year, and general inflation is starting to rise (that is the reason the Fed is raising interest rates). Let's say that overall inflation, including energy, goes up just 3% over wages between 2004 and 2006. This will increase the costs of the 72% of disposable income expenditures *not* included in the debt obligations. As far as the couple's financial numbers go, this is equivalent to a 3% reduction of money available, which would be similar in effect as raising the debt obligation another 3%, to 31%. For this example couple, let's redo the chart we showed in Figure 2-2 to show what this looks like versus historical changes in the debt obligation ratio. We see this below in Figure 2-8.

Example Couple with an Adjustable Rate Loan

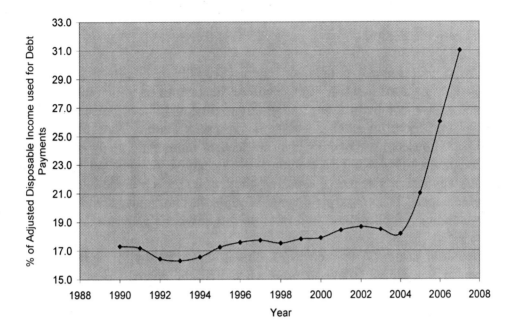

Figure 2-8

The projected debt ratio shown in Figure 2-8 will likely be even worse for many couples because besides going further in debt, the consumer has been supporting the spending spree by reducing his or her savings rate. Now that the savings rate is approaching zero, if the spending continues as it has since 1990, after year 2006 credit cards will have to fill the gap left by having no more savings to reduce. Things just don't look very good for the future.

The example couple I just described had an adjustable rate mortgage. So how many people are in similar circumstances? Well, half of all the mortgages in the United States were originated in 2003, either because of new mortgages or refinancing. This is $3.3 trillion dollars of mortgage debt that originated in 2003, which represented approximately 24 million total mortgage loans. 28% of the 2003 mortgages were adjustable rate mortgages, so there were 6.7 million adjustable rate mortgages in 2003 alone. If even half of these households get into severe payment problems with the expected higher interest rates, similar to what was shown for the example couple above, this would

31

mean that 3.35 million households would be facing bankruptcy by 2006 or 2007. With 2.6 people per household, this would more than double the already projected 3 million people expected to declare bankruptcy in 2006. And remember, we only included year 2003 mortgages. So, the example couple was not an extreme exception.

I showed the example couple as having $10,000 in credit card debt (the balance not paid off monthly, and therefore the amount on which interest must be paid). How common is this? Well, approximately 5% of households have $10,000 or more in unpaid balances on credit cards. That means over 5,500,000 households have this level of debt, or more. And many of these 5.5 million households will be common with the above 6.7 million households having adjustable rate mortgages, so they will get a double whammy on increased costs. Therefore, the example couple was not unusual and represents a large enough proportion of society to start us down the path to a depression.

Let's re-look at our GDP since 1950. This is shown below in Figure 2-9. It is shown in logarithmic scale to emphasize that the increase has been very uniform.

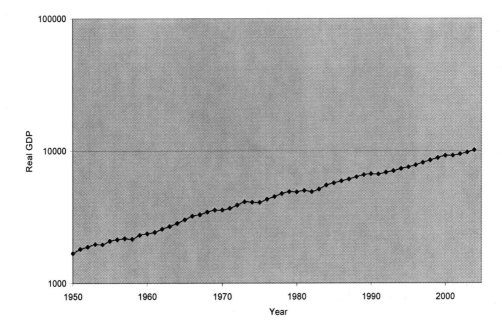

Figure 2-9

To show just how much the zealous consumer spending since 1990 has carried the economy, and how bad the United States economy *would* have been without the drawdown of the consumer's savings rate, let's go back and replay the GDP *without* the reduction of savings rate; in other words, what the GDP would have looked like if the consumer had kept saving at the 8% rate of 1990. We will assume that 70% of whatever extra the consumer spent eventually made its way to the GDP, because given the outflow of dollars from this country, not everything goes into our GDP. In Figure 2-10 below, I have also superimposed a straight line to make it easier to see the resultant change starting in 1990.

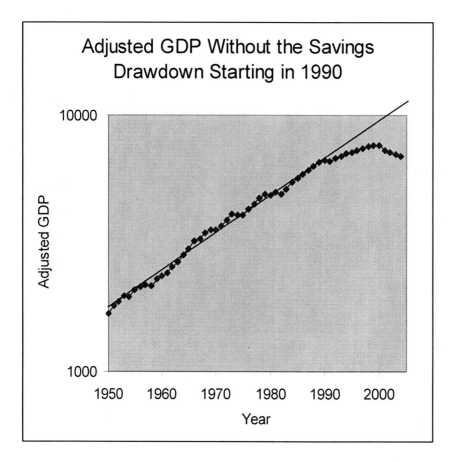

Figure 2-10

As you can see on the above chart, Figure 2-10, without the draw-down of the consumers' savings rate, the United States would have had a slowing economy since 1990. In fact, we would have been in a *depression* for the last four years, with a dropping GDP. Why did I use the term *depression* rather than *recession*? Because in the last 104 years, there was only one other time the GDP dropped four years in a row, as in Figure 2-10, and that was during the 1929 to 1933 depression. Note that I only included the savings draw-down in Figure 2-10. The credit card debt contribution is in addition to this. Also, I didn't subtract the effect of the cash-out refinancing that pumped an additional $96.5 billion back into the economy in 2002 alone! So the economy, without all the temporary cover from the consumers' excessive spending, has not been doing very well at all since the early nineties. What has been so gloriously touted as a great economy looks rather sick without the crutch of consumers going into debt and reducing their savings rate.

What caused the *real* economy (the one without all the consumer debt cover) to be so sick since the early nineties? Could it have been due to all the money that flowed into the dot-com companies that would have traditionally gone to investments in "regular" industry? Sure, e-Bay survived, but not too many other dot-coms did. Historically, a large number of new businesses fail, but most of them just lose the entrepreneur's life savings in the failed venture. Many of the tech businesses of the nineties garnered huge inputs of money and intellectual capital to pursue ideas that were not challenged with traditional tests of merit, and many of these investments never generated any earnings.

However, Figure 2-10 was just pretend. The consumer *did* draw down their savings, so we didn't have the depression, and the economy has *looked* okay. But now the savings rate is approaching zero, so the consumer can't use this reduction of savings much longer as a way of supporting his or her ever increasing spending habit. And with refinancing pretty much played out, the cash-out from refinancing will no longer be dumping additional funds into the economy. Also, consumer debt is pretty much maxed out. So let's look at what the *future* GDP is likely to look like if the consumer slowly starts to pay down his credit card debt (assuming pay-down at $1,000 per year for our earlier example couple) and people slowly start to save again, increasing their savings rate at 2% per year, until they get to 8%, the same rate it was in 1990. Below, in Figure 2-11, is the graph showing this future scenario, with a reference vertical line at year 2007.

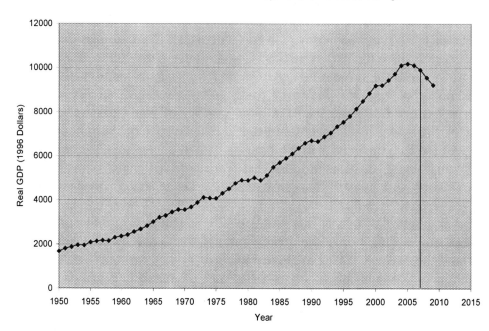

Predicted Real GDP With Slow Debt Payback and Increased Savings

Figure 2-11

I am not the only one to make this prediction about the GDP starting to level off, then turning downward as consumers return to their saving's mode. John Makin, former consultant to the US Treasury, writing for the American Enterprise Institute for Public Policy Institute for Public Policy Research, November 2004, predicts little GDP growth for 2005 due to increased savings, which is consistent with Figure 2-11 above.

Included in the assumptions for Figure 2-11 is that consumers will slowly return to saving. Why will they do this? After all, they have been relying on the stock market to make them rich, so why change? As I write this book, 2004 is coming to an end, and it has been a relatively good year for the stock market. However, this will be only the second time in the last five years that the stock market is up, and it is still about 20% below its 2000 high.

Investors will eventually realize that they are not getting rich in the stock market, and they had better start inputting extra funds into their savings if they want to have any chance of saving for their child's education or for retirement.

They will also begin to see that paying down their 20% interest-per-year credit card debt will benefit them far more than being in the stock market. In either scenario, the economy slows and the stock market goes down.

As you can see from Figure 2-11, starting in 2006, we will have a declining GDP. By 2007 we will be seeing the early signs of a depression. You can perhaps question the timing of the events triggering this curve, but the fact remains that the consumer has little savings rate left to reduce, and he or she is also near their absolute debt limit. Consumers will have to reduce their spending, and soon!

Since most people getting adjustable rate mortgages (ARMs) choose them so they can get as expensive of a house they can for their monthly payments, there is no way such people will be able to handle the increased debt burden that is forecasted without either dramatically reducing their spending, selling stocks to get needed funds, or giving up and going into bankruptcy or foreclosure.

Although the couple used for the prior example in this chapter was assumed to have had an adjustable rate mortgage, rather than a fixed mortgage, there are enough people in a similarly leveraged financial condition, with or without adjustable rate mortgages, that they will drive the country into a depression. "The State of the Nation's Housing 2003," from the Joint Center for Housing Studies of Harvard University, paints a dismal situation. It indicates that over 14 million households pay over 50% of their income on housing. This study also shows that, at the end of 2002, over 400,000 homeowners were in the foreclosure process. This record level of foreclosures is because of all the loans given to people with poor credit.

For anyone who thinks I exaggerate the situation, note that the inflation and mortgage rates I assume for 2006 are pretty much what those rates have historically been. There have been many periods within the last 25 years during which both interest rates and inflation have been *much higher* than I assumed, so the situation could get far worse. Certainly, the risk of foreign purchasers demanding very high interest rates on Treasury bonds is very real. Also, even with the interest rate hikes that have already occurred, many people with credit card debts and adjustable rate mortgages will find themselves well over their maximum debt limit.

We have a huge debt bubble that can not just keep growing. Governments can overspend for many years, with the inevitable bad effects delayed for years. But consumers soon will hit a maximum debt limit that can not be exceeded. They just won't be able to make their payments. *The above data indicates that 2006 will be the year that the consumers' rising debt can no longer fuel the economy, and the first real effect of the depression will be felt. Consumers might try to hold on a little longer, since spending is apparently as addicting as cigarettes or alcohol. So the effect may be delayed until 2007. But that is the latest the depression will start.*

In 2000 we saw the first inklings of the coming depression, when stock prices dropped. However, most of the losses were on paper only, and the immediate visible effects on the economy were few. It didn't stop us from going to war while at the same time reducing taxes and going further in debt. Few banks failed; nor did unemployment reach outrageous levels, at least not compared to historic levels. However, the stock market drop did show the first fissure in the belief that we had entered a new era where the market and economy would continue growing forever because of some super-power of the Fed to control the economy.

The debt bubble will be the trigger for the coming depression, and this downturn will affect many people. This is because the debt and housing bubbles are spread across all economic classes, whereas stock bubbles mostly affect the middle and upper income people only. Few classes will escape the ravages of this depression.

CHAPTER 3
So why will the Good Times End?

We have shown that, in the nineties, both stock prices and debt reached outlandish levels. Stock prices corrected some in 2000, but debt just kept soaring. So why won't stock prices return to their prior upward trend of the nineties, taking the DOW to 36,000 or even higher within several years, with this rising stock market then pulling the whole economy with it?

First, we have seen that stock prices rose in the nineties due to the combined effects of an increase in the population of people in the stock buying ages and an increased stock ownership of the general population. Let's look at both of these to see what is happening to each.

If you go back to the first chapter and look at the chart Figure 1-2, you can see that the growth of the population of stock buyers aged 30 through 54 has leveled off, and after 2005 it will begin to drop. Also, Figure 1-3 shows that the number of households holding mutual funds peeked in 2001. So there is no longer the strong demand for stocks facilitated by the growth in these two areas. Given a few more years, the reduction in the age 30 to 54 stock buyers will start having a negative effect on the market, causing it to drop. The effect of the debt bubble reaching maximum will likely cause the market drop to happen even sooner, but the reduced population of potential buyers will exacerbate the problem once the depression starts.

As I am writing this book, the Fed is raising interest rates, and mortgage rates are inching back towards historical levels. The effect of these increases in interest rates will be to quickly wipe out the recent small drop in the Financial Obligations Ratio that was shown in Figure 2-2. As was shown in Figure 2-6, by 2006 this ratio will be at an all-time high, and many people will have reached well beyond their highest sustainable debt ratio.

The Financial Obligations Ratio is not the only thing affecting the disposable personal income. Heating costs are predicted to rise 30% in 2005, and the oil shortage, due to a shortage of refineries, will continue to put cost pressure on all fuel users, private and corporate.

The value of the dollar against other currencies is falling. That will make imports more expensive. We are not just talking about big ticket items here. Look at how many everyday things, from clothes, to appliances, to electronics; are imported. The weaker dollar is beginning to make all of these things more expensive. As imports get more expensive, domestic companies, no longer restrained by lower-priced import competition, will start raising prices. This will fuel inflation.

Sure, if the price goes up enough, it may become economical to again make more products here in the United States, which will help reverse the current drop in manufacturing jobs in the United States. However, the product price rise would have to be substantial, and the net affect on the consumer will be much higher prices. All of this will put cost pressure on the consumer, who is already spending beyond his means.

Real incomes are not going up, and the reduction of manufacturing jobs is making the overall average pay of the remaining jobs lower than in the recent past. So people will either have to reduce spending or start draining their remaining existing savings, including selling stocks. Let's look at the effect of either option.

If people reduce spending, then industry will see reduced sales. To maintain profits and to match production demand, companies will raise prices and reduce their workforce, driving up unemployment and further reducing demand. Since many of those who will be unemployed have little ready savings, they will have to start selling stocks from their retirement savings. This selling pressure on stocks, along with the downward pressure on profits caused by the lower sales demands for goods, will cause stock prices to drop. This spiral will continue until stock prices and the business level have dropped to levels matched by earlier severe downturns or depressions.

The above scenario had people reducing their spending as their first response to their maxed-out debt level. If instead, they continue to spend and sell their stocks to continue their spending "habit," then the stock selling pressure will cause a related drop in the market, which will then lead the economic downturn rather than follow it. The net effect, however, is the same in that the stock market will go down dramatically.

Some people do not believe that this scenario is possible. They believe that the Fed has learned how to minimize downturns by controlling interest rates, or that they can, as a last resort, "print money." However, Fed Chief Alan Greenspan stated in 2002 that the Fed does *not* have the ability to stop bubbles or recessions. Extended downturns are either psychological or caused by some specific factor, like the debt bubble, and are little affected by any action of the Fed. The Fed can *delay* a downturn, but not stop it. In an economic downturn, people become very negative on the economy and the stock market, and then they retrench. The more the government attempts to reverse this negativity, the more people sense that things are *really* bad and are likely to get even worse. And printing excess money to solve the problem will cause rampant inflation, hurting those on a fixed income. Those on fixed incomes will then have to reduce *their* spending, which again causes a resultant market drop.

This inability of government policy to stop or reverse an economic downturn is evident if one looks at Japan since 1990. At that time the Japanese economy went into a severe funk, which continues to this day. See Figure 3-1 below.

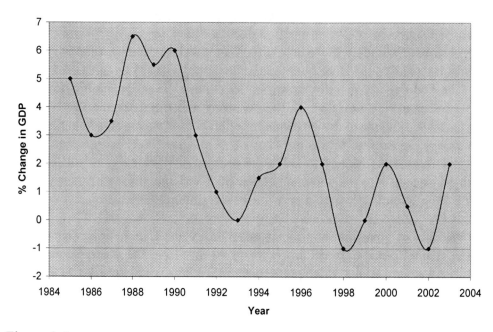

Figure 3-1

In response to this downturn, the Japanese government cut interest rates to zero and initiated massive spending programs, to no avail other than to create a huge debt versus its GDP (See Figure 3-2 below).

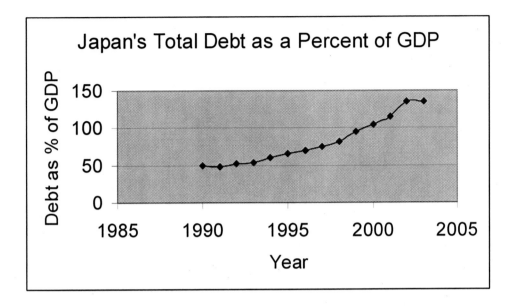

Figure 3-2

Note that the measures implemented to attempt to reverse Japan's slump were done in conjunction with the expertise of American economists, who were thought to have the formula to fight recessions. None of these steps have helped; in fact, they probably just made things worse by emphasizing how severe the problem was. The Japanese government's actions just exacerbated the already negative attitude of their population, and the Japanese people's response has been to further entrench.

Lest any of you forget, Japan was the economy that the USA was trying to emulate before Japan's 1990's downturn began. Japan had the computer expertise to use all of the information technology that has been so broadly advertised as the positive driver for the American economy. So if information technology was the positive driver for the American economy, how come it didn't help the Japanese?

Nothing stopped the Japanese consumer from entrenching and contributing to Japan's continuing economic downturn. It is worthwhile to look at what happened to the Japanese stock market as all this was going on. The Nikkei 225 Stock Index is shown in Figure 3-3 below.

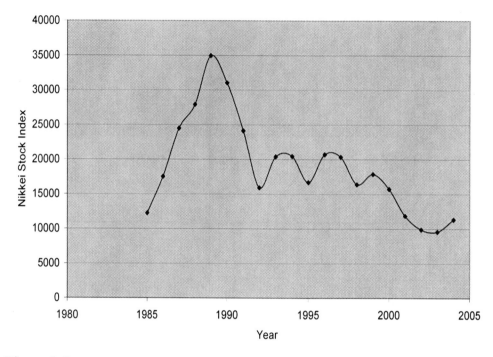

Japan's Nikkei 225 Stock Index

Figure 3-3

Note that the 71% drop in the Japanese stock market took about 13 years, and it had a plateau on its way down. The first drop was approximately 50% over a three year interval, and then it recovered some and stayed at a general level 40% below its high for five years. It then proceeded to drop 50% from that plateau.

In 2000 the United States stock market dropped about 44%, then recovered some to its current level (end of 2003), 25% below its high. If it follows the Japanese example, in about 2007 the market will again begin to drop, until the S&P 500 reaches 450 in year 2013.

Much of the Japanese economy of the nineties is now being mirrored in the current United States economy, just with a delay. Some people attribute the drop in the Japanese market to an aging of their population, and the United States is now entering a similar era. What has happened in Japan should not be dismissed lightly as not being applicable to the United States. Remember, in the eighties Japan's economy was the envy of the world. The Japanese are in many ways more educated than Americans, and they have a very stable government. They certainly had the technical expertise to use the advantages of the "new era" information systems, if that was the solution to their economic doldrums. It wasn't; nor was it the reason *our* stock market flourished in the nineties. It is important to remember that it was the increased demand for stocks that drove up stock market prices in the United States, not any real improvement in the United States economy.

Note that the debt chart in Figure 3-2 was for the Japanese *government* debt. The debt problem of the individual Japanese consumer was never as severe as that of the American consumer because the Japanese people never reduced their savings rate below 11%. The debt spending by the Americans has been the driver for the U.S. economy since 1990, and low interest rates have enabled this over-spending to go on longer than it would have otherwise. But this debt bubble has just delayed the inevitable American economic downturn. Due to this long delay, and the size of the personal debt bubble, by every measure the downturn in the American economy will be worse than the one being experienced by Japan. This is because the American consumers must both reduce their debt and begin to save before they can again even *start* to become a positive influence on the economy.

Getting back to the stock market, how far will the United States' stock market drop in the predicted depression? The stock market has always had a tendency to regress to the level such that stock prices are justified by competitive investments. It sometimes took many years, but the market has *always* regressed from overly high levels. Below, in Figure 3-4, let's re-look at an earlier chart showing the price/dividend ratio for the S&P 500 stocks.

Year-end Price/Dividend Ratio

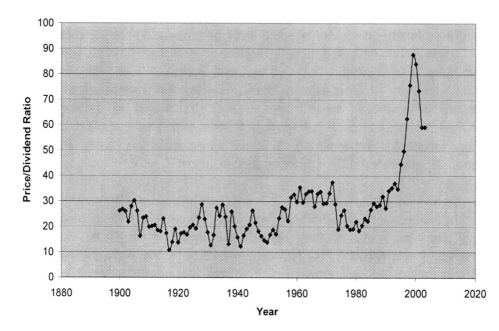

Figure 3-4

Note that a price/dividend ratio of 20, with the exception of the last 20 years, was pretty much the norm for the last 100 years. In the sixties, the ratio temporarily increased to about 35. But in the seventies, it had again returned to the general ratio of 20. The reason this regression tendency exists is that stocks must eventually compete with other investments. When stock prices are high, and if dividends have not increased proportionally, the price/dividend ratio becomes too high, and stocks are no longer competitive as a true investment. Stocks can continue rising in price for many years, but at some point a stock purchase is not investing. It is just gambling that some bigger fool will pay an even higher price for the stock in the future.

Why won't dividends increase in future years, thus making the current stock prices justifiable? First, the dividends would have to be 300% of current levels to justify current prices. Presumably, *real* corporate earnings would also have to be 300% of current levels for companies to afford such a dividend jump. Since even the continuance of current corporate earnings is at risk because of operating costs being postponed to the future, such an increase of earnings is highly unlikely. Nor is it likely that real corporate earning will be going up at all, given that consumers are going to have to curtail their spending as they approach their debt limits.

At the beginning of 2000, the dividend yield on the S&P 500 stocks was only slightly higher than 1%, versus the historical dividend yield of over 4%. Even at the end of 2003, the yield was less than 1.7%. Obviously, people were speculating on stock prices in the expectation of asset appreciation – the bigger fool thing; they were *not* investing for dividend income. Once the stock price speculation ends, stock prices will again drop sufficiently to put the dividend yield in line with other competing investment opportunities. In later chapters, we will discuss some rather sophisticated methods of determining the real (correct) value of stocks, but just using Figure 3-4 to monitor the price/dividend ratio will give you almost as good of a tool.

Early in 2000 it appears that some investors decided to take their money and run. No one knows for sure why they did this, but we already mentioned that the demand for stocks had already flattened due to the leveling off of the number of potential buyers. Also, most people were aware that stocks were outrageously overpriced, and some investors were just waiting for the slightest hesitation in the upward price trend to sell their stocks. However, the stock market did *not* drop far enough to lower the price/dividend ratio to its historical 20 level. At the end of 2003, the ratio was still 60, versus the historical 20 level.

Why did the market stop dropping before it got down to historical price levels? A probable reason is the effect of the continuing influx of money from the pension 401(k)'s. This continuing influx of funds into the market due to these savings plans is a relatively new phenomenon. Earlier downturns in the market did not have this stabilizing effect. People saving in their 401(k) plans do not make daily decisions as to their investments; their money is automatically invested in whatever was their investment choice when they set up their savings plan, and they don't change their investment choices often.

If people take money out of a 401(k) savings before they are 59 ½ years of age, they pay a substantial tax penalty. So people are hesitant to remove funds from their IRAs. The effect of the continuing 401(k) stock investments puts a damper on any extended market drop. However, continuing periods of poor market performance *will* eventually cause people to *change* their 401(k) investment choices to other investments, like treasury bonds. Switching investment options within a 401(k) plan does not garner a tax penalty.

Books on the Stock Market

There are many books on the stock market. However, most of these books assume that the world will repeat, at least in regards to the perceived nineties' stock market performance. They blindly assume that the stock market has always been the best long-term investment, disregarding the fact that in the last century there were several extended periods of twenty years or so when stocks were *not* the best investment. This blind assumption makes all the conclusions and advice in these other books questionable.

One thing seems to stand out in most of the books on the stock market that I used for reference. Even those pushing stocks for long-term investments indicate that, in the future, stocks will not be as profitable as they were in the past. They tend to almost hide this conclusion (with the exception of *Irrational Exuberance*, *Valuing Wall Street,* and *Financial Reckoning Day*) and immediately go back to examples of buying stocks for the long term. Assuming historical 3.5% inflation, here is a summary of the predictions of real stock performance from those reference books that *did* choose to make a prediction. Note that in many cases, the values shown required some interpretation on my part, partly because the authors often gave alternate scenarios of a sudden drop in market prices or a level market for many years, and partly because inflation was included in some estimates.

In addition to the listed reference books, investment manager Robert Arnott and Vanguard's retired founder John Bogle have both stated in articles and interviews that they expect future returns to equal 7% to 7 ½% (including inflation). I have included their predictions in the below summary.

BOOKS/ARTICLES	FUTURE STOCK YIELD without INFLATION
Winning with the Dow's Losers	3.5%
Yes, You Can Time the Market	0%
The Four Pillars of Investing	3.5%

Valuing Wall Street	2.5%
Winning the Loser's Game	4.0%
Financial Reckoning Day	Negative
Irrational Exuberance	1%
Robert Arnott and John Bogle Articles	3 ½ to 4%

Reiterating, the above estimates are for "real" gains, which do not include inflation.

The Median (middle value) of these predictions is 3.5%, versus the historical 6.5% real stock performance. The baseline TIPS (Treasury Inflation Protected Securities) we used in a prior chapter are assumed to be paying 3%, with basically no risk and in addition to any inflation. The median prediction made by the reference books for future yields is only slightly greater than the assumed yield for TIPS, and the ½% difference would not justify the higher risk of stocks.

None of this precludes stocks as a possible great investment in the future. If the market were to take a *huge* dive, and you were not already invested, it may be that the market would then again be viable, and you would be in a position of having capital available to take advantage of this opportunity. All of the above books allow for this scenario.

Some people interpret the limited market drop in 2000 as some verification that things are "different this time," and that regression to the mean is no longer valid. However, former market drops after bubbles often came in several spaced and delayed downward steps. This was also true in the recent Japanese market drop, which you saw in Figure 3-3. Everyone is aware of the October 1929 market drop in the United States, but not everyone is aware that the market recovered most of this drop in the months following. The total large market drop following the initial 1929 drop actually took years, with several partial recoveries along the way. It takes a long time before investors finally give up and accept that a market is tanking. But once investors finally accept this, the market often drops below the traditional mean because everyone has become so frightened and negative that no one wants to buy stocks.

Based on Figure 3-4, we would estimate that the market price/dividend ratio, which was at 60 at the end of 2003, will eventually drop below its historical 20 level in a severe downturn of the economy. This would be at least a 67% stock price reduction versus 2003 stock prices, which would make the S&P 500 be priced at 370. Note that later in the book we will finalize the exact price/dividend buy ratio we want to use for reference.

As mentioned in the previous chapter, the exact timing of this coming market drop is difficult to ascertain. But looking at the continuing rise in bankruptcies and the financial obligations ratio, it appears that many people are at, or close to, their debt limits. The increase of interest rates and energy costs, along with the continuing spending rate, will soon push many of these people well *over* their limits. It is difficult to imagine that these people will not reach a critical point by 2007, and that the downward spiral will not then begin.

As mentioned earlier, the total predicted stock market drop will not happen in just one downward spike. The market will drop somewhat, and some investors will think the bottom has been reached. These investors will then buy stocks, causing a slight market upturn. However, the debt will still be there, and the market recovery will be short, followed by another market drop. Each successive drop to a lower price level will sour more investors, until finally no one wants to buy stocks. Then the bottom will be reached. Watching the price/dividend ratio will be one way to sense when the market is getting close to its bottom, or at least close enough to again consider buying stocks. The smart investor will buy when everyone else is sour on the stock market.

CHAPTER 4
What Will the Coming Depression Be Like?

Investors really *want* the stock market and the economy to go up! If *willing* the stock market to go up worked, the resultant market gain would be dramatic. And obviously no one wants the country to sink into a severe depression. This positive desire is blinding people to economic realities. But the excesses of the last 15 years have a severe and inevitable price that must be paid. Neither individuals nor the country can keep spending beyond their means forever. *Everybody* knows that, but few want to face the reality of what's coming. Because individual debt has some maximum point, and because consumer debt spending and drawing down the savings rate close to zero has fueled the recent economy, there *will be* a slowdown when the debt level reaches maximum. This will trigger the depression. Someone can argue about the timing or severity, but a slowdown *will* happen. Some will think this chapter is like Chicken Little. So be it!

Stocks can stay overpriced for many years, as they have in the past. Overpriced stocks alone will not *cause* a downturn in the economy. Many economists were burned in the middle nineties because they predicted an economic slowdown based on overly high stock prices. The slowdown didn't happen, so they were ostracized. Something other than excessive market prices must be the trigger to a downturn; but the degree that the stock market is overpriced *will* determine how far the market will fall once the downturn starts.

Let's walk through what is going to happen in the next several years. Don't write me letters about specific details in this prediction. The intent is to show what type of things are possible, not that everything will happen exactly as or when forecasted. This is a frightening scenario, but similar things have happened in our country, or in other countries, during past periods of severe economic stress. People act very irrationally when their economic world comes crashing down around them, which is exactly what happens to those severely hurt in a depression. And the people likely to be hurt in the coming depression, because it will include a large number of the middle class, will have far more potential to do real damage than those hurt in the first Great Depression.

Sometime in 2006 consumers will reach their maximum debt level, and the resultant slowdown of the economy will begin to be felt in 2006 or 2007. The consumers reaching their maximum debt level will only partly be caused by their continued spending. Their general living cost will have been raised by outside forces, and this will hasten the time of their hitting their maximum debt. In fact, even if consumers start reducing their spending in 2005, it will be too late. Their other costs, like energy, medical costs, and all imported goods, will have gone up so much that consumers will not even be able to sustain payments on their current debts. As I am writing this, home heating costs are predicted to rise 30% this winter, and the dollar versus the euro has dropped 34% in the last several years. The dollar versus the yen is at new lows, and the Chinese have indicated that they may disassociate the value of their currency from the dollar, which is predicted to increase the price of goods from China by 40%. The costs of living for consumers will rise rapidly.

In response to the terrorists' attacks, America has gone to war several times and has implemented costly procedures to protect the "homeland." Rather than funding these wars and their related costs with tax increases and a general tightening of the belt on spending, which is what has happened historically in times of war, instead the United States lowered taxes, and consumers went on a spending spree. You don't need a doctorate in economics to see the folly in this. This is akin to someone responding to a family financial crisis by having the wife quit her job and taking out a loan to buy a 7-series BMW. You may be able to temporarily get by, and even appear to be doing very well, but this is not a viable long-term solution.

The continuing excessive government debt, even though it does not have the defined maximum of an individual's debt, is nevertheless starting to contribute to a financial slowdown. The people who have been loaning money to the U.S. government are primarily the Chinese, Japanese and Europeans. Since the value of the dollar versus their currencies keeps dropping, the Japanese and Europeans are actually losing on their investments. They are therefore starting to insist on higher interest on these loans. Fed Chief Greenspan warned of this in November 2004. The resultant expected higher interest rates will cause everyone in America to have higher loan payments, because it makes both the United States and the individual debtors' interest payments higher. The increased debt burden will cause the consumer to reduce spending, which will slow the economy. The government will either have to raise taxes or borrow even more money to stay solvent. If the government tries to reduce spending by shrinking the size of the government bureaucracy, the resultant increase of people out of work will also slow the economy.

As interest rates go up on Treasury bills and other debt instruments, these investments become more attractive, and some money will flow out of the stock market to these other securities. In the long run, the stock market must compete with other investment options, so the stock market will go down in price to make the dividend payout more attractive in relation to the stock price.

Companies have been optimizing bottom lines rather than investing for future businesses, so it seems less likely that there are any great new technologies that are in the wings ready to rescue us. In the last century, we had world-changing inventions that were consumer and industry game-changers, such as telephones, radios, automobiles, airplanes, televisions, transistors, microchips, computers, and such. The continuing increase in computer speed may allow people to download high-resolution pictures of their grandchildren at faster speeds, and to accumulate even more data, but the higher speeds have no obvious big advantage for most industries or consumers. There are no apparent breakthrough technologies ready to reignite our economy. That doesn't mean there won't be great innovations in the future, but invention has not been the recent priority of industry; its priority has been making profits look good.

Companies will respond to any slowdown with layoffs to lower their expenses, and they will implement price increases in an attempt to maintain profits (and their salaries). They will not expand to go after new business because even in the recent relatively good times, companies have found that it is easier and less risky just to push harder on current people and businesses, using creative accounting when required. They haven't believed the government's economic data that we have turned the corner on the economy, so they have been conservative on any expansion plans.

If this sounds like the makings of a perfect storm, it is. None of the above is new information, but it is now coming to a head because the savings rate is approaching zero, and the consumer debt is maxed out. Debt will be the trigger that causes it all to crash. Then all the evils we have fed on for the last fifteen years will begin to feed on us. Some will blame the government and some will blame the terrorists. But *we* are the villains here. Few have not participated in the excesses, and few will be spared the hurt the country will go through.

There will be several apparent *recoveries* as the depression marches down its path, with glimmers of hope led by those who have not yet given up on the stock market or the economy. The TV stock analysts will continue to ask "experts" if the market has now bottomed out, and the experts will assure everyone that it has, and that those who are maintaining their buy-and-hold investment philosophies will be rewarded. Perhaps they will, but not in *this* life!

The problem with any depression scenario is that it is self-energizing. As unemployment goes up, the economy gets weaker, causing companies to downsize further and therefore adding to the roles of the unemployed. As sales go down, profits also go down. Dividends will have to be cut, since there will be no earnings to support the current dividends. Slowly, people will lose faith in the market, sell some stocks, and drive prices down even further.

Come 2008 the number of people giving up on making house payments will skyrocket. Since many of the recent mortgage loans were adjustable rate, or had little or no collateral, banks will be forced to foreclose on the homes and sell them, causing a glut of homes on the market and a deflation of home values. In the 2000 market drop, almost no banks went belly up because people had not bought stocks on leverage. This is not true in housing, where people and banks *are* leveraged. As the current inflated home values go down, many people will have mortgages greater than the value of their homes, and they will willingly give their homes back to the bank rather than fight their mortgage payments. Unless the federal government comes to their rescue, many banks will fail in this downturn. This is because banks got too confident and optimized bottom line results, with little consideration for the risks they were taking with marginal mortgage loans.

You will be able to get a great deal on a used SUV, especially a Hummer! The automotive market will be for cars getting great gas mileage, and Detroit will again be caught off guard and all geared up for the gas guzzlers. Sound familiar? This will cause massive layoffs at Detroit carmakers, and all the under-funded automakers' pension funds will become zero-funded. Millions of Japanese high mileage cars with new technologies, like hybrid engines, will have been on the road for many years. But the American automakers, with little on-road experience with these new technologies, will be a car-generation or two behind. And hydrogen cars, despite Detroit's hype, are far from ready for production.

The war in Iraq will become a full blown civil war, with American soldiers in the middle between the Sunnis, Shiites and Kurds. Shiites will be in control, and the Sunnis and Kurds won't like it. Deaths and costs will skyrocket. There will be anti-war marches, much like in the Vietnam conflict. The President will want to send in more troops and start the draft if necessary. After all, he got reelected largely on his steadfastness and his aggressive war on terror, in which he has successfully included the Iraq war. But Congress will have had it. In a very open and heated battle between the White House and the Congress, Congress will refuse further war funding, bringing the soldiers home. An Iranian type religious anti-American government will forcefully take over Iraq and with ruthless power put the country under control. Bush's administration will be the goat for all the country's economic problems, but the problem started under Clinton's regime. However, the tax reduction and the war in Iraq *have* made the problem worse.

By 2010 the United States government will be in huge trouble. They will try government make-work programs to stimulate the economy (similar to the massive programs Japan initiated), but the United States will have entered the depression with so much debt that they will have trouble getting the money to support these make-work programs, even at the high interest rates being offered on Treasury bonds. The government will eventually resort to printing money, because that is the only economic trick that has not been tried in Japan, and because the Fed has already stated publicly they will do that before they ever allow deflation. This will cause worldwide turmoil in the financial markets. Unemployment will be well over 10%, and protest marches on Washington by various groups will become commonplace.

The new presidency and the Congress will both be Democratic, but they will find themselves having to take actions very alien to the Democratic Party. Because of reduced tax income, the Democrats will have to reduce spending across the board, including social programs. Government will have to be downsized, with massive layoffs. Foreign countries will require a balanced budget plan before they will loan us any more money. We will protest but give in, having no choice. We will be treated with distain, just as *we* previously treated third world countries with out of control economies.

Retirement age will be changed immediately to age 70, since this will reduce social security retirement costs starting the following year. A law will be passed that companies can not lay off any more people due to reduced sales; companies *will* be allowed, however, to reduce salaries or work hours.

The birth rate will go to zero, and much to the consternation of the Right to Life people, the rate of abortions will increase. No one will want to bring a child into the very tenuous economy that will be gripping the United States.

In 2012 China will invade Taiwan, and the United States will only be able to rant and rave. The world will no longer take the military threats from the United States seriously because Congress will not be ready to take on another war. China and India will start to be the dominant forces in the world, politically and militarily.

By 2013 people in America will have given up. Unemployment will be over 15%, and the stock market will be down over 70% from its 2003 price level. With everything looking so glum, at last the country will slowly start to rebuild. This will also be the time to get back into the stock market.

The debt problem will begin to slowly diminish because with inflated dollars, both the consumer debt and the government debt will seem smaller, and they will be paid down with a dollar worth far less than it is now. The winners in this exchange will be the debtors. The losers will be all the countries that loaned money to the United States, everyone who bought non-inflation-adjusted bonds or saved money in a bank, and those who are on fixed incomes, like retirees on a pension.

It will be a simpler country that comes out of the depression. Perhaps looking at England can give some hints. The United States consumer will no longer be trying to buy whatever is new and cool. They will just be trying to get by, getting their pleasures from more simple things, like a walk in the park or playing cards. Plasma TV's and such will no longer be affordable, nor will they be a priority. Foodstuffs and a comfortable survival will be the goal. High school students, poor dears, will have to take the bus to school, rather than drive their family's third car. The joys of sex will again have to be learned in the back seat of the family car, rather than in the teenager's own car. Of course, this is only after the teenager convinces his parents that he or she needs the car to go to the library. Some things just seem predestined to go around.

Car pooling will again become popular. The stock market will be akin to poison for most people. We will no longer be the world's policeman or act so morally superior in our dealings with other countries. Perhaps the terrorists will then no longer consider us their number one target. We will withdraw from many trade relationships with other countries, having set up trade barriers in response to our country's huge financial and unemployment problems. Equally, the world will withdraw from us. They will be looking at us as another world power has-been. We will have paid back debts with dollars that had lost much of their worth, and the world will be in turmoil, since so much of the world's economy previously revolved around a stable dollar.

There will be cries to go back to a gold-backed dollar. Young people will rebel en-mass against the debt that is being left them. There will be much negativity towards recent immigrants because they will be blamed for the unemployment. Immigration will be stopped.

Shareholders will force down the often obscene salaries of corporate managers and directors. Everyone living in wealthy developments will feel vulnerable, and private security businesses will be one of the few businesses prospering. Alcohol sales will jump, as they do in most downturns.

Environmental concerns will take a back seat to getting industry running. The Democrats, much to their own dismay, will weaken pollution limits to promote industrial growth. The number of people attending college will drop dramatically because of the costs, and those attending will often have to work part time to help make expenses. Some colleges will fold. Government loans for education will be long gone. When job openings occur in industry, the lines of applicants will be long, with people having doctorates competing with high school dropouts even for manual labor jobs.

Automobiles will become extremely small, and many families will only be able to afford one. Multiple TVs and video games will become things of the past. Books will go up in sales. Religion will become even stronger, and some of these religious folks will use the economic downturn as a way of "proving" their 'God's wrath' theories. Communists, socialists, revolutionaries, fascists, Nazi's, skin-heads, white-power groups, black-power groups, and other fanatics will come out of the walls; and they will all get an inordinate amount of support from the populace. This will *not* be a very happy country!

Protest groups will have a new and powerful means to rally forces against the government. The internet will be used to coordinate protest marches and other mischief. This will enable quick and, at times, violent reaction to any event that some group finds distasteful. Mob mentality will be easier to excite and riots easier to incite, because large numbers of people can be rallied on very short notice when an event is still at an emotional high. Since no one can verify the veracity of items posted, half-truths and pure fabrications will sometimes trigger mass reactions. The quickness of this digital communication will often preclude the real truth from interceding.

The care of the aged, which is now thought of as a looming problem for the future, will be less of a problem because it will be literally unfunded. People will have to care for their elderly parents at home, rather than hiding them away in a nursing home. With the rarity of jobs available, few families will have two wage earners, so this home care will be possible, even if not desired. No longer will most of our medical expenses be spent on the last year of life, keeping someone alive who often has minimal quality of life. When the elderly get sick, the government will support only minimal care. Talk of euthanasia will become commonplace, even though the practice won't be implemented, at least not openly. The care of the increasing number of elderly with Alzheimer's will trigger many of these discussions.

As for other medical costs that are currently paid by Medicare and Medicaid, forget it. Hospitalization and medicines will be tightly rationed and only given to those with prospects for a quick and complete recovery. Other than for the very wealthy, who, as always, can survive any downturn, the nursing homes remaining will be sorry affairs indeed.

Some people who thought they had retired well, with comfortable fixed pensions, will be close to poverty. Their pensions will be small compared to the cost of everything in the now inflated dollar. Many pension plans will have failed because the parent companies could no longer afford their costs.

Few people will fly anywhere, even on business. Energy costs and the costs of making flights terrorist-resistant will make flying too expensive. Many airlines will have failed and gone out of business. Few people will take distant vacations, since they won't be able to afford them. People will be closing up parts of their large houses to save energy. Houses will be cold in the winter and hot in the summer to save energy costs. People won't be able to downsize because the market for houses will have tanked.

Some readers will think I am being too negative. Not so! Here is negative: Terrorists attack the oil facilities in Saudi Arabia in 2006, or overthrow their government. Now *that* would be negative because all of the world's economies would be put in turmoil. And I won't even go into the type of terrorist attacks on the United States that can cause massive disruption.

The dollar can be so devalued by our government using their printing presses with abandon that our whole monetary system fails. A dictatorial government will then be voted in that restricts freedoms in order to get our country back on a firm financial footing. Remember, Germany elected Hitler in the midst of an economic crisis. And despite what we want to believe, the Germans were just as civilized and educated as Americans are now. Now *that* is being negative!

Sadly, I think I was being realistic and rather optimistic in my earlier predictions.

CHAPTER 5
What Else May Trigger the Depression

When someone is working on an industrial process or a system, either to fix a problem or to find out what is critical, they try to identify the Key Process Input Variables (KPIVs). These are the things that are most likely to influence a change. Note that it is the *key* input variables that are of interest, *not* all the sundry input variables that, although theoretically possible to be an influence, do not generally play a critical role. If you analyze every theoretically possible influence, you get inundated with detail and data. Similarly, in this case we want to know the KPIVs likely to trigger an economic depression and whether any of these identified KPIVs are at a state, or a condition, such that they could indeed actually be the trigger for the depression.

The KPIV that we have identified as most likely to trigger the depression is consumer debt. This key process input variable was identified as most critical because it already is well on its way to dramatically blow by its sustainable maximum. When this happens only bad things can follow. Those bad things are, as far as their effect on the economy, a slow down in spending, the selling of stocks, and/or the declaring of individual bankruptcy. These, in turn, will then trigger a whole myriad of other bad things.

We also discussed that stocks being overpriced was *not* a KPIV, at least as far as triggering a depression. Stocks can be overpriced for many years, as they were in the late nineties, without triggering much of an economic slowdown at all. Even with the market drop in 2000, no great economic downturn occurred. In fact, consumers just kept spending and waiting for the stock market to recover. However, once the depression actually is in full bloom, the degree to which stocks are overpriced *will* determine how far the stock market will fall.

There *are*, however, additional KPIVs whose effects could trigger a depression. Although the timing of these other KPIVs are likely to be later than the effect of consumer debt, events can happen that will increase their urgency and cause one or more of them to be the depression trigger. The additional KPIVs are the wars in Iraq and Afghanistan, terrorists, energy prices, a drop in the dollar's value, the deficit, the balance of payments, inflation, and interest rates. These KPIVs are not all independent, and many are likely to act in concert. The fact that there are so many other KPIVs just about ready to explode makes it very difficult not to believe that a depression is close. The timing prediction of 2006 or 2007 may be off a year, but the depression is coming. We will discuss each of the aforementioned additional KPIVs in the rest of this chapter.

WARS IN IRAQ AND AFGHANISTAN

Even those who support the war in Iraq do not see a quick ending. As time goes on, the possibility of a civil war between different factions within Iraq gets more likely. It appears that we will be in Iraq for many years, and perhaps with far greater troop strength than is currently deployed. Even maintaining current troop levels is a long-term issue, given the number of National Guard and Reserve forces involved. To get additional personnel to join the military, or even to keep manpower at the current levels, it appears that the military will have to offer greater incentives, both in sign-on bonuses and salaries. And many military experts have been vocal in estimating that it will take a tripling of forces in Iraq to get the country under control. They make a point that only about 30,000 or 40,000 of the troops in Iraq are actually in action; the rest are support troops. So the size of the force active in trying to keep the country in control is not much larger than the size of New York City's police force.

A tripling of force level would require huge additional funding and a probable return of the draft. All of this will add to the costs of running government and create huge amounts of unrest. In any case, if the loss of life keeps rising as it has been, the country will begin to back off in their support of the war. Since President Bush has shown no sign of backing away from his commitment, no matter how bad things become in Iraq, this could cause major attitude problems within the country. Already, people are getting disconcerted about the cost and length of the war, and a 2005 poll on the net showed that only 25% of those polled thought that the war was worth the cost in lives and dollars.

Afghanistan superficially looks more promising, but the people really in control of the country are the drug lords. The amount of poppy being grown in Afghanistan is feeding 70% to 80% of the world market for poppy-related drugs. Opiates come from the seed pod of the poppy, which is then converted to opium. Codeine and morphine are derived from opium, and other drugs, such as heroin, are processed from morphine or codeine. The profit these drug lords are making will make it very difficult for the government of Afghanistan to stop this trade, especially since growing poppy is the main income source for the country. Stopping the drug lords may require a substantial increase in military backup from the United States, and it will have to be a long term commitment because the minute we look away the drug lords will again reassert their control.

There are 20,000 drug-induced deaths every year in the United States, and the UN estimates 100,000 drug-induced deaths per year world wide. If America leaves the current situation in Afghanistan in place, an argument can be made that far more lives will be lost in America every year due to increased drug problems related to drug availability than were lost in the terrorists' twin towers and Pentagon attacks. The United States will be *forced* to get more aggressively involved in stopping the drug war lords.

All of these wars will eventually wear down America's confidence, affecting both the economy and stock market. This may take several years, but it won't be too much behind the timing of the debt depression trigger.

TERRORISTS

Terrorists are a great unknown. The terrorists are learning a dangerous lesson in Iraq – that they can make and use homemade bombs almost with impunity. There is no reason to go for the sophistication of weapons of mass destruction. If they go after the Saudi oil fields and refineries with these homemade bombs, they will bring America and the world to its knees. Also, there are many oil refineries in the United States protected only rudimentarily. Even a reasonably short interval of oil interruption will have huge negative affects on the American economy, and an extended oil interruption will be devastating.

Terrorists are the wild card in the economy because they are so unpredictable, and their acts are potentially so disastrous. The timing of when another major attack on the United States may occur is just unknown, but it certainly could precede the debt trigger.

There is some thought that our war activities in Iraq are just exacerbating the terrorist problem. Even though our intent of going into this war may have been noble, some Moslem nations read our actions as religious persecution. This is being used as a means of stirring up Moslem youth against America throughout the world, which, if it continues out of control, could affect our economic well being in many countries.

ENERGY PRICES

Energy prices have gone up 25% in 2004, and a shortage of refinery capacity portends bad omens for the immediate future, especially with China's growing thirst for oil. And we have no one to blame for this but ourselves. OPEC gave this country headaches many years ago, and in response, for a few years after the OPEC oil embargo, the United States made real progress on becoming less dependent on foreign oil. Our cars began to get decent gas mileage, people insulated their homes and replaced inefficient windows, and some people even car-pooled. Industry made great strides on energy efficiency, and we were beginning to wean ourselves, at least a little, from foreign oil. Alternate energy sources, such as windmills and solar panels, even got government financial support.

Then, most everything related to energy efficiency stopped. OPEC started to act friendlier, and their lobby in Washington assured us that everything was now okay. We no longer felt at risk from the oil producing countries. We stopped requiring ever higher gas mileage from cars, and in fact, SUV's and big pickups began to dominate the market. Federal funding of new energy sources was either reduced or eliminated. We are now firmly back into the grips of foreign oil.

It was mentioned above that terrorists may attack the Saudi oil refineries. Equally possible is an overthrow of the Saudi government because they have a lot of unrest within their country. The President has made no secret that he wants to sow the seeds of discontent through all the dictatorships that are in the Middle East. However, one of the worst dictatorships is the Saudi government, and Bush may get more than he bargained for if the people in Saudi Arabia decide to get rid of the Saudi family. There is a good chance that whatever government replaces the Saudi's would not have as chummy of a relationship with the United States, and they may even take great satisfaction in reducing the availability of oil to the United States.

DROP IN DOLLAR VALUE

The dollar value has dropped dramatically against most of the world's currencies. This issue is interwoven with all the other KPIVs that can trigger a depression. As mentioned in Chapter 2, this could eventually sour foreign investors on buying Treasury bonds at their current yields, forcing those yields to rise. Those with adjustable rate mortgages, which are generally tied to the Treasury security yields, could find their monthly payments almost doubling, eventually leading to foreclosure on their homes.

One of the reasons oil prices are going up has nothing to do with the availability of oil. It is because oil is priced in dollars. As those dollars lose purchasing power in Europe, the Saudi family can no longer afford as many European products, so they raise oil prices. They are looking to keep their purchasing power the same in Europe, so as the dollar goes down in value, the price of oil will continue to go up.

Imports will become more expensive. Go into Wal-Mart and see how many things are imported, and realize what will happen to the cost of living as the prices on these items increase. Of course, if imports get expensive enough, at some point it then becomes economically viable for United States companies to produce the goods, and that would theoretically help the employment picture in the United States. However, it will take many years of higher import costs before American industry will take a risk of adding capacity. A higher cost of living will come much quicker. And this higher cost of living will cause people to reduce their spending, reducing demand and thus removing the motivation for industry to add capacity.

As the price of imports goes up, the industries in the United States no longer have to price-compete against low-cost imports. The American industries will then feel free to raise prices to help their bottom lines. Here comes inflation!

RECORD BUDGET GAP

The government is doing pretty much what the consumers are doing: spending much more than their income. Now, this problem started well before Bush got into office, although his administration did make it worse. The Clinton administration got a lot of positive press for running a surplus, but to some degree that is part of the price we are paying now. If Greenspan had followed through on his concern in December 1996, where at a speech to the American Enterprise Institute, he made his now famous "irrational exuberance" comment regards the stock market, he would have raised interest rates at that time, or done other things to slow the economy. We probably would have had a mild recession in the late nineties, and Clinton would not have had budget surpluses, since those surpluses were caused by the exorbitant taxes raised from those who cashed in on the over-heated stock market. But the consumer spending spree would probably not have occurred, and we would not be listing consumer debt as the most likely trigger for the coming depression.

Certainly, some of the government overspending was going to occur in any case. When we went into the war with Iraq, the administration ignored those who said it would cost $200 billion. The administration said $50 billion. But at the time I am writing this, the costs are well over $200 billion. There is no end in sight to this war spending.

In 2002 our government gave tax relief to many of its people, especially the wealthy. Now, if this tax reduction had been matched with a similar cut in government spending, it truly would have been a tax break. However, the government reduced no costs and took out a loan to give this tax relief, because the government was already spending more than it had before giving this tax break. This would be like an uncle, who you were quite sure was in debt, sending you a $1,000 check through the mail with a nice note saying that he liked you and just wanted you to have it because he thought you could use it. Then, sometime later, you find that somehow he had taken a loan out in your name, and you or your children will have to repay it someday with interest. You *then* find out that this uncle *also* sent a similar note to a wealthy cousin, who you never really liked, and that the uncle had given *him $5,000* that you and your children will *also* have to help repay. Would you really feel good about these "presents" from your uncle? The taxpayers in the United States seemed to like *their* presents from their Uncle Sam. Even those who got little benefit from the tax reduction seemed to support it.

In the past, when this country went to war, the populace was expected to carry part of the load. In World War II, women went to work in factories, production of automobiles was pretty much put on hold, critical things were rationed, and ordinary people were drafted. The two recent wars in the Middle East, however, were accompanied by a lowering of interest rates and taxes, and resulted in a spending spree by consumers. The cost of the war will be paid by future generations. However, the idea is apparently that the future generations won't *have* any more wars because the Middle East will be democratic, peaceful, and maybe even converting to Christianity. So presumably the future generations will be more than happy to pay the debt for this latest war-to-end-all-wars.

People who live in the United States either think that our government is immune to the possibility of a complete meltdown of our money system, or they are totally unaware that a currency not backed by gold has always succumbed to an overspending situation followed by the printing of money, thereby destroying the currency. They seem unawares that our currency has been without at least some gold backing for less than forty years. Nor do they seem aware that, in an earlier life, their Fed Chief Alan Greenspan was a currency-backed-by-gold fanatic, and many years ago he wrote a paper saying that the very things that are currently happening in our economy were inevitable for a currency not backed by gold. Maybe Greenspan is just trying to prove the points he made in his earlier paper!

BALANCE OF PAYMENTS

In 2003 the United States imported more goods than they exported, and the account deficit for the United States was $531 billion. This deficit was financed by foreigners, mostly the Japanese. This causes multiple problems, certainly not the least of which is that the money we send to other countries to buy *their* goods could be better used to supply employment to our citizens.

Why do people in the United States buy foreign goods? Well, obviously one reason is status. Many people would much rather drive a German or English luxury automobile than a Cadillac because of the image thing. But there are also some very real reasons people buy foreign goods. With very few exceptions, if someone wants a performance sedan that is fun to drive, they have to go to Germany. If they want the smell of fine leather and the richness of real wood in an automobile with classic styling, they buy a Jaguar. If they want great gas mileage in a reasonably priced and superbly built automobile, they go to Japan. Of course, there are exceptions to this, and some of this attitude is left over from the sixties, when American automobiles had real quality issues. But those negative attitudes were based on real experiences, which take years to forget. Every year automobiles are rated for quality by various consumer groups, and to this day, few American automobiles are generally very high on that list. So the problem has not completely vanished.

Of course, the other reason people buy imported goods is low cost. People can put American flags on their automobiles and support foreign wars that have little justification, but when it comes to buying an item made in the good-old-USA, or a less expensive one made overseas, we know which one wins.

Just like high stock prices, the trade deficit alone will probably not be the trigger for a depression. But it will contribute to how bad the recession will be. And if we don't even have an industry that makes what the American consumer wants to buy, it will be more difficult to climb out of a depression.

INFLATION

Inflation is the 700 pound gorilla, and he (she?) will probably demonstrate his terror by driving the debt bubble to untenable levels. We already covered how the Fed is raising short term interest rates, affecting credit cards and home equity loans. We also saw how the CMT rate is increasing, which will cause an increase in adjustable mortgage rates. The declining value of the dollar against foreign currencies will make imports more expensive. Everything points to inflation. As we have mentioned earlier, in the seventies we had inflation well over 10% for several years, so inflation can be devastating, especially to people on fixed incomes.

Now, the flip side is deflation. From 1930 through 1932, prices deflated approximately 25%, and it wasn't until the forties that this was reversed. However, in the coming depression this is unlikely to happen for two reasons. First, in 2002 the Fed, through its governor Benjamin Bernanke, announced to the world that they would print money before allowing deflation to happen. That certainly would stop deflation, but just like chemotherapy on many types of cancers, the side effects may not be trivial. In fact, the cure could indeed kill the patient by ruining the viability of the U. S. currency. Currency maintains its value only by its relative scarcity. This is especially true for any currency without gold backing, which has been the case with the U.S. currency since 1968, when Nixon pulled the final plug on gold. Too much currency in the market makes its value go down, which leads to inflation.

The other reason that deflation is less likely than it was in the 1929 depression is that industry has not increased capacity, or hired additional workers, for many years. Industry has not been convinced that there truly has been an economic recovery, so their response to any increase in orders has been to work their current employees additional hours or to outsource to other countries. They didn't add excess capacity. Also, there has been no great buildup of inventory. So when the depression comes, industry will not be forced to lower prices to keep excess capacity utilized or to get rid of excess inventories. They *will* downsize their labor force, but since they are already at a lean level, the effect will not be as dramatic as in the 1929 depression.

The exception to the no-deflation statement above will probably be in housing. In this century home building has been rampant, and prices have been inflating dramatically. This is likely to be corrected in the initial few years of the depression. There truly has been a housing price bubble. This deflation in housing could be quite dramatic in some housing markets where prices have exploded, and the deflated values of these homes could end up being far less than their mortgages. This could cause many people to walk away from their mortgages, leaving the banks with a large number of homes they need to unload on the market, starting a spiral of downward housing prices. This will have no affect on those who are able to keep their homes. And this may offer some relative bargains for those who are living in apartments as the depression progresses and have the resources to purchase a home. Deflation will probably be limited to housing. Most things will inflate.

Again, inflation alone probably won't trigger inflation. It will do its nasty thing through consumer debt.

INTEREST RATES

Interest rates by themselves won't cause a depression. But as we saw in Chapter 2 on consumer debt, the increased interest rates on credit cards, home equity loans, and mortgages, especially on adjustable rate mortgages, can easily push someone from being borderline-economically to being in deep financial trouble. Also, interest rates are not independent of inflation. Some of the time there is a response delay from one to the other, but they generally track together.

CHAPTER 6
Could This Book Be Completely Wrong?

Of course this book could be wrong! There is an overwhelming amount of data on the economy, and trying to sort and pick what is critical is not without some risk. However, I think if anyone looks at the supporting data in this book, and the logical continuity of the story told, they will agree that the likelihood of this book being completely wrong is quite low. Sure, the timing of the forecasted depression could be off a year, and the severity of the downturn is open for disagreement. But it is very difficult to see how the next few years can be too much different than forecasted. When I was trying to write this chapter, I kept coming up with additional scenarios on how things could be worse than what I predicted, but I found few scenarios on how things could be much better.

Of course, there is always the possibility of a miracle. Bill Gates and his billionaire friends could decide that it is not in their best interests for this country to get into a severe funk, and they could get together and offer to relieve the consumers of some of their debt. But even under such an unlikely scenario, the most it would do is delay the depression. As long as the consumer keeps spending more than what he or she makes, we will be heading for a recession or depression. That is what makes the arguments presented in this book so compelling.

Kurt Richebacher, former chief economist of the Dresdner Bank, and author of the monthly newsletter "The Richebacher Letter", discussed the United States economy during an interview. He said that credit can't keep an economy growing, and he believes that a debt crisis is coming. He thinks that encouraging debt as a way of growing an economy is insanity. Richebacher also believes that the refinancing that occurred due to the lower interest rates has made the debt bubble much worse.

Peter Schiff, CEO and chief global strategist of Euro Pacific Capital, in a January 2005 article on AOL, said that Americans have been going into debt for many years, but in the last five years it has gotten much worse. In agreement with this book, he thinks that, to keep investment coming from abroad, interest rates will have to rise substantially.

Perhaps an innovation will save the United States' economy. No one can preclude that possibility. Maybe somewhere in this country there is some clever inventor who has a device that makes energy out of water. The process only works here in the United States, and it is cheap and easy to develop. We will no longer be dependent on foreign oil; in fact we will be exporting this energy to the Middle East because it is so cheap and so clean. But I am not aware of any invention of the sort, or of any other new technology that will be a game changer and save our economy, so this possibility is not included in my reasoning. And any innovation that has not yet gotten the attention of the press is probably many years away from becoming commercially viable, and even more years away from having a major economic influence. It certainly isn't obvious that we are going to be rescued by innovation.

Consumers could again do the refinance-their-home thing, as long as mortgage rates remain low. This could again allow them to switch from high interest credit card debt to lower mortgage rate debt. However, this option is ending as mortgage rates rise, and in any case, this would only be a temporary fix as long as the consumer persists in spending more than he or she earns.

Consumers could slow down their spending just enough to keep their debt payments barely manageable, and they could just continue on at a zero savings rate. But this would still cause the economy to slow, not quite as much as the scenario I showed earlier in the book of paying down the debt and starting to save, but it would still be a slowdown. This would perhaps cause a longer recession that just goes on seemingly forever. However, when you consider how *any* slowdown will cause a spiral of lower earnings, market drops, unemployment, foreclosure of homes, more bankruptcies, etc.; it is hard to envision anything but a full blown depression.

Maybe interest rates on the treasury securities won't go up because foreign investors feel that their other investment options all have even *bigger* risks than investing in our bonds, even at a low interest rate. Then, the payments on adjustable rate mortgages would not go up. But the 1-year Constant Maturity Treasury (CMT) index, which is related to the average yield on U.S. Treasury securities, has already started to rise. And we saw that just the fact that the consumer is reaching zero on his savings rate will cause either a slowing of spending or an even greater increase of debt. Consumers will eventually have to slow their spending, and this will cause a downturn of the economy.

Maybe the Fed will reverse its direction on increasing short term interest rates, if it senses a slowing of the economy. This reversal, however, would cause panic in the financial markets because it would signal that the Fed is getting bad vibes on the economy. The stock market's reaction would be to drop precipitously, in which case the market drop could become the depression trigger.

Companies no longer invest much for the future, at least compared to what they did in years past. The stock market is overpriced. Our country spends more than it brings in with taxation, and our trade deficit just keeps getting worse. Terrorists are driving our country's direction, and our president keeps reminding us to be fearful. We go to wars that are not winnable, and we are slowly selling off our country's assets to Europe, Japan, and China. Social Security Retirement, Medicare, and Medicaid are getting ready to pounce on our economy.

But it will likely be consumer debt that will trigger the coming depression. Unless this book is completely wrong!

CHAPTER 7
Can't the Fed Stop the Coming Depression?

First, let's describe what the Fed (Federal Reserve System) is, and the limits of its influence on the economy. The Fed was established by Congress in 1913 as a means to foster a sound money and financial system. It basically is the central bank of the United States.

The Fed has twelve regional Reserve Banks and a Board of Governors appointed by the president. They have a Federal Open Market Committee, with twelve members that set the overnight Fed Funds Rate. They also influence how much money is in the market, and therefore the interest rates, by buying and selling government bonds. When they buy bonds they are injecting more money into the economy, which tends to make money available for borrowing at lower rates, stimulating the economy. The Fed selling bonds does the opposite.

Alan Greenspan is the Chairman of the Board of Governors and is the most publicly visible of all the Board members. When Alan speaks, the world listens! A negative comment from Chairman Greenspan, like when he made his infamous comment on "irrational exuberance" at a dinner at the American Enterprise Institute in 1996, can cause a tremor in stock markets around the world.

Although the Fed is technically not a branch of the federal government and can operate independently, since all of the members of the Board of Governors are appointed by the president and confirmed by the Senate, they *are* influenced by political pressure, especially when a considered action by the Fed may slow the economy. Also, they are probably not immune to their star status when the economy seems to be humming.

It was mentioned above that the Fed influences interest rates by adjusting the Fed Funds rate, and by buying or selling government bonds. But there are powerful outside influences beyond the Fed's control that also affect interest rates. One of the biggest risks on current Treasury security yields, which Greenspan warned of recently, is that the Europeans and Japanese, who are buying many of these securities, will start to demand higher rates to balance out the huge losses they are experiencing through the value drop of the dollar versus their currencies. The Fed has little control over this. And perhaps an even bigger risk is that these countries start to sell back their current holdings in our stocks and bonds. Where would the United States get the money? The stock market would crash because of the sell pressure, and the government would have to print money to put liquidity in the market, causing worldwide panic in the dollar, and causing inflation. Again, these events are largely out of the Fed's control.

If you read Woodward's *Maestro: Greenspan's Fed and the American Boom*, you will get an insider's look at the workings of the Fed, and it does not always give you a warm and fuzzy feeling. There is much dissention within the Board of Governors when actions are called for, with other members of the Board often having to dissuade Greenspan from following his first reactions to a problem. Also, their actions often seem to be very short-sighted, just delaying a problem into the future, when it then worsens.

The Fed's actions since the early nineties are indicative. They lowered the Fed's fund rate to 3 percent in 1992, over-stimulating the economy, especially the stock market. This is what eventually triggered Greenspan's comment on "irrational exuberance" at a dinner at the American Enterprise Institute in 1996. He knew that stock prices were getting outrageously high, and Alan warned that "we should not underestimate or become complacent about the complexity of the interactions of the asset markets and the economy." Yet, while he was making this statement, the Fed was allowing the M3 money supply, which had been reasonably stable for five years, to start rising dramatically. This was like pouring gasoline on a fire that was already burning out of control. Apparently due to political pressure, and despite Greenspan's publicly expressed concern, the Fed did nothing to dampen the "irrational exuberance" on stock prices, and the stock market continued to rise for another four years. This certainly felt fine to everybody during those years, but it is like someone over-indulging on rich meals for years – eventually a price would have to be paid.

In 2000 the market made a downward correction. Some like to refer to this as the Dot-Com Crash, but that is an over-simplification. Almost all stocks were affected, not just the new technology stocks. Stock prices had just gotten so high that some investors decided to cut and run.

The stock market drop in 2000 did not trigger much of an economic slowdown because it had nothing to do with the basic economy. Even the 9-11 terrorist attack, which came shortly after the market drop began, did not trigger much of a recession. But to make *sure* it didn't, the Fed lowered interest rates dramatically. This was supposed to encourage spending by consumers (who were already spending too much), which would then cause industry to expand and begin hiring more employees, thus getting the economy back to the high-growth it had in the past. But this did not work. Yes, it got the consumers to refinance their homes and go even further in debt. But this influx of consumer money did nothing but keep the GDP growing at its prior rate. It did not stimulate the economy to expand. Neither did the tax reduction put in place by Congress. Consumer debt and the reduction in the savings rate are the only things that have kept the economy afloat.

Since the lower interest rates did not have their intended effect of causing the economy to expand, the Fed is now raising interest rates back up because they have a fear of inflation. But this increase in interest rates will drive the consumer over his debt maximum and will trigger the depression.

So the Fed, by first over-stimulating the economy in 1992, and then by not slowing it in 1996 when they saw it was spinning out of control, avoided a probable minor recession in the mid-nineties. By lowering interest rates dramatically early in this century, they again avoided a recession and set the United States up for a major depression starting in 2006 or 2007.

PART II
The Market is Bad Now,
But It Could Be Good in the Future

CHAPTER 8: Detail on the Current Market being a Bad Buy
Even without the forecasted depression, at current stock prices, TIPS would be a better investment than the stock market.

CHAPTER 9: When to Get Back Into the Stock Market
The stock market becomes reasonably priced when the S&P 500 price/dividend ratio is 17.2 or less.

CHAPTER 10: Once You are Back in the Stock Market
Index funds are a better investment than actively managed mutual funds. But buying the most recent stocks added to the Dow, when the S&P 500 price/dividend is 17.2 or below, may be better than either.

CHAPTER 8
Detail on Why the Stock Market Is
Currently Such a Bad Investment

As I was writing this book and discussing the subject with others, it seemed like I had little trouble getting people to believe that we are on the edge of a coming depression. They knew that they or their acquaintances had been living beyond their means and had been borrowing to their maximum limits. They also knew there would be a price to be paid, although I don't think they fully appreciated how high that price will be.

The thing I had the most trouble with was convincing people that the stock market is currently a very bad investment. The media has done phenomenally well on convincing people that a buy-and-hold strategy in the market is the best and only way that people should invest long-term. The old saw of buying low and selling high is apparently felt to be invalid. The investment gurus have convinced people that this approach might cause people to miss the biggest market jumps because they may be out of the market. On account of this belief that the stock market is always best, *this chapter will get into some detail on why the market is sometimes just over priced, and like anything else in the world when it is dramatically overpriced, it is then a very bad buy!*

Market Myths

Market Myth #1: The stock market has always been the best place for the long-term investor.

Between 1982 and 2000, the stock market had an unusually large and sustained upward trend. These recent 18 years are *not* typical of most market time periods! Within the last 100 years, there have been several periods of twenty years when the market was *not* the best investment.

Market Myth #2: The stock market is a long term investment vehicle, with most investors getting the benefits of many years of accumulated capital appreciation through compounding and reinvestment.

Intended or not, few investors leave their money in the stock market for extended periods. They usually have some reason to withdraw funds. Even if a savings program does persist for a large number of years, since investment input is spread throughout the time period, only a small portion of the invested funds get the full benefits of long-term appreciation and reinvestment.

Market Myth #3: Although the risk due to market volatility is high for short-term investors, longer term investors are not affected by this risk.

Although longer term investors are *less* affected by market risk (price variability) than short-term investors, the investment horizon for most investors is not long enough to discount the risk completely.

We will be spending some time trying to dispel these myths.

In the data below, I will show why, even if we weren't on the edge of a depression, the stock market would still be a bad investment at this time.

Before we get into any more detail on the stock market, it is time to further define TIPS, the Treasury Inflation Protected Securities we alluded to in several earlier chapters.

TIPS, Treasury Inflation Protected Securities, have only been available since 1997. TIPS can be bought and sold through a broker or bank, but they will charge a fee. They can be bought directly from the government for no fee. For information you can call 800-722-2678, or log onto www.publicdebt.treas.gov. They can be purchased in minimum denominations of $1,000, in $1,000 multiples.

The rate of interest to be paid on a TIPS investment is established at the time of purchase and stays constant for the life of the security. However, every six months, the face value of the security is indexed with inflation, and the interest rate is then paid on this adjusted security value. This insulates the effective rate of interest on the security from inflation.

TIPS are also available as a stock security (TIP is the stock symbol) or in mutual funds. Buying TIPS as a stock security does increase volatility somewhat because the fund in which the security is held can decide to sell the security rather than hold it to maturity. Holding a security to maturity is the only way to guarantee the principal.

TIPS have an interest rate assigned at time of purchase, which since their introduction, has varied anywhere from 1.7% to 4%, based on the auction results which determine this interest rate. 3% is the assumed interest rate for calculations in this book. The base purchase value of the TIPS is adjusted semi-annually based on the inflation rate. So if you purchase a TIPS for $1,000, and inflation goes up 4% the first six months, then the security base value becomes $1,040 for the next six months, to adjust for inflation. The next six month's interest rate will then be calculated using $1,040 as a base, not $1000. This semi-annual adjustment goes on for the life of the TIPS, and after maturity you get the accumulated inflated value of the TIPS. TIPS are exempt from state and local income taxes. In the unlikely event that there is deflation during the term of the security, the US Treasury guarantees the full original principal at maturity.

There can be some negatives, like you are taxed annually on any gain in the inflated value of the TIPS. But this negative is cancelled if you have them in a Roth IRA (which will be discussed in a later chapter) or in any other tax-shelter. For now, know that these are a low risk, conservative saving means, and TIPS will be used for baseline comparisons throughout the book.

There is another similar government savings instrument that offers identical inflation-protection. They are Series I Savings Bonds. These have some advantages over TIPS, if someone is saving outside of an IRA or Roth tax-sheltered mode, in that the interest and inflation adjustments on the Series I Savings Bonds are accumulated tax-free as the bond builds to maturity. Also, some people may qualify for tax relief, if the gains are used for college expenses. The Series I Savings Bonds have no secondary market such as TIPS, but they can be "put" back (sorry, a government term) into the US Treasury, with some possible loss of interest, if someone needs to get their money out before maturity.

There are subtle individual advantages for both TIPS and Series I Savings Bonds. A case can be made that the Series I Savings Bonds are best for the period of time when you are *saving for* retirement, since no regular payout of interest occurs, whereas the TIPS may be best for the years of actual retirement when you are counting on using the interest for income purposes. However, the differences between the two are small enough that both can be considered equivalent as far as their effect on the savings analysis being done in this book. Know that Series I Savings Bonds are considered an equivalent investment wherever TIPS are referred to in this text; it is for simplicity only that I refer to TIPS throughout the book.

Inflation has to be a big concern. That is why we have chosen to use TIPS as our baseline savings. Inflation has been relatively low in recent years, but in the years 1973 through 1981, inflation averaged over 9% per year. That means that in those nine years a fixed amount of money lost over half its value. There is no reason to take that kind of risk on savings, when TIPS will protect you from such a devastating loss.

Note that although TIPS are *almost* a zero-risk investment, they are not totally without risk. Let's assume you buy a TIPS paying 3% interest, and for some reason immediately after you bought this security, the stock market and the economy just started to take off, with real earnings and dividends rising dramatically while inflation remained low. As we have noted in this book, we find this scenario highly unlikely, but it is theoretically possible. In the situation just described, the value of the TIPS security, if you had to sell before maturity, would likely have gone down because of the higher gains being realized in the stock market. We have to really stretch to envision this happening, but as we said, it is possible. Also, if the interest rates on more recent TIPS are dramatically higher than on the TIPS you purchased, the value on the earlier TIPS will be reduced if you have to sell. Holding them until maturity would still guarantee the principal, but you would have been getting a lower interest rate during that hold period versus the later TIPS.

Now, let's get back to the stock market.

Modeling the Past Stock Market Performance at Current Dividend Yields

When one looks at the gains that were made on the stock market in the last 103 years, we find that roughly 1/3 of the gains came from inflation, 1/3 came from the stock prices going up *in excess of* inflation, and 1/3 came from dividends. Since the percent dividend is now substantially lower than it was in the past, this means that if the market price continues at its current level, the dividend portion of future gains will be much less than in the past. So let's see if we had a similar stock performance as in the last 103 years, but at our current lower dividend rate, how our investment would look versus a 3% TIPS alternative investment. After all, we are starting at the lower dividend baseline if we enter the stock market at this time, and a repeat performance on the stock market is a fairly optimistic outlook.

Below, in Figures 8-1 through 8-3, we are going to do a "pretend" model of the stock market since 1900. In doing this "model", we are going to do a "replay" of the exact S&P 500 performance, including the same inflation numbers as the last 103 years, but *at current dividend rates*. The dividend yield for the last 7 years has been 1.43%, which is far less than historical dividend yields. This is mostly a reflection of the extremely high price of stocks, rather than some dramatic change in dividend policy. Without a *dramatic* drop in stock prices, this dividend ratio is likely to stay the same for the immediate future. When we "replay" the last 103 year's S&P 500 performance, we are going to assume this 1.43% dividend yield, then compare the stock market performance versus the almost zero risk 3% TIPS performance. Again, the only difference from the prior market performance is to incorporate recent dividend yields onto the past 103 year's stock market performance.

The numbers within each of the tables are the total gains for the accumulative number of appropriate years. For example, in Figure 8-1, the first number under "5 yr TIPS" is 1.263. That means that if TIPS had been available at that time, and they were paying an assumed 3% interest, their total gain, including inflation, between the years 1900 and 1905, would have been 26.3%. Equally, the first number under "5 yr S&P" is 1.491. That means that the total gain on the S&P 500 for the five years between 1900 and 1905, with 1.43% dividends, would have been 49.1%. In 1906, the five year previous gain for TIPS would have been 28.9%; whereas the five year previous gain for the S&P 500 would have been 32.9%.

5 Year Replayed "Buy-and-Hold" with 1.43% Dividend Yields

Replay Year	5 year TIPS	5 year S&P	Replay Year	5 year TIPS	5 year S&P	Replay Year	5 year TIPS	5 year S&P
1900			1935	**0.998**	0.940	1969	**1.393**	1.166
1901			1936	1.113	2.270	1970	**1.442**	1.070
1902			1937	1.271	1.643	1971	**1.439**	1.364
1903			1938	1.227	1.404	1972	**1.444**	1.314
1904			1939	1.210	1.412	1973	**1.497**	1.008
1905	1.263	1.491	1940	**1.184**	0.845	1974	**1.582**	0.800
1906	1.289	1.329	1941	**1.280**	0.543	1975	**1.602**	1.051
1907	**1.300**	0.876	1942	**1.355**	0.995	1976	**1.626**	1.130
1908	1.300	1.476	1943	**1.432**	0.948	1977	**1.676**	0.865
1909	**1.353**	1.340	1944	**1.464**	1.141	1978	**1.681**	1.058
1910	**1.322**	1.018	1945	1.486	1.762	1979	**1.695**	1.690
1911	**1.289**	0.994	1946	1.594	1.890	1980	**1.781**	1.616
1912	1.284	1.533	1947	1.591	1.681	1981	**1.848**	1.224
1913	**1.310**	0.956	1948	**1.591**	1.398	1982	**1.799**	1.588
1914	**1.255**	0.766	1949	**1.525**	1.355	1983	1.715	1.842
1915	**1.279**	1.125	1950	**1.579**	1.262	1984	1.577	1.663
1916	**1.407**	1.155	1951	1.420	1.668	1985	1.458	1.671
1917	**1.606**	0.778	1952	1.318	1.865	1986	1.356	2.121
1918	**1.887**	1.057	1953	1.290	1.752	1987	1.364	1.886
1919	**2.133**	1.318	1954	1.307	2.305	1988	1.372	1.808
1920	**2.146**	0.771	1955	1.240	2.392	1989	1.381	2.269
1921	**1.711**	0.802	1956	1.206	2.108	1990	1.411	1.678
1922	**1.423**	1.397	1957	1.231	1.615	1991	1.438	1.849
1923	**1.214**	1.182	1958	1.243	2.389	1992	1.417	1.893
1924	1.064	1.232	1959	1.273	1.787	1993	1.395	1.803
1925	1.072	2.011	1960	1.285	1.372	1994	1.370	1.395
1926	1.185	1.979	1961	1.257	1.646	1995	1.325	2.002
1927	1.186	2.143	1962	1.238	1.694	1996	1.328	1.907
1928	1.146	2.999	1963	1.237	1.459	1997	1.313	2.391
1929	1.153	2.224	1964	1.228	1.519	1998	1.299	2.829
1930	1.046	1.291	1965	1.235	1.708	1999	1.299	3.434
1931	**0.962**	0.646	1966	**1.268**	1.205	2000	1.309	2.301
1932	**0.885**	0.419	1967	1.289	1.641	2001	1.292	1.664
1933	**0.902**	0.445	1968	1.327	1.486	2002	**1.290**	0.973
1934	**0.910**	0.475				2003	**1.297**	0.971

Figure 8-1

Noting the **bold** numbers that indicate when the prior five year TIPS beat the prior five year S&P 500 stocks, 46% of the time the prior five year TIPS beat the prior five year stock market results, when the last 103 years of the stock market were replayed at the current 1.43% dividend yields.

Again, the numbers within the table are the total gains for the accumulative number of appropriate years. For example, in Figure 8-2 below, the first number under "10 yr TIPS" is 1.669. That means that if TIPS had been available at that time, and they were paying an assumed 3% interest, their total gain, including inflation, between the years 1900 and 1910, would have been 66.9%. Equally, the first number under "10 yr S&P" is 1.518. That means that the total gain on the S&P 500 for the ten years between 1900 and 1910 was 51.8%. In 1911, the ten year previous gain for TIPS would have been 66.1%; whereas the ten year previous gain for the S&P 500 was 32.1%.

10 Year Replayed "Buy-and-Hold" with 1.43% Dividend Yields

Replay Year	10 yr TIPS	10 yr S&P		Replay Year	10 yr TIPS	10 yr S&P		Replay Year	10 yr TIPS	10 yr S&P
1900				1935	1.044	1.214		1969	1.711	1.772
1901				1936	1.071	1.468		1970	1.780	1.828
1902				1937	**1.125**	0.688		1971	**1.825**	1.645
1903				1938	**1.107**	0.625		1972	1.861	2.156
1904				1939	**1.101**	0.671		1973	**1.987**	1.499
1905				1940	**1.182**	0.795		1974	**2.204**	0.932
1906				1941	**1.425**	1.233		1975	**2.309**	1.125
1907				1942	**1.721**	1.635		1976	**2.339**	1.542
1908				1943	**1.758**	1.332		1977	**2.420**	1.136
1909				1944	**1.771**	1.612		1978	**2.517**	1.067
1910	**1.669**	1.518		1945	**1.759**	1.489		1979	**2.680**	1.351
1911	**1.661**	1.321		1946	**2.040**	1.027		1980	**2.852**	1.698
1912	**1.669**	1.343		1947	**2.155**	1.673		1981	**3.004**	1.384
1913	**1.702**	1.410		1948	**2.279**	1.326		1982	**3.016**	1.373
1914	**1.698**	1.027		1949	**2.233**	1.546		1983	**2.883**	1.949
1915	**1.690**	1.145		1950	**2.345**	2.224		1984	2.673	2.811
1916	**1.813**	1.148		1951	2.264	3.153		1985	2.597	2.700
1917	**2.062**	1.193		1952	2.096	3.135		1986	2.506	2.597
1918	**2.471**	1.011		1953	2.053	2.451		1987	2.454	2.994
1919	**2.676**	1.010		1954	1.993	3.123		1988	2.354	3.330
1920	**2.745**	0.868		1955	1.958	3.019		1989	2.179	3.774
1921	**2.407**	0.926		1956	1.713	3.516		1990	2.058	2.803
1922	**2.284**	1.087		1957	1.622	3.012		1991	1.950	3.923
1923	**2.292**	1.250		1958	1.603	4.186		1992	1.933	3.571
1924	**2.270**	1.623		1959	1.664	4.119		1993	1.914	3.260
1925	**2.302**	1.551		1960	1.594	3.281		1994	1.891	3.165
1926	**2.028**	1.587		1961	1.516	3.469		1995	1.869	3.360
1927	1.687	2.993		1962	1.524	2.736		1996	1.909	3.525
1928	1.392	3.545		1963	1.538	3.485		1997	1.861	4.527
1929	1.227	2.740		1964	1.563	2.714		1998	1.812	5.101
1930	1.122	2.596		1965	1.587	2.342		1999	1.779	4.792
1931	1.140	1.279		1966	1.594	1.984		2000	1.735	4.608
1932	**1.050**	0.897		1967	1.596	2.780		2001	1.715	3.173
1933	1.034	1.335		1968	1.641	2.168		2002	1.694	2.327
1934	1.049	1.057						2003	1.685	2.747

Figure 8-2

Noting the numbers in **bold**, in this case 48% of the time the prior ten year TIPS beat the prior ten year S&P 500 stock market results, when the last 103 years of the stock market were replayed at the current 1.43% dividend yields.

Again, the numbers within the table are the total gains for the accumulative number of appropriate years. For example, in Figure 8-3 below, the first number under "20 yr TIPS" is 4.582. That means that if TIPS had been available at that time, and they were paying an assumed 3% interest, their total gain, including inflation, between the years 1900 and 1920, would have been 358.2%. Equally, the first number under "20 yr S&P" is 1.317. That means that the total gain on the S&P 500 for the twenty years between 1900 and 1920 was 31.7%. In 1921, the twenty year previous gain for TIPS would have been 299.8%; whereas the twenty year previous gain for the S&P 500 was 22.3%.

20 Year Replayed "Buy-and-Hold" with 1.43% Dividend Yields

Replay Year	20 yr TIPS	20 yr S&P	Replay Year	20 yr TIPS	20 yr S&P	Replay Year	20 yr TIPS	20 yr S&P
1900			1935	**2.404**	1.883	1969	2.847	7.297
1901			1936	2.172	2.329	1970	2.837	5.998
1902			1937	1.898	2.059	1971	2.766	5.705
1903			1938	1.541	2.217	1972	2.837	5.900
1904			1939	1.350	1.839	1973	3.054	5.222
1905			1940	1.326	2.063	1974	**3.445**	2.531
1906			1941	**1.624**	1.578	1975	**3.664**	2.634
1907			1942	**1.807**	1.467	1976	**3.729**	3.058
1908			1943	**1.817**	1.778	1977	**3.863**	3.159
1909			1944	**1.858**	1.704	1978	**4.130**	2.312
1910			1945	**1.837**	1.807	1979	**4.586**	2.394
1911			1946	**2.184**	1.507	1980	**5.077**	3.103
1912			1947	**2.424**	1.151	1981	**5.481**	2.275
1913			1948	**2.523**	0.829	1982	**5.612**	2.961
1914			1949	**2.458**	1.038	1983	**5.727**	2.920
1915			1950	**2.772**	1.767	1984	**5.891**	2.621
1916			1951	3.225	3.887	1985	**5.996**	3.037
1917			1952	3.609	5.125	1986	**5.863**	4.005
1918			1953	**3.608**	3.263	1987	**5.940**	3.402
1919			1954	3.530	5.034	1988	**5.924**	3.552
1920	**4.582**	1.317	1955	3.443	4.496	1989	**5.840**	5.099
1921	**3.998**	1.223	1956	3.494	3.609	1990	**5.869**	4.760
1922	**3.813**	1.460	1957	3.495	5.039	1991	**5.857**	5.427
1923	**3.901**	1.763	1958	3.654	5.551	1992	**5.830**	4.903
1924	**3.854**	1.667	1959	3.715	6.368	1993	5.519	6.352
1925	**3.891**	1.777	1960	3.738	7.297	1994	5.056	8.899
1926	**3.676**	1.821	1961	3.432	10.94	1995	4.854	9.072
1927	3.479	3.571	1962	3.196	8.580	1996	4.785	9.157
1928	3.440	3.582	1963	3.156	8.540	1997	4.567	13.56
1929	**3.283**	2.766	1964	3.116	8.478	1998	4.265	16.99
1930	**3.079**	2.252	1965	3.107	7.073	1999	3.876	18.08
1931	**2.744**	1.185	1966	2.730	6.973	2000	3.569	12.92
1932	**2.399**	0.976	1967	2.589	8.375	2001	3.345	12.45
1933	**2.369**	1.669	1968	2.631	9.076	2002	3.275	8.310
1934	**2.381**	1.716				2003	3.225	8.956

Figure 8-3

Figure 8-3 numbers in **bold** show that 54% of the time the 20 year prior TIPS beat the prior S&P 500 stock market 20 year results, when the last 103 years of the stock market were replayed at the current 1.43% dividend yields.

The 20 year hold result wasn't only due to the earlier dates of the replayed years. Look at the most recent 30 years in the above spreadsheet, and you will see that 63% of the time the TIPS out-performed the stock market. Dividends have been an important element in market gain, and with the current high stock market prices, the effect of the dividends is reduced dramatically. That makes the TIPS option very attractive. Approximately half the time, in an equivalent market of the last 103 years, you would have beaten the market with an almost zero risk investment, when you assume dividends similar to present!

> "A sacred tenet of economics is that return is directly proportional to risk. On that basis, stocks have the most risk, corporate bonds next, and Treasury Bills (cash) have the lowest risk."

It appears that this "sacred tenet of economics" may not apply at the very high market prices we are currently experiencing! 3% TIPS, an almost zero-risk investment, beat the stock market return 54% of the time on a 20 year hold, when the last 103 years of stock market performance were "replayed" with current dividend yields! Later in the book, we show that even if the TIPS are paying as little as 1.5%, the relative advantage of TIPS doesn't change much because of its tie to inflation, which is often the largest portion of its yield.

So even if we weren't expecting a severe depression, and instead the future stock market repeats exactly as it has for the last 103 years, but with current dividend yields, the market would be no better investment than the nearly zero-risk TIPS. With the risks inherent in the stock market, this data indicates that investing in the stock market at current stock prices is a bad choice, whether or not you believe we are heading into a depression.

Is the Market Overpriced?

In an earlier chapter, we used the price/dividend ratio to determine that the current stock market is dramatically overpriced, at least versus historical values. There are other more esoteric ways to evaluate the fair market value of the stock market, which we will now review. These other methods are being shown only to emphasize that, no matter what method we use for this evaluation, we find that the stock market is currently way over priced. As we already stated, the price/dividend ratio is a fully acceptable way of determining the correct market price, and it is the key measurement we use in this book. So those of you without a keen interest in the other methods can just quickly gloss over the details of the other methods discussed in this chapter.

One way to estimate the correct stock market value is based on an expected Future Discounted Dividend Stream. Two of the reference books, Smithers and Wright's *Valuing Wall Street* and Bernstein's *The Four Pillars of Investing,* use this method. The other method is to estimate the stock market's value by determining the market companies' replacement value. Both Smithers and Wright's *Valuing Wall Street* and Stein and DeMuth's *Yes, You can Time the Market* use similar methods related to fundamental values. You can refer to these books for more detail. I will briefly review both methods here to give the reader some understanding of each.

70 years ago, Irving Fisher, former professor at Yale, came up with a way to evaluate individual stocks, or in our case, the S&P 500 index. It is similar to what we discussed earlier, that a company is worth its Future Discounted Dividend Stream. The formula derived by Irving Fisher is:

Market Value = Current Dividend / (DR – Dividend Rate of Growth).

Let me explain each of the terms in this formula.

Market Value is, in this case, the fair market price of the S&P 500 stock index. Once we calculate this value, we can then compare it to the actual price of the S&P 500 that is announced daily, when they report how the stock market did. In this case, we are trying to calculate what the price, or Market Value, *should* be, based on the Current Dividends being paid by the companies in the S&P 500, and how much those dividends are increasing every year, which is the Dividend Rate of Growth.

The DR is the yield we expect from the stock market to make it a viable investment. Because the stock market is generally thought to have more risk and variation than many alternate investments, people won't normally invest in the stock market unless its expected yield is higher than more conservative investments, like government bonds. In very positive investment time periods, where people feel very good about the stock market's likelihood to go up, they may assume a small amount of stock market risk and therefore a smaller DR. In hard times, like in the midst of a depression, when investors are sour on the market, investors may demand a very large market risk adjustment, which makes the DR higher. We will evaluate the Market Value with two extremes of DR, which includes the assumed market risk.

First, let's see how the market is priced if we assume a positive investor attitude. We have assumed throughout this book that on the average, we can get 3% from TIPS, a very low risk investment. We will assume for this analysis that future inflation will be 3.5% (the same as historical), and we want an added 1.5% for stock market risk. This sums to 8.0%. This is our DR. This is a very low DR because it assumes that people *want* to invest in the stock market and are not requiring it to pay more than 1.5% over a conservative investment like TIPS. When the stock market is very popular, as it was in the nineties, the DR is small. Let's now calculate what the price of the S&P 500 should be under this positive investment attitude, which in early 2005 is still the current investment attitude towards the stock market.

Historical dividend growth (Dividend Rate of Growth) has been 4.2%. For those inquisitive types, we calculated this number using the Key Numbers shown in the Appendix. Using Excel, we multiplied the % dividend times the S&P 500 price for both the values in years 1900 and 2003, to get the dividend values for both years, which are 103 years apart. If you multiply the year 1900 dividend value times 1.042 to the 103rd power, you will see that it equals the dividend value in year 2003. The 1.042 value is where the 4.2% Dividend Rate of Growth value came from. While doing the above calculation, we also determined the Current Dividend to use in the equation, which is the year 2003 dividend value, which was obtained by multiplying the % dividend in year 2003 (1.69, from the Appendix) times the year 2003 S&P 500 price ($1112, from the Appendix), giving $18.79.

Plugging these values into the above equation we get:
Market Value = Current Dividend / (DR – Dividend Rate of Growth)
Market Value = $18.79 / (0.08 – 0.042)
Market Value = $494, versus the $1112 S&P price at the end of year 2003.

On the above basis, the market was 125% overpriced at the end of year 2003, even when assuming a very positive investor attitude.

If investors become sour on the stock market, which will happen if investors begin to believe that we are going to be in a depression soon, then the investors will not want to invest in the market unless they foresee profits far in excess of what they could get on a more conservative investment such as TIPS. We will now recalculate the Irving Fisher formula for Market Value, with a negative attitude towards the market.

With a negative attitude on the stock market, the investor will demand more than an added 1.5% premium for market risk. Let's assume that the investor demands an extra 4%. This means that the new DR will be 3% TIPS, plus 3.5% inflation, plus 4% extra for stock market risk. This sums to 10.5%, or 0.105.

The other values in the equation stay the same as in the earlier chapter.
Market Value = Current Dividend / (DR – Dividend Rate of Growth).
Market Value = $18.79 / (0.105 – 0.042).
Market Value = $298, versus the $1112 S&P price at the end of year 2003.

On the above basis, the market, as of the end of year 2003, was 273% overpriced. This is more likely to be the value of interest because we want to know how far the market will drop in the midst of a depression, when the investors will truly be negative.

Note that there have been periods in the past where investors have demanded a DR value *far greater* than the 0.105 we used in the above calculation.

Another way to evaluate an investment is to determine its replacement cost versus its selling price. In the case of the S&P 500, the assumed replacement price would be either the internal book value of all the companies in the S&P 500 or the government's value on what these companies are worth. They both give similar results.

In *Valuing Wall Street*, using the government's estimates on company values, Andrew Smithers and Stephen Wright concluded that the market was approximately 2.25 times overpriced at the end of 1998. Adjusting these numbers to the S&P 500 price at the end of 2003, we conclude that the market was 190% overpriced at the end of 2003, which is midway between the 125% overpriced market value we found using Fisher's Future Discounted Dividend Stream method with a positive-market DR and the 273% overpriced market value we calculated using Fisher's Future Discounted Dividend Stream method with a more negative-market DR.

One other very simple way of evaluating the market is to use a concept called regression to the price mean. As stated earlier, the real gain on the stock market (not including inflation) for the first half of the last century was 5%. Between 1951 and 1982, it was 6%. So for the first 82 years of the last century, the average real gain on the stock market was 5.4%. For the last 20 years, the real stock market gain has been 10%. Since we have seen nothing that justified the recent jump in stock prices, this means that the price of stocks has been growing an excess of 4.6% (10% - 5.4%) for each of the last 20 years and would now be expected to regress to the price mean.

Let's see how much it should regress. Given that the market price has been increasing excessively at a 4.6% rate for 20 years, if we take 1.046 to the 20th power, we get 2.46. This means that the market is overpriced by 146%.

Let's summarize all the methods we used in this chapter to evaluate if the market was overpriced at the end of 2003:

METHOD	AMOUNT OVERPRICED
Market Value via Future Discounted Dividend	273% (negative attitude)
Replacement cost versus its S&P 500 selling price	190%
Regression to the price mean	146%

All the above results show that the market is anywhere from 146% to 273% overpriced at the 1112 price of the S&P 500 at the end of 2003. This can be compared to our price/dividend ratio analysis that showed the market as being at least 200% overpriced, which is just about the same as the 203% average of the above numbers.

Just for reference, we saw earlier that, using the Japanese stock market as an example, the market is 250% overpriced. Also, we saw that, calculating the Future Discounted Dividend Stream with a sour investor attitude, the market is 273% overpriced. Both of these numbers reflect the investor attitude that will exist near the bottom of the depression. These numbers indicate that an extremely conservative investor could wait until the market drops even lower than our earlier price/dividend numbers suggest. We will be calculating a more exact price/dividend ratio that does indeed come closer to the 250% overpriced number which we identified in the Japanese example.

Determining Market Return

There is a formula known as the Gordon Equation, which is based on the earlier discussed Fisher's Future Discounted Dividend Stream method. This Gordon Equation enables us to predict what market overall return, or DR, we can expect from a given dividend yield and dividend growth rate.

Gordon Equation:
Market Return = Dividend Yield + Dividend Growth Rate

As we saw earlier in this chapter, the recent dividend yield has been 1.43%, and the dividend growth rate has been 4.2%. Plugging these numbers into the Gordon Equation we get:

Market Return = 0.014 + 0.042 = 0.056, or 5.6%.

If we assume inflation is approximately 3.5% (historical) of that number, it gives us a real (without inflation) yield of about 2%. Note that this is less than the 3% we have assumed for the near-zero risk TIPS. So at the current stock market price, we should assume that we will only make 2% per year (without inflation) from any stock market investment.

As we said earlier in the book, just because the stock market is overpriced does not necessarily mean that its price will be coming down anytime soon. Markets can stay overpriced for many years. The market drop will be caused by some other event, which in this case we suspect will be the consumer debt getting too high. However, once the market *does* start to drop, the above evaluation tools give us some idea on how *far* the market will drop. This is useful if we have intent of buying back into the market once it is reasonably priced.

CHAPTER 9
When to Get Back Into the Stock Market

As we concluded in earlier chapters, all analyses indicate that the market is dramatically overpriced, and that TIPS (Treasury Inflation Protected Securities) are currently a much better investment choice than the stock market. For the price of the stock market to get down low enough to be back into its historical price/dividend range, it would have to drop at least 67% from its end of 2003 S&P 500 level of 1112. As we will see later in this chapter, a conservative approach is to not get back into the market until the price/dividend ratio is 17.2 or less. The "sell" trigger, once the stock market started to rise, would then be a price/dividend ratio of 28. This sell trigger, and how it was quantified, will also be discussed later in this chapter.

Since dividends have historically risen at a 4.2% rate, we can extrapolate the likely S&P 500 price equivalence for the above 17.2 and 28 price/dividend buy and sell triggers. These values are shown in Figure 9-1 below. These extrapolated prices can be used as a trigger that you are getting close to an entry or exit point on the stock market. You will then want to calculate the actual price/dividend value.

APPROXIMATE S&P 500 TRIGGER PRICE TO GET INTO THE MARKET AND ALSO TO GET BACK OUT

Year	S&P 500 Buy Price	S&P 500 Sell Price
2005	336	547
2006	351	571
2007	365	595
2008	381	620
2009	397	646
2010	413	674
2011	430	702
2012	448	732
2013	467	763

Figure 9-1

We noted in an earlier chapter that if our stock market follows the Japanese example, in about 2007 the U.S. market will begin to drop until the S&P 500 reaches 450, in year 2013. Coincidently, in the above chart we identified almost the same target for year 2013 using a totally independent approach.

Using the numbers in the above table, Figure 9-1, if in 2007 the market drops far enough that the S&P 500 stock index is below 365, it would be time to look at reentering the stock market. At that point, you would want to calculate the actual price/dividend value to assist on this decision. This additional calculation is needed in case companies are doing so poorly that they reduce their dividends. Then, say in 2008, the market gets above 620. It would then be time to consider getting back out of the market and back into TIPS. It is very possible that in 2009 the market could then drop below 397, and you would again reenter the market, selling in year 2010 if the S&P 500 index goes over 674. During the turmoil of the coming depression, these kinds of wild market swings could very well happen, but you only want to participate when the market drops to a historically acceptable level, using the values in Figure 9-1 as a guide. Again, as the stock prices approach those in table 9-1, it would be wise to calculate the *actual* price/dividend ratio to verify the 17.2 price/dividend ratio to buy, or to verify the 28 price/dividend ratio to sell, since some companies may have been forced to reduce dividends, making the actual trigger prices of the S&P 500 lower than what are indicated in Figure 9-1.

Does Market Timing Work?

What was shown above is a form of market timing, which many books say can't be done. Certainly with the recent performance of stocks, you would have done well versus other investments at most buy dates early in the nineties. But those who bought the S&P 500 in year 2000 at a value over 1500 may be in for a long wait to get *their* money back.

Part of the reasoning for people saying that market timing doesn't work is that no one knows how to sell at the *absolute top* or buy at the market's *absolute bottom*. In this book we are only talking about buying when stocks *are at a relative low, not an absolute low.* And we use historical data and logic on the market's real worth to determine what these buy and sell values are as we approach decision points as to whether we should be in or out of the stock market.

Why don't more people invest this way? Well, the very effective marketing campaigns put on by stock brokers encourage a buy-and-hold strategy. They obviously are *not* going to support any method that would keep someone out of the market for almost 20 years, which a relative price/dividend strategy would have done several times in the last 103 years. Brokers do not make money when people are not in the stock market.

The other reason people don't invest this way is that mutual funds control 90% of the stocks traded. And as we discussed earlier, the mutual funds managers are only interested in short term profits. They can not keep their investors' money out of the stock market for multiple years because they are measured on "how they play the market" each year, which requires them to be *in* the market.

Let's use the price/dividend ratio, which we discussed earlier in the book, to see if buying stocks when they are at a relatively low price is better than buying them at a relatively high price. The answer to this may seem obvious, but the buy-and-hold philosophy says that there is no difference – that you can *not* time the market using market price or any other tool, and therefore you would be better off just ignoring price when you are considering investing in the market.

Below, in Figure 9-2, are the "ordered" end-of-the-year price/dividend ratios since 1900, listing them from the highest price/dividend ratio down to the lowest. I highlighted in **bold** the lowest 16 price/dividend ratios since 1900, which is the range in which we would think that stocks would be a relative good buy. For those statistically oriented, this represents price/dividend ratios lower than one sigma below the mean.

"Ordered" Price/Dividend ratios since 1900

Price/Dividend		Price/Dividend		Year	Price/Dividend
87.72		28.01			20.20
84.03		28.01			20.16
75.76		27.70			19.88
73.53		27.40			19.69
62.50		27.32			19.27
59.17		26.88			19.12
59.17		26.81			19.12
49.75		26.74			19.05
44.64		26.53			19.01
37.45		26.32			18.94
37.04		26.18			18.83
35.46		26.18			18.59
35.21		26.04			18.48
34.84		25.91			18.21
34.13		24.51			18.18
34.01		24.27			17.79
33.90		23.98			17.76
33.78		23.87			17.45
33.22		23.53			17.33
33.00		23.42		**1953**	**17.12**
32.89		23.36		**1951**	**16.86**
32.68		23.26		**1923**	**16.86**
31.95		23.15		**1932**	**16.72**
31.55		22.99		**1942**	**16.56**
30.21		22.32		**1948**	**16.34**
29.76		22.22		**1907**	**16.31**
29.59		22.03		**1940**	**15.80**
29.33		21.88		**1949**	**14.71**
29.24		21.55		**1918**	**13.97**
29.15		20.75		**1950**	**13.89**
28.90		20.70		**1920**	**13.76**
28.74		20.62		**1937**	**13.19**
28.57		20.49		**1931**	**12.69**
28.57		20.37		**1941**	**12.24**
28.01				**1917**	**10.75**

Figure 9-2

So we would buy stocks if the price /dividend ratio was 17.2 or below.

This presents a problem. If we look at the dates that represent the price/dividend values of 17.2 or below in Figure 9-2, the most recent date is 1953. That means we would have been out of the stock market for 50 years, which may reduce risk but also precludes many potential gains from being in the stock market.

But we must realize that the data shown in Figure 9-2 is end-of-the-year values (we couldn't show all 26,780 daily values in the chart), and we know that there is much price variation of the market within each year. Indeed, when we look at individual day data for the last 53 years, we see many additional years when the price/dividend ratio *was* below 17.2 at some time during the year. We don't have this daily data for the years of 1900 to 1949, but we extrapolated the same price variation we saw in the most recent 53 years and used this for our assumptions on the 1900 to 1949 daily data. With the daily data, we see that by using a price/dividend buy trigger of 17.2, we would be able to invest in the market right up to the 1986 jump in stock prices.

Earlier in the book, we estimated that the stock market would drop at least 67% from its end-of-2003 level. Using the 17.2 price/dividend ratio, the drop would actually be 71%.

We have already determined that TIPS are the best investment when compared to the current over-priced stock market. Now we want to find some savings "Formula" that allows us to get some of the greater stock market yields when the market is reasonably priced, but gets us out of the market in higher priced market periods. The goal is to see if we can come up with a way to match the earlier stock market yields (even with their former higher dividends), but with the lower risk of being out of the market much of the time. The savings Formula must take us out of the market whenever the market is overpriced, putting the investment into TIPS during these periods.

We have determined that a price/dividend ratio of 17.2 is a reasonable low level that we want to test as to when the market is a "good buy." We now need a test high-level at which we would want to sell our stocks. Let's re-look at an earlier chart, Figure 9-3, that we showed regarding year-end price/dividend levels.

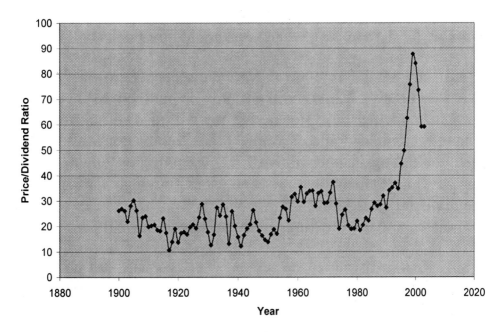

Year-end Price/Dividend Ratio

Figure 9-3

The "relative high" on the price/dividend ratio has had three different general levels within the last 103 years. By looking at Figure 9-3, through the fifties, and again from 1975 through the eighties, it appears that the relative high was close to 30. In the sixties, the relative high was about 35. Then, in the nineties, it just took off, with the price/dividend ratio in 2000 being almost 300% of the relative high for the first 55 years.

However, we have already discussed that the stock market has recently been extremely over-priced, so we don't want to use recent highs as a sell-criteria. Just looking at the chart, it appears that a value of 28 may be a good test number. Since this is 63% higher than our buy value of 17.2, it would certainly represent a reasonable gain. We also are aware that, due to the daily price variation we discussed earlier, that we will be hitting the 28 price/dividend sell value more often than the above year-end values on Figure 9-3 indicate.

So, here is the savings Formula (we will use this capitalized term several times throughout this book) we want to test.

Formula: for determining when you should buy stocks or TIPS.

We will buy stocks anytime the price/dividend ratio on the S&P 500 is at or below 17.2. We will not only be putting new investment money into buying these stocks, but we will also sell all the TIPS we have accumulated and use those funds to buy stocks. When the price/dividend again goes above 17.2, we will stop buying stocks with new investment money and start buying TIPS. If the price/dividend goes above 28, we will sell all the stocks we have accumulated and use the funds from the sale to buy TIPS.

We will use past data to test the above savings Formula, and just for the purpose of keeping score, we will assume that we are saving 100 dollars every year in equivalent 2003 dollars. We will be comparing the Formula-driven trade results to a similar $100 annual investment in the S&P 500. We will start in 1907, because that is the first year that the price/dividend is below 17.2, and we can therefore start everything at a zero base.

Here in Figure 9-4 is the data from that test comparison:

Comparing Formula Buys versus Regular S&P 500-Only Buys

Year (bold when buy stocks)	New TIPS	Accumulated Formula S&P	Accumulated TIPS	Accumulated Formula TIPS+S&P	Accumulated S&P500 only
1907	0.00	4.71		4.71	4.71
1908	4.87	6.82	4.87	11.69	11.69
1909	4.87	8.14	10.15	18.29	18.81
1910	0.00	23.09	0.00	23.09	22.47
1911	0.00	29.51	0.00	29.51	28.85

1912	5.25	31.91	5.25	37.16	36.44
1913	0.00	39.72	0.00	39.72	38.30
1914	0.00	43.75	0.00	43.75	42.39
1915	5.58	59.42	5.58	65.00	63.14
1916	0.00	76.83	0.00	76.83	74.44
1917	0.00	63.74	0.00	63.74	61.95
1918	0.00	87.50	0.00	87.50	85.26
1919	0.00	113.77	0.00	113.77	111.08
1920	0.00	102.89	0.00	102.89	100.71
1921	0.00	128.44	0.00	128.44	125.95
1922	0.00	172.50	0.00	172.50	169.34
1923	0.00	186.77	0.00	186.77	183.52
1924	0.00	244.83	0.00	244.83	240.73
1925	9.55	324.89	9.55	334.44	319.60
1926	0.00	389.18	0.00	389.18	373.44
1927	9.77	537.88	9.77	547.65	516.52
1928	9.55	0.00	799.86	799.86	758.92
1929	9.44	0.00	837.98	837.98	701.58
1930	0.00	819.02	0.00	819.02	534.77
1931	0.00	470.83	0.00	470.83	310.51
1932	0.00	437.72	0.00	437.72	291.41
1933	7.23	0.00	683.93	683.93	452.93
1934	7.29	0.00	722.10	722.10	449.76
1935	7.40	0.00	772.72	772.72	667.62
1936	7.62	0.00	814.71	814.71	892.12
1937	0.00	870.16	0.00	870.16	583.59
1938	7.95	1153.32	7.95	1161.27	776.11
1939	0.00	1152.74	0.00	1152.74	772.74
1940	0.00	1041.09	0.00	1041.09	700.44
1941	0.00	923.71	0.00	923.71	624.02
1942	0.00	1123.96	0.00	1123.96	762.07
1943	0.00	1418.54	0.00	1418.54	964.81
1944	9.61	1704.64	9.61	1714.25	1162.47
1945	9.83	0.00	2341.81	2341.81	1593.22

1946	10.05	0.00	2846.72	2846.72	1469.09
1947	0.00	3195.57	0.00	3195.57	1555.07
1948	0.00	3367.79	0.00	3367.79	1645.52
1949	0.00	3980.75	0.00	3980.75	1951.81
1950	0.00	5189.86	0.00	5189.86	2551.30
1951	0.00	6438.41	0.00	6438.41	3172.09
1952	0.00	7636.89	0.00	7636.89	3769.98
1953	0.00	7570.18	0.00	7570.18	3744.51
1954	0.00	11538.7	0.00	11538.7	5715.00
1955	14.74	0.00	15217.1	15217.1	7537.04
1956	14.79	0.00	16142.7	16142.7	8072.63
1957	15.24	0.00	17110.1	17110.1	7240.16
1958	15.68	0.00	17940.3	17940.3	10410.2
1959	15.95	0.00	18804.9	18804.9	11678.9
1960	16.23	0.00	19641.1	19641.1	11747.4
1961	16.45	0.00	20378.6	20378.6	14917.2
1962	16.56	0.00	21278.2	21278.2	13628.1
1963	16.78	0.00	22283.3	22283.3	16738.1
1964	17.06	0.00	23185.2	23185.2	19504.5
1965	17.22	0.00	24343.9	24343.9	21936
1966	17.56	0.00	25933.8	25933.8	19746.8
1967	18.16	0.00	27518.3	27518.3	24500.3
1968	18.71	0.00	29661.3	29661.3	27221
1969	19.60	0.00	32408.9	32408.9	24945.8
1970	20.81	0.00	35207.3	35207.3	25949.3
1971	21.97	0.00	37435.5	37435.5	29682.2
1972	22.69	0.00	39856.4	39856.4	35343.0
1973	23.46	0.00	44545.4	44545.4	30175
1974	0.00	51403.11	0.00	51403.1	22214
1975	28.65	70568.46	28.65	70597.1	30512.6
1976	30.64	87483.97	61.54	87545.5	37844
1977	32.13	81255.36	99.64	81355	35167.8
1978	0.00	86740.41	0.00	86740.4	37513
1979	0.00	102919.64	0.00	102920	44531.2
1980	0.00	136414.63	0.00	136415	59047.9

1981	0.00	129746.23	0.00	129746	56188.4
1982	0.00	157754.12	0.00	157754	68347.1
1983	53.88	193389.47	53.88	193443	83816.6
1984	55.92	205578.33	113.55	205692	89131.1
1985	58.13	270859.54	179.40	271039	117467
1986	60.34	0.00	321724	321724	139453
1987	61.00	0.00	345703	345703	146836
1988	63.71	0.00	371416	371416	171287
1989	66.52	0.00	399886	399886	225628
1990	69.61	0.00	436370	436370	218696
1991	73.86	0.00	462906	462906	285394
1992	76.13	0.00	490297	490297	307215
1993	78.34	0.00	518560	518560	338257
1994	80.49	0.00	548068	548068	342804
1995	82.64	0.00	578505	578505	471705
1996	84.74	0.00	615166	615166	472895
1997	87.55	0.00	644181	644181	773747
1998	89.05	0.00	673979	673979	994962
1999	90.48	0.00	712382	712382	1204408
2000	92.91	0.00	757973	757973	1094847
2001	96.06	0.00	795184	795184	964812
2002	97.88	0.00	831709	831709	751229
2003	100.0	0.00	874792	874792	965401

Figure 9-4

Here are some explanations of Figure 9-4. The first column on the left is the year, with those years when Formula *stocks* were being purchased in **bold**. These would be years when the price/dividend ratio dropped below 17.2 and we are only buying stock. These purchase years represent 39% of the studied years.

The second column from the left is the dollar value of the "new TIPS" being purchased. Both the TIPS and the S&P 500 are purchased in $100 amounts every year, in year 2003 dollar equivalents.

The third column from the left is the accumulated dollar value of the Formula S&P stock purchased. Note that in years 1928, 1933, 1945, 1955, and 1986; this went to zero. These were years when the daily price/dividend rose to 28 (after earlier being below 17.2) and triggered the selling of all accumulated stocks. Above a price/dividend ratio of 28, we are just buying TIPS.

The fourth column is the accumulated dollar value of the TIPS. Note that in years shown in **bold**, this number drops to zero, since any TIPS that have been accumulated are sold, and all resultant funds are being used for stock purchase.

The last two columns on the right are the running totals of the dollar values for the Formula mix total versus the total S&P500-Only results. This is where we keep score.

Figure 9-5 is a logarithmic graph showing these last two columns' results

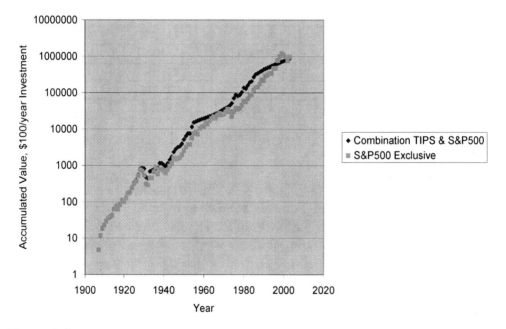

Figure 9-5

It certainly looks like we were successful in coming up with a savings Formula which keeps up with the stock market but with less risk, since when using the Formula, we are only in the stock market about half the time. The other half of the time we are buying the almost zero risk TIPS. The Formula results were generally ahead of the S&P 500 results, except for the most recent few years. However, if the market drops over 70%, as we are predicting, the Formula method will be 60% ahead of the market. This is because the Formula, per our plan, has been keeping us out of the recent over-heated market. When the stock market drops, the TIPS will then be sold, and the funds can then be used to re-enter the market. The purchase price of buying TIPS, especially if we buy it as a stock security, is no different than buying an S&P 500 index fund, so purchase costs can be ignored in the comparison.

Although using an investment window of 97 years, as we did above, is good for analyzing general concepts, it *doesn't* reflect the realities of shorter investment windows. Shorter investment windows more reflect the way an actual investor saves. So, in Figure 9-6 below, let's look at the results of this savings Formula versus the S&P 500 in five year investment scenarios, where we are investing $100 every year for five years. As a means of keeping score, we assume the investment is in year 2003 equivalent dollars.

Comparison of Formula Buy versus Straight S&P 500 Buy
5 Year Investment, $100 (year 2003 $) Every Year, 3% TIPS
Best results in **bold**

Year End	Formula Gains	Formula Results	S&P Results	S&P Gain
1911	0.0229	**29.51**	28.85	
1912	0.0256	**28.60**	27.89	
1913	0.0527	**26.39**	25.07	
1914	0.0296	**25.96**	25.21	
1915	0.0309	**33.91**	32.89	
1916	0.0431	**35.84**	34.36	
1917	0.0104	**27.30**	27.02	
1918	0.0103	**34.59**	34.24	
1919	0.0103	**41.34**	40.92	
1920		38.17	38.17	
1921		48.46	48.46	
1922		59.70	59.70	

1923		59.77	59.77	
1924		70.91	70.91	
1925	0.1263	**85.15**	75.60	
1926	0.1388	**79.82**	70.09	
1927	0.2862	**103.25**	80.28	
1928	0.3160	**121.22**	92.12	
1929	0.5583	**106.47**	68.33	
1930	0.5589	**71.78**	46.05	
1931	0.4029	**38.40**	27.37	
1932	0.0933	**30.67**	28.05	
1933	0.0359	**46.62**	45.00	
1934	0.0587	**48.51**	45.82	
1935		50.53	**63.93**	0.2653
1936		46.04	**68.75**	0.4932
1937	0.1184	**41.37**	36.99	
1938	0.3053	**58.69**	44.96	
1939	0.3652	**54.86**	40.18	
1940	0.3023	**47.39**	36.39	
1941	0.1857	**41.22**	34.77	
1942	0.1902	**48.79**	40.99	
1943		51.37	51.37	
1944	0.1602	**69.56**	59.96	
1945	0.1353	**84.85**	74.74	
1946	0.4705	**89.59**	60.92	
1947	0.4967	**88.41**	59.07	
1948	0.4118	**84.14**	59.60	
1949	0.0827	**73.56**	67.95	
1950	0.0127	**87.28**	86.19	
1951		99.48	99.48	
1952		104.42	104.42	
1953		89.35	89.35	
1954		112.68	112.68	
1955		125.21	125.21	
1956		113.17	**114.03**	0.0076
1957	0.1451	**102.53**	89.54	
1958		88.37	**103.66**	0.1731
1959		84.43	**102.01**	0.2082
1960		85.40	**95.91**	0.1230
1961		86.39	**110.97**	0.2845

1962		87.82	**89.33**	0.0171
1963		89.29	**101.33**	0.1348
1964		90.30	**108.53**	0.2019
1965		91.93	**109.04**	0.1861
1966	0.0065	**94.56**	93.95	
1967		97.09	**104.99**	0.0814
1968		101.04	**108.10**	0.0699
1969	0.0961	**106.16**	96.85	
1970	0.0994	**111.24**	101.19	
1971	0.0322	**114.92**	111.34	
1972		118.75	**129.07**	0.0869
1973	0.1344	**128.09**	112.91	
1974	0.5605	**142.24**	91.15	
1975	0.6302	**210.89**	129.37	
1976	0.6361	**266.80**	163.06	
1977	0.7149	**276.18**	161.05	
1978	0.6310	**288.50**	176.89	
1979	0.6745	**328.66**	196.27	
1980	0.4682	**362.93**	247.20	
1981	0.2266	**291.15**	237.37	
1982		278.22	278.22	
1983	0.1691	**372.43**	318.55	
1984	0.3549	**433.47**	319.92	
1985	0.4535	**575.00**	395.60	
1986	0.4534	**598.64**	411.89	
1987	0.5409	**590.64**	383.32	
1988	0.2996	**520.94**	400.84	
1989		441.47	**453.09**	0.0263
1990		375.76	**400.62**	0.0661
1991		385.67	**473.25**	0.2271
1992		398.11	**457.99**	0.1504
1993		410.45	**456.85**	0.1130
1994		423.13	**442.44**	0.0456
1995		436.99	**541.36**	0.2388
1996		451.27	**505.11**	0.1193
1997		460.10	**722.36**	0.5700
1998		468.62	**787.60**	0.6807
1999		481.19	**761.20**	0.5819
2000		496.63	**593.10**	0.1943

2001	0.1383	**507.53**	445.85	
2002	0.4324	**515.69**	360.02	
2003	0.1062	**526.83**	476.25	

72% of the 5 year periods, the Formula equaled or beat the S&P 500.
On the average, the Formula method beat the S&P 500 by 1.9% per year.
47% of the time the Formula was completely out of the stock market.

Figure 9-6

So if we look at investing when our time period is five years, the Formula based investment equaled or beat the straight S&P 500 investment 72% of the time. In addition, the Formula method averaged almost 2% greater returns per year. On this basis, the market timing per the Formula is far superior to just blindly investing in the S&P 500, when the investment period is five years. In addition, since the Formula investment method was out of the stock market almost half the time, this is a far lower risk method than being in the market continuously.

Note that nothing about this method involves any trick on "beating the market." In fact, if you look at the detail within the above spreadsheet, you will see that there are 12 incidences where both methods were buying stocks for the whole five year period, and their returns were identical. The only reason the Formula method beats the straight S&P 500 investment is because it stays out of the market when it is high priced, instead investing in TIPS. This method works strictly because of market timing.

The five year investment period being so good is of special interest because many people start out with the intent of saving for a longer period, but because of some unforeseen reason, they have to withdraw their savings early. The Formula method reduces the risk that they will lose substantial amounts of money if they have to cut their investment window short.

Now let's look at a similar comparison, in Figure 9-7, when the investment window is 10 years.

Comparison of Formula Buy versus Straight S&P 500 Buy
10 Year Investment, $100 (year 2003 $) Every Year, 3% TIPS
Best results in **bold**

Year End	Gain	Formula Results	S&P Results	S&P Gain
1916	0.0322	**76.83**	74.44	
1917	0.0333	**55.54**	53.75	
1918	0.0312	**69.75**	67.64	
1919	0.0201	**84.31**	82.65	
1920	0.0190	**72.09**	70.75	
1921	0.0183	**85.77**	84.23	
1922	0.0046	**108.01**	107.51	
1923	0.0047	**109.97**	109.46	
1924	0.0048	**134.11**	133.47	
1925	0.0568	**177.63**	168.08	
1926	0.0521	**196.55**	186.82	
1927	0.0981	**257.06**	234.08	
1928	0.0941	**338.38**	309.27	
1929	0.2491	**318.34**	254.86	
1930	0.6107	**260.38**	161.66	
1931	0.5785	**127.09**	80.51	
1932	0.5315	**105.65**	68.98	
1933	0.5036	**142.11**	94.52	
1934	0.5634	**133.13**	85.16	
1935		113.12	**115.91**	0.0247
1936		108.04	**141.32**	0.3080
1937	0.1028	**98.82**	89.61	
1938	0.1381	**133.85**	117.61	
1939	0.1202	**128.60**	114.80	
1940	0.1239	**112.37**	99.98	
1941	0.1362	**91.10**	80.18	
1942	0.1524	**99.90**	86.69	
1943	0.1590	**120.86**	104.28	
1944	0.2604	**147.83**	117.28	
1945	0.2210	**187.58**	153.63	
1946	0.5256	**212.64**	139.38	
1947	0.6002	**223.28**	139.53	
1948	0.4097	**203.04**	144.03	
1949	0.3768	**227.33**	165.11	

1950	0.3485	**272.16**	201.82	
1951	0.3176	**298.97**	226.90	
1952	0.2838	**312.82**	243.66	
1953	0.2458	**276.25**	221.73	
1954	0.0524	**323.83**	307.71	
1955	0.0085	**378.78**	375.59	
1956		360.60	**363.61**	0.0084
1957	0.1643	**334.86**	287.60	
1958		298.87	**349.60**	0.1697
1959		267.07	**330.27**	0.2366
1960		246.31	**289.47**	0.1752
1961		228.65	**320.11**	0.4000
1962		214.81	**256.77**	0.1953
1963		198.61	**266.99**	0.3443
1964		193.99	**277.95**	0.4328
1965		197.38	**287.24**	0.4553
1966		204.10	**240.15**	0.1766
1967		210.27	**264.89**	0.2598
1968		219.49	**272.24**	0.2403
1969		231.98	**235.13**	0.0136
1970	0.0614	**243.78**	229.67	
1971		251.01	**252.03**	0.0041
1972		258.96	**279.98**	0.0812
1973	0.2028	**279.39**	232.29	
1974	0.7519	**310.16**	177.04	
1975	0.7482	**433.29**	247.84	
1976	0.7566	**534.74**	304.41	
1977	0.7922	**517.75**	288.90	
1978	0.6965	**537.09**	316.59	
1979	0.6197	**612.54**	378.19	
1980	0.5585	**773.80**	496.50	
1981	0.4790	**707.61**	478.46	
1982	0.3944	**822.64**	589.94	
1983	0.4245	**1014.59**	712.27	
1984	0.5308	**1088.94**	711.36	
1985	0.4616	**1294.57**	885.71	
1986	0.3201	**1319.10**	999.28	
1987	0.2243	**1199.18**	979.49	
1988	0.1478	**1205.57**	1050.30	

1989		1219.54	**1261.32**	0.0343
1990	0.1139	**1265.18**	1135.78	
1991		1246.29	**1314.78**	0.0550
1992		1235.11	**1258.79**	0.0192
1993		1137.20	**1247.36**	0.0969
1994		1027.73	**1129.94**	0.0995
1995		934.77	**1404.46**	0.5025
1996		963.42	**1288.43**	0.3374
1997		982.78	**1874.77**	0.9076
1998		1001.72	**2130.34**	1.1267
1999		1030.81	**2314.67**	1.2455
2000		1068.81	**1848.93**	0.7299
2001		1090.49	**1475.90**	0.3534
2002	0.0456	**1109.36**	1061.02	
2003		1134.71	**1240.08**	0.0929

66% of the 10 year periods, the Formula beat the S&P 500.
On the average, the Formula method beat the S&P 500 by 0.9% per year.
48% of the time the Formula was completely out of the stock market.

Figure 9-7

If we look at investing when the time period is ten years, the Formula based investment beat the straight S&P 500 investment 66% of the time. In addition, the Formula method averaged almost 1% greater returns per year. On this basis, the market timing per the Formula is superior to just blindly investing in the S&P 500 when the investment period is ten years. In addition, since the Formula investment method was out of the stock market almost half the time, this is a far lower risk method than being in the market continuously.

Now let's look at a similar comparison in Figure 9-8 when the investment window is 20 years.

Comparison of Formula Buy versus Straight S&P 500 Buy
20 Year Investment, $100 (year 2003 $) Every Year, 3% TIPS

Best results in **bold**

End Year	Formula Gain	Formula Results	S&P Results	S&P Gain
1926	0.0421	**389.18**	373.44	
1927	0.0650	**510.28**	479.15	
1928	0.0604	**706.25**	666.00	
1929	0.1979	**703.42**	587.23	
1930	0.5382	**651.82**	423.76	
1931	0.5220	**356.64**	234.33	
1932	0.4917	**313.57**	210.20	
1933	0.4819	**456.87**	308.30	
1934	0.5719	**451.61**	287.31	
1935	0.1286	**458.27**	406.05	
1936		460.70	**516.91**	0.1220
1937	0.4500	**454.55**	313.47	
1938	0.4602	**563.56**	385.96	
1939	0.4508	**513.31**	353.82	
1940	0.4364	**404.35**	281.50	
1941	0.4169	**313.38**	221.18	
1942	0.3969	**344.42**	246.57	
1943	0.3757	**390.50**	283.85	
1944	0.3854	**436.63**	315.17	
1945	0.2462	**502.95**	403.57	
1946	0.6055	**561.95**	350.02	
1947	0.5715	**560.83**	356.88	
1948	0.5305	**568.66**	371.56	
1949	0.5006	**646.08**	430.55	
1950	0.4947	**802.93**	537.18	
1951	0.4942	**904.44**	605.32	
1952	0.4947	**963.81**	644.81	
1953	0.4900	**897.71**	602.51	
1954	0.4976	**1277.86**	853.26	
1955	0.4690	**1566.17**	1066.13	
1956	0.4048	**1538.28**	1095.01	
1957	0.6521	**1505.81**	911.44	
1958	0.1067	**1361.40**	1230.19	
1959	0.0267	**1324.68**	1290.27	

1960	0.0556	**1262.37**	1195.86	
1961		1163.41	**1364.25**	0.1726
1962		1076.75	**1120.97**	0.0411
1963		1003.73	**1242.35**	0.2377
1964		838.61	**1313.15**	0.5659
1965		798.42	**1366.05**	0.7109
1966		778.85	**1118.78**	0.4364
1967		744.71	**1227.60**	0.6484
1968		709.97	**1177.24**	0.6582
1969		688.96	**933.92**	0.3556
1970		682.23	**863.42**	0.2656
1971		668.22	**883.57**	0.3223
1972		658.70	**940.60**	0.4280
1973		673.93	**709.91**	0.0534
1974	0.5021	**737.66**	491.08	
1975	0.5558	**1002.17**	644.14	
1976	0.6027	**1219.52**	760.94	
1977	0.7049	**1135.44**	666.00	
1978	0.7064	**1174.98**	688.59	
1979	0.6930	**1344.83**	794.35	
1980	0.6882	**1712.99**	1014.71	
1981	0.6530	**1572.82**	951.48	
1982	0.6351	**1842.26**	1126.70	
1983	0.6431	**2221.52**	1352.02	
1984	0.6408	**2323.48**	1416.05	
1985	0.6146	**2958.93**	1832.65	
1986	0.5760	**3329.94**	2112.97	
1987	0.5671	**3412.63**	2177.67	
1988	0.4063	**3497.45**	2487.00	
1989	0.1342	**3591.83**	3166.80	
1990	0.2589	**3732.83**	2965.12	
1991	0.0080	**3763.64**	3733.79	
1992		3784.94	**3899.69**	0.0303
1993		3809.78	**4111.25**	0.0791
1994		3836.49	**3856.87**	0.0053
1995		3646.22	**4950.55**	0.3577
1996		3481.72	**4667.81**	0.3407
1997		3213.92	**7023.65**	1.1854
1998		3186.12	**8218.19**	1.5794

1999		3200.24	**9034.67**	1.8231
2000		3263.33	**7525.33**	1.3060
2001		3228.43	**5913.90**	0.8318
2002		3201.72	**4134.77**	0.2914
2003		3050.64	**4795.52**	0.5720

66% of the 20 year periods, the Formula beat the S&P 500.
On the average, the Formula method beat the S&P 500 by 0.6%
per year.
47% of the time the Formula was completely out of the stock
market.

Figure 9-8

When our investment time period is twenty years, the Formula based investment beat the straight S&P 500 investment 66% of the time. In addition, the Formula method averaged 0.6% greater returns per year. On this basis, the market timing per the Formula is superior to just blindly investing in the S&P 500 when the investment period is twenty years. In addition, since the Formula investment method was out of the stock market almost half the time, this is a far lower risk method than being in the market continuously.

You can see that the per-year advantage of the Formula method diminishes as the years of investment increase. This is consistent with the general guideline that market variability becomes less of a concern as the number of investment years increases. However, since the Formula method still performed better than the straight S&P 500 stock buying method in the twenty year investment window, market timing wins! Also, as we stated earlier, many investors start out with the intention of investing for twenty or more years, then the real-world causes them to withdraw savings for some unforeseen need. Using the formula makes it far less likely that they will lose money on an early withdrawal.

1.5% TIPS

All of the previous examples used a 3% TIPS interest assumption. However, we said earlier in the book that the interest rate on TIPS can vary. Let's redo the above Formula test with TIPS paying 1.5% (plus inflation), which is lower interest than TIPS have historically paid. Figure 9-9 below shows the results of the savings Formula versus the S&P 500 in five year investment scenarios, where we are investing $100 every year for five years. To keep score we assume the investment is in year 2003 equivalent dollars.

Comparison of Formula Buy versus Straight S&P 500 Buy
5 Year Investment, $100 (year 2003 $) Every Year, 1.5% TIPS
Best results in **Bold**

End Year	Formula Gain	Formula Results	S&P 500 Results	S&P 500 Gain
1911	0.0146	**29.27**	28.85	
1912	0.0163	**28.35**	27.89	
1913	0.0466	**26.24**	25.07	
1914	0.0266	**25.88**	25.21	
1915	0.0277	**33.81**	32.89	
1916	0.0374	**35.65**	34.36	
1917	0.0081	**27.23**	27.02	
1918	0.0080	**34.51**	34.24	
1919	0.0080	**41.25**	40.92	
1920		38.17	38.17	
1921		48.46	48.46	
1922		59.70	59.70	
1923		59.77	59.77	
1924		70.91	70.91	
1925	0.1263	**85.15**	75.60	
1926	0.1368	**79.68**	70.09	
1927	0.2838	**103.06**	80.28	
1928	0.3113	**120.79**	92.12	
1929	0.5313	**104.63**	68.33	
1930	0.5183	**69.92**	46.05	
1931	0.3764	**37.67**	27.37	
1932	0.0855	**30.45**	28.05	
1933	0.0334	**46.51**	45.00	

1934	0.0458	**47.91**	45.82	
1935		49.42	**63.93**	0.2938
1936		44.75	**68.75**	0.5365
1937	0.0860	**40.17**	36.99	
1938	0.2847	**57.76**	44.96	
1939	0.3511	**54.29**	40.18	
1940	0.2957	**47.15**	36.39	
1941	0.1830	**41.13**	34.77	
1942	0.1875	**48.67**	40.99	
1943		51.37	51.37	
1944	0.1602	**69.56**	59.96	
1945	0.1333	**84.70**	74.74	
1946	0.4515	**88.43**	60.92	
1947	0.4626	**86.39**	59.07	
1948	0.3856	**82.58**	59.60	
1949	0.0737	**72.95**	67.95	
1950	0.0099	**87.04**	86.19	
1951		99.48	99.48	
1952		104.42	104.42	
1953		89.35	89.35	
1954		112.68	112.68	
1955		125.21	125.21	
1956		111.78	**114.03**	0.0201
1957	0.1201	**100.30**	89.54	
1958		85.98	**103.66**	0.2057
1959		81.98	**102.01**	0.2443
1960		82.93	**95.91**	0.1565
1961		83.88	**110.97**	0.3230
1962		85.26	**89.33**	0.0476
1963		86.69	**101.33**	0.1689
1964		87.66	**108.53**	0.2381
1965		89.25	**109.04**	0.2217
1966		91.82	**93.95**	0.0232
1967		94.29	**104.99**	0.1136
1968		98.14	**108.10**	0.1016
1969	0.0649	**103.14**	96.85	
1970	0.0683	**108.10**	101.19	
1971	0.0030	**111.67**	111.34	
1972		115.39	**129.07**	0.1186

1973	0.1026	**124.49**	112.91	
1974	0.5172	**138.29**	91.15	
1975	0.6055	**207.70**	129.37	
1976	0.6218	**264.46**	163.06	
1977	0.7028	**274.24**	161.05	
1978	0.6139	**285.47**	176.89	
1979	0.6562	**325.07**	196.27	
1980	0.4587	**360.59**	247.20	
1981	0.2235	**290.43**	237.37	
1982		278.22	278.22	
1983	0.1691	**372.43**	318.55	
1984	0.3524	**432.66**	319.92	
1985	0.4470	**572.44**	395.60	
1986	0.4405	**593.32**	411.89	
1987	0.5069	**577.62**	383.32	
1988	0.2629	**506.21**	400.84	
1989		427.79	**453.09**	0.0592
1990		365.09	**400.62**	0.0973
1991		374.76	**473.25**	0.2628
1992		386.81	**457.99**	0.1840
1993		398.77	**456.85**	0.1456
1994		411.05	**442.44**	0.0764
1995		424.42	**541.36**	0.2755
1996		438.30	**505.11**	0.1524
1997		446.84	**722.36**	0.6166
1998		455.09	**787.60**	0.7307
1999		467.30	**761.20**	0.6289
2000		482.31	**593.10**	0.2297
2001	0.1054	**492.86**	445.85	
2002	0.3910	**500.78**	360.02	
2003	0.0743	**511.63**	476.25	

Figure 9-9

Investing when our time period is five years, with 1.5% TIPS, the Formula based investment equaled or beat the straight S&P 500 investment 71% of the time. In addition, the Formula method averaged 1.4 % greater returns per year. On this basis, the market timing per the Formula is far superior to just blindly investing in the S&P 500 when the investment period is five years. In addition, since the Formula investment method was out of the stock market almost half the time, this is a far lower risk method than being in the market continuously.

Again, nothing about this method involves any trick on "beating the market." In fact, if you look at the detail within the above spreadsheet, you will see that there are 12 incidences where both methods were buying stocks for the whole five year period, and their returns were identical. The only reason the Formula method beats the straight S&P 500 investment is because it stays out of the market when it is high priced, instead investing in TIPS at 1.5% interest (plus inflation). This method works strictly because of market timing.

Just as was true when we looked at the 3% TIPS comparison, the five year investment period being so good is of special interest because many people start out with the intent of saving for a longer period, but because of some unforeseen reason have to withdraw their savings early. The Formula method reduces the risk that they will lose substantial amounts of money if they have to cut their investment window short.

Now let's look at a similar comparison, in Figure 9-10, when the investment window is 10 years using 1.5% TIPS.

Comparison of Formula Buy versus Straight S&P 500 Buy
10 Year Investment, $100 (year 2003 $) Every Year, 1.5% TIPS
Best results in **bold**

End Year	Formula Gain	Formula Results	S&P 500 Results	S&P 500 Gain
1916	0.0251	**76.31**	74.44	
1917	0.0260	**55.15**	53.75	
1918	0.0271	**69.47**	67.64	
1919	0.0174	**84.09**	82.65	
1920	0.0165	**71.91**	70.75	
1921	0.0159	**85.57**	84.23	
1922	0.0036	**107.90**	107.51	
1923	0.0036	**109.86**	109.46	
1924	0.0037	**133.97**	133.47	
1925	0.0568	**177.63**	168.08	
1926	0.0513	**196.40**	186.82	

1927	0.0973	**256.86**	234.08	
1928	0.0927	**337.95**	309.27	
1929	0.2298	**313.43**	254.86	
1930	0.5627	**252.62**	161.66	
1931	0.5348	**123.56**	80.51	
1932	0.4928	**102.98**	68.98	
1933	0.4688	**138.83**	94.52	
1934	0.5103	**128.61**	85.16	
1935		108.66	**115.91**	0.0668
1936		103.00	**141.32**	0.3720
1937	0.0493	**94.03**	89.61	
1938	0.0930	**128.55**	117.61	
1939	0.0807	**124.07**	114.80	
1940	0.0892	**108.90**	99.98	
1941	0.1089	**88.91**	80.18	
1942	0.1340	**98.31**	86.69	
1943	0.1471	**119.63**	104.28	
1944	0.2535	**147.02**	117.28	
1945	0.2167	**186.92**	153.63	
1946	0.5044	**209.68**	139.38	
1947	0.5588	**217.50**	139.53	
1948	0.3777	**198.43**	144.03	
1949	0.3479	**222.55**	165.11	
1950	0.3223	**266.87**	201.82	
1951	0.2946	**293.75**	226.90	
1952	0.2643	**308.07**	243.66	
1953	0.2302	**272.78**	221.73	
1954	0.0467	**322.08**	307.71	
1955	0.0066	**378.07**	375.59	
1956		355.70	**363.61**	0.0222
1957	0.1338	**326.09**	287.60	
1958		287.64	**349.60**	0.2154
1959		254.44	**330.27**	0.2980
1960		232.68	**289.47**	0.2441
1961		214.60	**320.11**	0.4916
1962		200.81	**256.77**	0.2787
1963		185.62	**266.99**	0.4384
1964		181.31	**277.95**	0.5330
1965		184.49	**287.24**	0.5569

1966		190.78	**240.15**	0.2588
1967		196.55	**264.89**	0.3477
1968		205.21	**272.24**	0.3266
1969		216.94	**235.13**	0.0838
1970		228.04	**229.67**	0.0071
1971		234.85	**252.03**	0.0732
1972		242.32	**279.98**	0.1554
1973	0.1260	**261.56**	232.29	
1974	0.6412	**290.56**	177.04	
1975	0.6633	**412.24**	247.84	
1976	0.6899	**514.41**	304.41	
1977	0.7405	**502.81**	288.90	
1978	0.6550	**523.94**	316.59	
1979	0.5893	**601.07**	378.19	
1980	0.5366	**762.90**	496.50	
1981	0.4636	**700.27**	478.46	
1982	0.3833	**816.06**	589.94	
1983	0.4150	**1007.85**	712.27	
1984	0.5196	**1080.96**	711.36	
1985	0.4535	**1287.36**	885.71	
1986	0.3130	**1312.01**	999.28	
1987	0.2023	**1177.66**	979.49	
1988	0.1129	**1168.85**	1050.30	
1989		1168.46	**1261.32**	0.0795
1990	0.0559	**1199.27**	1135.78	
1991		1169.88	**1314.78**	0.1239
1992		1149.68	**1258.79**	0.0949
1993		1056.79	**1247.36**	0.1803
1994		956.78	**1129.94**	0.1810
1995		874.74	**1404.46**	0.6056
1996		901.68	**1288.43**	0.4289
1997		919.64	**1874.77**	1.0386
1998		937.19	**2130.34**	1.2731
1999		964.28	**2314.67**	1.4004
2000		999.65	**1848.93**	0.8496
2001		1019.85	**1475.90**	0.4472
2002		1037.40	**1061.02**	0.0228
2003		1061.11	**1240.08**	0.1687

Figure 9-10

If we look at investing when the time period is ten years with 1.5% TIPS, the Formula based investment beat the straight S&P 500 investment 64% of the time. In addition, the Formula method averaged 0.4% greater returns per year. On this basis, the market timing per the Formula is superior to just blindly investing in the S&P 500 when the investment period is ten years. In addition, since the Formula investment method was out of the stock market almost half the time, this is a far lower risk method than being in the market continuously.

Now let's look at a similar comparison in Figure 9-11 when the investment window is 20 years with 1.5% TIPS.

Comparison of Formula Buy versus Straight S&P 500 Buy
20 Year Investment, $100 (year 2003 $) Every Year, 1.5% TIPS
Best results **bold**

End Year	Formula Gain	Formula Mix Results	S&P 500 Results	S&P 500 Gain
1926	0.0382	**387.72**	373.44	
1927	0.0608	**508.29**	479.15	
1928	0.0576	**704.33**	666.00	
1929	0.1783	**691.95**	587.23	
1930	0.4901	**631.47**	423.76	
1931	0.4755	**345.76**	234.33	
1932	0.4486	**304.50**	210.20	
1933	0.4398	**443.90**	308.30	
1934	0.5066	**432.85**	287.31	
1935	0.0684	**433.82**	406.05	
1936		430.46	**516.91**	0.2008
1937	0.3383	**419.51**	313.47	
1938	0.3517	**521.69**	385.96	
1939	0.3457	**476.14**	353.82	
1940	0.3370	**376.36**	281.50	
1941	0.3246	**292.97**	221.18	
1942	0.3114	**323.35**	246.57	
1943	0.2976	**368.33**	283.85	
1944	0.3144	**414.27**	315.17	

1945	0.1925	**481.25**	403.57	
1946	0.5254	**533.92**	350.02	
1947	0.4863	**530.44**	356.88	
1948	0.4542	**540.31**	371.56	
1949	0.4311	**616.18**	430.55	
1950	0.4298	**768.08**	537.18	
1951	0.4365	**869.56**	605.32	
1952	0.4458	**932.24**	644.81	
1953	0.4475	**872.13**	602.51	
1954	0.4601	**1245.82**	853.26	
1955	0.4360	**1530.94**	1066.13	
1956	0.3564	**1485.21**	1095.01	
1957	0.5741	**1434.67**	911.44	
1958	0.0424	**1282.40**	1230.19	
1959		1232.06	**1290.27**	0.0472
1960		1159.94	**1195.86**	0.0310
1961		1057.01	**1364.25**	0.2907
1962		968.19	**1120.97**	0.1578
1963		894.03	**1242.35**	0.3896
1964		744.37	**1313.15**	0.7641
1965		703.82	**1366.05**	0.9409
1966		681.60	**1118.78**	0.6414
1967		647.11	**1227.60**	0.8970
1968		614.03	**1177.24**	0.9172
1969		594.23	**933.92**	0.5717
1970		587.18	**863.42**	0.4704
1971		574.50	**883.57**	0.5380
1972		566.54	**940.60**	0.6603
1973		581.79	**709.91**	0.2202
1974	0.2993	**638.04**	491.08	
1975	0.3683	**881.39**	644.14	
1976	0.4288	**1087.23**	760.94	
1977	0.5419	**1026.93**	666.00	
1978	0.5582	**1072.95**	688.59	
1979	0.5614	**1240.29**	794.35	
1980	0.5713	**1594.43**	1014.71	
1981	0.5528	**1477.41**	951.48	
1982	0.5489	**1745.11**	1126.70	
1983	0.5703	**2123.05**	1352.02	

1984	0.5801	**2237.51**	1416.05	
1985	0.5641	**2866.52**	1832.65	
1986	0.5337	**3240.66**	2112.97	
1987	0.5116	**3291.80**	2177.67	
1988	0.3440	**3342.63**	2487.00	
1989	0.0737	**3400.23**	3166.80	
1990	0.1803	**3499.64**	2965.12	
1991		3492.13	**3733.79**	0.0692
1992		3474.15	**3899.69**	0.1225
1993		3457.71	**4111.25**	0.1890
1994		3441.44	**3856.87**	0.1207
1995		3244.71	**4950.55**	0.5257
1996		3075.70	**4667.81**	0.5176
1997		2820.72	**7023.65**	1.4900
1998		2774.02	**8218.19**	1.9626
1999		2766.54	**9034.67**	2.2657
2000		2802.70	**7525.33**	1.6850
2001		2759.07	**5913.90**	1.1434
2002		2724.99	**4134.77**	0.5174
2003		2603.70	**4795.52**	0.8418

Figure 9-11

When our investment time period is twenty years with 1.5% TIPS, the Formula based investment beat the straight S&P 500 investment 63% of the time, and on the average, the Formula method and the S&P 500 stocks returns were the same. On this basis, the market timing per the Formula is better than just blindly investing in the S&P 500 when the investment period is twenty years because the Formula investment method was out of the stock market almost half the time. This is a far lower risk than being in the market continuously. Also, as we stated earlier, many investors start out with the intention of investing for twenty or more years, then the real-world causes them to withdraw savings for some unforeseen need. Using the formula makes it far less likely that they will lose money on an early withdrawal, since the five year investment using the Formula beat the S&P 500 even with a 1.5% TIPS.

The lower TIP interest rate did not substantially change the favorable outcome of the Formula approach to investing versus the straight S&P 500 stock investment. This is because when the Formula takes you out of the market because the market is too high, the important thing is to make sure your money is in an investment that at least keeps up with inflation. The inflation portion of the income on TIPS does that.

In Smithers and Wright's *Valuing Wall Street,* the authors state that, when using a buy-and-hold strategy, investors never lost money when they were invested in stocks for 20 years. This could very well be true, but the above data shows that the Formula method, using a combination of stocks and TIPS, is even better!

A concern on any method of investing is that once the method is published it will no longer be valid because "everyone" will do it, canceling its advantage. Well, in this case, not to worry. Mutual funds will never buy into any method that would keep someone out of the stock market as long as twenty years, which the Formula method does. Even for individual investors, very few people would be able to "stand" being out of the market as it was in the nineties, when it looked like everybody was making a killing in the market!

If the market does drop enough to again be viable (per the Formula), and if the total real yield on the market is again 5.5%, which was the historical real gain, then using the above results indicates that retirement savings requirements, which will be covered in Part III, would be reduced substantially. However, it is important that ready funds be available to take advantage of this reduced market price. Also, these intervals of the market being relatively low in price may not always be in effect when savings are taking place, so you should *not* include them in your base retirement savings plan assumptions. If the opportunity of the low priced market *does* occur, and you get the extra gains from investing into that lower-priced market, then you can reduce the annual savings requirements for the remaining years of your savings.

In Smithers and Wright's *Valuing Wall Street,* it is emphasized that people nearing retirement age, or already in retirement, are at high risk using stock market yields as a source of retirement income. The potential gain for a retiree who is drawing down his principal is small compared to the downside risk of a market drop. Again, *Valuing Wall Street* states that, as you get close to retirement, you should only be invested in stocks if you are sure that the market isn't overpriced. I take that concept further and propose that near or during retirement someone should only consider investing *extra* funds in the stock market, and then only when the market is relatively *undervalued per the above Formula*!

We have been using the price/dividend ratio as a trigger to buy or sell stocks. Here is a web source for dividend information:

"Global Financial Data – Data Download/Graphing System",
http://www.globalfindata.com/cgi-bin/data_downloader2.cgi?description=UK+Consumer+...

This web site is also listed in the Appendix. The data from this site will assist in calculating the S&P 500 price/dividend ratio.

CHAPTER 10
Once You Are Back in the Stock Market

In the previous chapter, we determined that once the market drops we could use the price/dividend ratio, or the chart (figure 9-1) showing the equivalent S&P 500 price, to determine when to buy and when to sell stocks. We now want to discuss very briefly some general knowledge related to the stock market.

Index Funds versus Actively Managed Mutual Funds:

A stock index is a measure of the stock performance of a select group of companies that are supposed to be representative of the total stock market. For example, the Dow Jones Industrial Stock Index is a group of 30 company stocks picked by journalists at the Wall Street Journal. A stock index is just a score card on how well that particular group of stocks is doing at any given moment. A stock index *fund* allows someone to buy stocks in the same balance as the stocks represented by that particular index. For example, if someone buys an index fund based on the Dow Jones, they are buying shares in all the companies in the Dow Jones index and in the same proportion. An index fund makes no attempt to evaluate the individual merits of each stock within the index, so the management costs of running an index fund are very low compared to an actively managed mutual fund.

Actively managed mutual funds, where fund managers evaluate the merits of each stock, and the buying or selling of them accordingly, generally charge between 1% and 2% for this service. What do the share holders of a mutual fund get in return? On the average, they get performance *worse* than the overall market average! Even for those actively managed funds that happen, *by chance*, to beat the market in a given year, those *lucky* mutual funds are unlikely to do it the following year. There have been countless studies that confirm these findings. In the long run, actively managed mutual funds just do not perform as well as the general market!

More than a few books speak quite disparagingly about the relatively poor performance of actively managed funds and question the analytical skills of the active-fund managers, since a non-managed stock index can so readily beat them. But the relatively poor performance of actively managed mutual funds compared to index funds shouldn't be surprising. An index fund is indirectly using the average judgment of *all* the active fund managers, since the active fund managers, as a group, determine the prices of most stocks on the market. Any time a stock's price is felt to be out-of-line, at least compared to other stock prices at the time, some mutual fund buys (or sells) that stock until the price is again neutral in their collective judgment. They buy if the stock is seen as under-priced and sell if they feel the stock is over-priced.

So it's not luck, nor is it a mystery, why index funds do so well compared to actively managed mutual funds. An index fund's stocks are bought and sold at the collective (market) price, in balance with the index's stock loading, and the index fund share holders get the service of price-determination by mutual fund managers for free.

In fact, if all the investors got wise together and bought index funds rather than actively managed mutual funds, the field of active fund manager "experts" would no longer exist, and the stock market prices would become more chaotic. Only the individual investors would be determining a stock's current price, without the detailed analysis currently being done by professionals. Not to worry, though! The marketing skills of people selling actively managed mutual funds far exceed any book's ability to get the message across to people that they are wasting their money buying actively managed mutual funds. There are currently more actively managed mutual funds than there are individual company stocks to buy, and that is unlikely to change any time soon.

Newspapers are happy to report the names of the current crop of successful (i.e. beat the average mutual fund) actively managed mutual funds, especially if they were better than the average fund several years in-a-row. It doesn't matter that this performance of "successful" mutual funds can easily be explained by simple probability. If a lot of actively managed mutual funds are "playing" the market, statistically some are bound to do better than the others, even sometimes for multiple years. In fact, with the large number of actively managed mutual funds, it is likely that some fund will beat the average fund 10+ years in a row due to chance alone. After all, the odds of getting ten-heads-in-a-row on ten flips of a coin are one-in-1024, and there are more than

1024 actively managed mutual funds. Since each mutual fund has an approximate 50% chance of beating the average mutual fund in any given year, one is likely to beat the average fund 10 times in-a-row by chance alone.

The fund managers of the "better-than-average" mutual funds then get their "well-earned" millions of dollars in bonuses. Many of the mutual funds that are unlucky enough to be below average several years in-a-row will just sort of vanish, so their results will no longer be seen as a blemish on the brokerage firm's mutual fund list. *Sweet game*!

As we have shown, an alternative to buying an actively managed mutual fund is buying an index fund that matches its stock mix to an index. Some of the indexes from which you can choose to match are the Dow Jones Industrial, the S&P 500, the Russell 3000, and the Wilshire 5000. So if you want to buy into the general stock market, choose an index fund, not an actively managed mutual fund.

Random Walk:

The term "random walk", made famous by Burton Malkiel's *A Random Walk Down Wall Street*, which was published over 30 years ago, basically means that a stock's price movement is truly random, and that any prior change in a stock's price has no influence on whether its future price will be higher, lower, or the same. This is analogous to the concept of each flip of a coin being truly independent of the results of any previous coin flip.

The Efficient Market Theory:

The Efficient Market Theory assumes that all stocks are perfectly priced at all times, based on all information available, and that all information is instantly known by all. The effect of this theory is that no stock is more of a bargain than any other stock, since any difference between stocks related to current or future performance, perceived or real, is already incorporated into a stock's price, and any new information will be instantly adjusted-for. Therefore, no arbitrage situation ever arises such that someone could make a profit by buying an under-priced stock because of some important knowledge positively affecting the company's future and selling shortly when the price reacted to this information. The Efficient Market Theory assumes that *everyone* becomes aware of any important piece of knowledge affecting the company at the same time, and the price instantly corrects without any individual being able to gain from the knowledge.

In the earlier discussion on index funds, it was stated that "any time a stock's price is felt to be out-of-line, at least compared to other stock prices at the time, some mutual fund buys (or sells) that stock until the price is again neutral in their collective judgment." This process is pre-assumed in an Efficient Market.

The effect of the Random Walk and the Efficient Market Theories is that the price of a stock is always correct. If both of these theories are 100% correct, then there is never a "good buy" or "bad buy" on a stock or on the market in general; nor is there a "good time" or "bad time" to buy stocks. Indeed, throwing darts at a financial page on random days would be just as effective as any other investment method!

The Random Walk and Efficient Market Theories may be generally valid, but at times, non-random events seem to drive stock prices. On October 19, 1987, Black Monday, the market dropped 23%! Were the stocks properly priced, per the Efficient Market Theory, before or after the drop? Once the market started this severe drop, was every "next price" during the following hours truly as random as the Random Walk Theory maintains?

The Efficient Market Theory seems valid in keeping individual stock prices in-line with each other at any given point in time. But it does not seem effective in keeping the *total* market "logically" priced at all times.

Most methods that attempt to "beat the market" violate the Random Walk Theory and/or the Efficient Market Theory, since they attempt to "time" the market or make some judgment on stock prices being over or under priced.

Below, Figure 10-1, is a chart showing the S&P 500 total return for the last 103 years. Total return means that dividends and inflation are included.

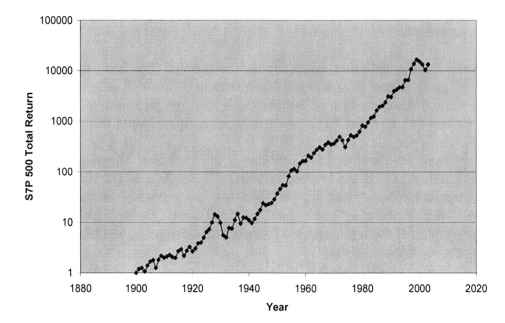

Figure 10-1

These results of the S&P 500 total return, shown on a semi-log plot (Figure 10-1), certainly don't look random. The chart appears to have a long-term upward trend. This graph and the other above observations call into question the validity of both the Random Walk and Efficient Market theories.

Buying Individual Stocks versus Buying an Index Fund

Even though index funds readily beat actively managed mutual fund performance, index funds may not be your best investment strategy once the market becomes reasonably priced. First, index funds still have some degree of stock turnover as companies are moved into and out of the fund portfolio. Since 1931, 38 stocks have moved in and out of the Dow, and the Dow is by far the most stable of the indexed funds. This stock movement does add to fund management costs.

Here are a few examples of stocks that may be good short term stocks, but stocks that you would probably be wise to stay away from as a long-term investor. With index funds you will be buying many of these stocks, since they are included in many index funds. I will use stocks included in the Dow Jones Index Fund as examples because the stocks I mention will then be familiar to most of you. Note that since I first wrote this chapter, two of the six stocks I mention (AT&T and Kodak) have been taken off the Dow. This is because people on the Wall Street Journal, who decide the makeup of the Dow, no longer felt that these companies were indicative of the general market. I left the discussion of these two companies in the chapter because I believe that this recent action by the journalists at the Wall Street Journal supports my point that some stocks in indexes are NOT good long term buys because the companies are no longer dynamic. My analysis just happened to beat the "Wall Street Journal" people to this conclusion.

AT&T Previously a powerhouse, AT&T no longer leads in anything, and all parts of their business are under attack by more aggressive competitors. AT&T pays a good yield and is not at risk of going bankrupt anytime in the near future, but it may not be a good long-term stock purchase.

Boeing Co. Anything related to aircraft is at risk since the terrorist attack of 9/11. Airplanes will always be susceptible to terrorist attacks, so air travel will continue to be under pressure. If airlines don't have customers or profits, they don't buy new planes. The United States military air-power is clearly superior to everyone in the world, so future plane purchases by the military will be at risk of budget pressures. Not a good long-term stock.

Eastman Kodak This company is primarily in the photographic film business, which is slowly being replaced by digital. Although Kodak is making an attempt to enter the digital market with its own line of digital cameras, they are behind the development curve and will not lead the market. They were too slow to react to the realities of the market place. Not a good long-term stock.

General Motors GM is losing market share every year. To get sales they are discounting cars to the point that their profits per vehicle are very low. They have billions of dollars of obligations for pensions and health care benefits. They have outmoded and under-utilized plants they can't close because of union contract agreements. Their dividend is great, so they attract short-term buyers. But in the long run, their poor performance in the market will eventually force them to reduce this dividend. This is *not* a good long-term buy. This is now especially true because the Chinese have announced that they are going to enter the United States automobile market in 2007, with automobiles priced 30% less than the competition.

IBM   Another former powerhouse, IBM has trouble growing revenues. They are growing profits by cost cutting, but somewhere along the way this well will dry up, and the fact that their business is not growing will catch up. This is NOT a good long-term buy.

McDonald's   No one can go into a McDonald's restaurant and not see that their star has faded. What was once a dynamic restaurant chain, clean, with uniformly hot food, with people smiling and working very hard, has now become mediocre by any measure. They keep searching for the new Big Mac that will make their business take off, but they haven't found it. Their expansions overseas have not met expectations, and they are slowing growth in that direction. Competitors have managed to give the public a perceived healthier and better product, served in a cleaner environment. McDonalds' long-term future just doesn't look that great.

The above listed six stocks of concern until recently represented 20% of the Dow Jones stock mix. This means that for anyone buying a Dow index, one out of every five stocks being purchased were stocks that may not have represented a good long-term purchase.

There is another problem with buying an index fund. There is one area where mutual fund managers may *not* be the primary element determining stock price. This is on stocks that become "fad" stocks. AOL was an example of this during the recent bubble. Its price was bid up to levels that could never be justified by *any* future business forecast. Again, index funds may have some "fad" stocks included, which you buy automatically with the index fund.

Buying Individual Stocks

An option to index funds is buying individual stocks. Most books on investing stress diversification. So if you choose to buy individual stocks, purchase a different stock each time. Don't get enamored with one or two stocks. Once your portfolio has six or more stocks, you are getting sufficiently diversified. Note that when buying stocks, try not to buy stocks in similar fields. For example, buying stocks of two automobile manufacturers, or two financial organizations, would be limiting your diversification. Sometimes stocks move together for reasons not outwardly apparent, as you will see below in the comparison of Wal-Mart and Johnson & Johnson. It may be worthwhile to look at the stock prices for the last five to ten years to make sure you don't buy stocks whose prices move in lock-step.

Here is an example (Figure 10-2) where the two stock prices have *not* moved in concert and would therefore be viable stocks to be purchased for diversity. The two stocks are 3M and Microsoft.

MMM and Microsoft Stock prices

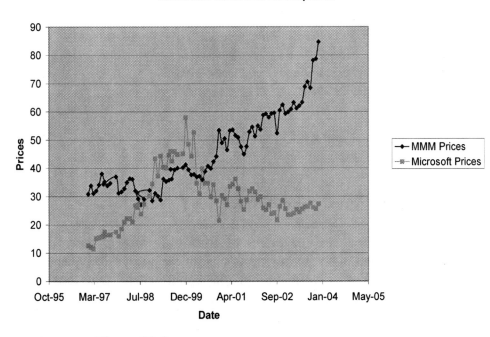

Figure 10-2

Below, in Figure 10-3, are shown two stocks that would *not* do well as far as diversity, since they both track somewhat together. The two stocks are Wal-Mart and Johnson & Johnson. Note that it is not outwardly obvious that these two stocks should track together.

Wal-Mart and Johnson & Johnson Stock Prices

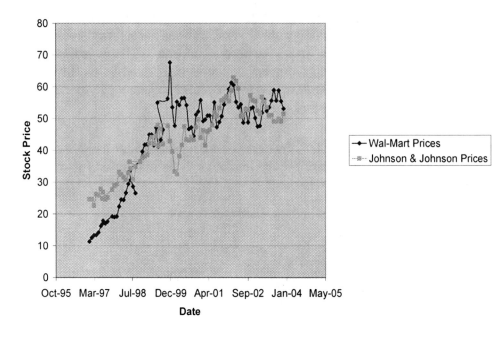

Figure 10-3

Which Individual Stocks Should You Buy?

We already mentioned that the prices of stocks are largely determined by mutual fund managers, who are buying stocks for the short-term, generally for less than one year. Your investment horizon would generally be longer. You want to be able to buy stocks with long-term potential so you can hold them long enough to qualify for the capital gains tax, but these stocks aren't always easy to find without massive amounts of detailed research.

What if you could get a group of "experts," who had no bias to sell you stocks, to select stocks that were great substantial companies that are stable, represent this country's industry, and are likely to continue to grow and prosper for many years? Incidentally, it would be nice if they would do this for free.

Well, the expert-picked stocks are already out there for you to use. The stocks in the Dow are picked by the staff of the "Wall Street Journal" for the reasons just discussed. So, why not just buy a Dow Index fund? We already mentioned the problems of company changes in the index, fad stocks, and stocks no longer viable long-term. The companies representing the Dow, as is true with any company, have an earnings life-cycle, where the company is initially growing and dynamic, then mature and stable, and then slowly dying as new and more aggressive companies take their place. When a company becomes part of the Dow, it usually stays on the Dow until it is clearly in the dying stage. That is why, of the list of six problem stocks just discussed, two were just removed from the Dow. They were dying (or, at least having some respiratory problems). Below, in Figure 10-4, is a visual representation of a company's life cycle.

Typical Earnings Life-Cycle of a Company

EARNINGS

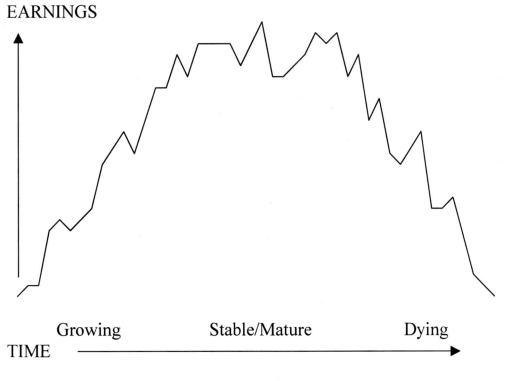

Figure 10-4

You would like to buy stocks in the early growing stage of the life cycle. To do this, buy the stocks that were *most recently added* to the DOW. You can look on the net to see the most recent additions. Here are the most recent at the time of this book's writing.

2004   American International Group, Pfizer, Verizon Communications.
1999   Home Depot, Microsoft, Intel.
1997   Wal-Mart, Travelers Group, Hewlett-Packard, Johnson & Johnson.
1991   Caterpillar, Walt Disney, J. P. Morgan
1987   Coca-Cola
1985   McDonald's, Philip Morris (Altria)
1982   American Express
1979   IBM, Merck
1976   3M
1959   Alcoa, Owen's-Illinois, Swift & Co

Let's look at how these stocks have done against the S&P 500 for five and ten year holds. I am only showing the ones for which I have data that includes the effect of dividends and splits, and have sufficient data for the ten year holds. For this example, I assume purchase of the stock the year after they were added to the Dow.

Gain % after 5 year holds:

Buy Year	Company	S&P 500	Company	Company/S&P 500
1977	3M	94%	575%	6.12
1980	IBM	98%	393%	4.01
1983	American Express	103%	614%	5.96
1986	McDonald's	104%	143%	1.38
1986	Philip Morris (Altria)	104%	1973%	18.97
1988	Coca-Cola	97%	654%	6.74
1992	Caterpillar	152%	389%	2.56
1992	Walt Disney	152%	148%	0.97
1992	J. P. Morgan	152%	226%	1.49

Testing for significant differences between the S&P 500 gains vs. the gains on the most recent adds to the Dow for a five year hold, using the S&P 500 as the population, we can be 99% confident that the superior results of the recent adds to the Dow were *not* due to random cause. Random cause means "just due to luck".

Gain % after 10 year holds:

Buy Year	Company	S&P 500	Company	Company/S&P 500
1977	3M	315%	9728%	30.9
1980	IBM	268%	778%	2.90
1983	American Express	302%	1857%	6.15
1986	McDonald's	238%	737%	3.10
1986	Philip Morris (Altria)	238%	6094%	25.6
1988	Coca-Cola	480%	3224%	6.72
1992	Caterpillar	144%	375%	2.60
1992	Walt Disney	144%	76%	0.53
1992	J. P. Morgan	144%	169%	1.17

Testing for significant differences between the S&P 500 gains vs. the gains on the most recent adds to the Dow for a ten year hold, using the S&P 500 as the population, we can be 97.5% confident that the superior results of the recent adds to the Dow were not due to random cause.

Note that for both the five year and ten year holds, the individual stocks beat the S&P 89% of the time, and often by a substantial amount.

Let's look at the 10 year charts for each of these individual stocks and see if we can glean even more insight on these stocks. They are plotted logarithmically, so that a constant increase will appear as an upwardly sloped line. Below are Figures 10-5 through 10-13.

S&P 500 Total Return vs. 3M Total Return , with 1977 as Base 1

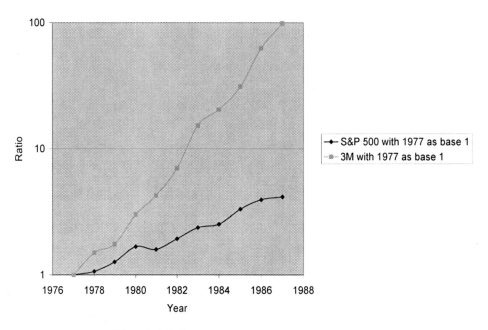

Figure 10-5

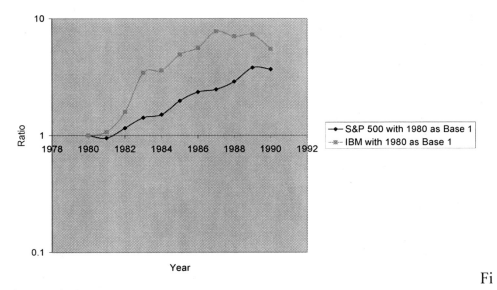

Figure 10-6

Fi

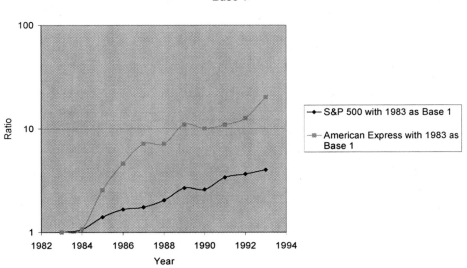

Figure 10-7

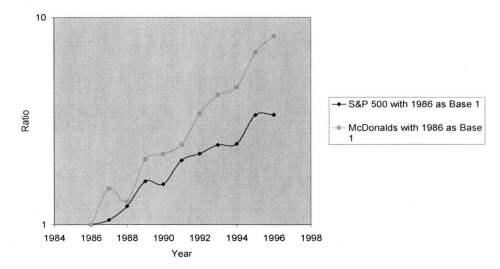

Figure 10-8

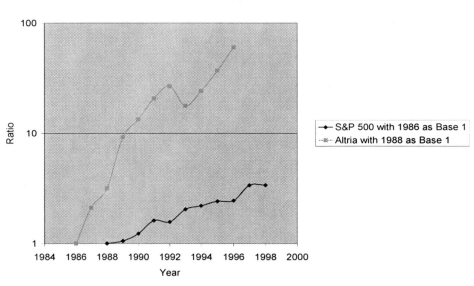

Figure 10-9

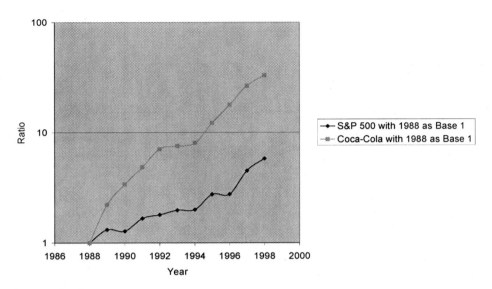

Figure 10-10

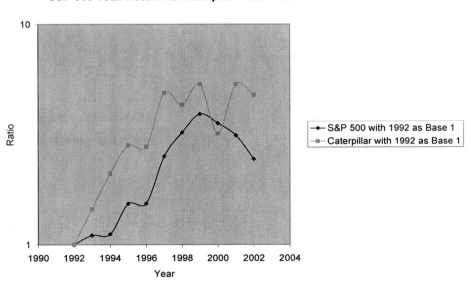

Figure 10-11

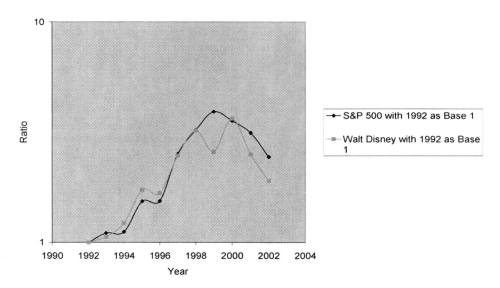

Figure 10-12

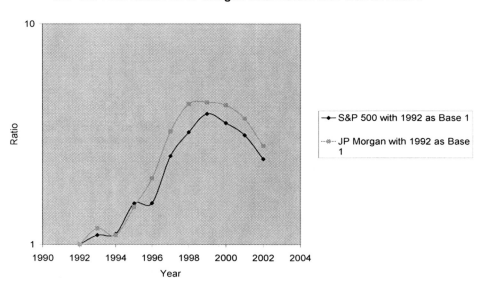

Figure 10-13

You can see that Walt Disney was the only stock that did not beat the S&P 500 for the 10 year hold period. It was also the only company stock that was not substantially ahead of the S&P 500 after five years, so perhaps this should have served as a warning that this stock was not without issues. However, for the ten years, it still had a return of 6.5% per year, which is not a disaster. Here are the annual yields of the above nine company stocks vs. the S&P 500 for the related ten year hold period.

Years	S&P 500 Annual Yield	Company	Company Annual Yield
1977-1987	15.2%	3M	58%
1980-1990	14.0%	IBM	18.5%
1983-1993	15.0%	AmericanExpress	35%
1986-1986	13.0%	McDonald's	23.3%
1986-1996	13.0%	Altria	50%
1988-1998	19.2%	Coca-Cola	42%
1992-2002	9.3%	Caterpillar	17.0%
1992-2002	9.3%	Walt Disney	6.5%
1992-2002	9.3%	JP Morgan	10.9%

The average annual percentage that the company stocks beat the S&P 500 was 16.0%.

The above comparisons were based on buying the most recent addition to the Dow in the year following its acceptance into the Dow. However, we said earlier that we only wanted to buy stocks when the overall market was low priced. That is why we developed the Formula based on the price/dividend ratio. Let's see how the most recent additions to the Dow do when purchased per the dates shown as Formula buy-years, using the previous Formula low price trigger, as shown on Figure 9-4, rather than automatically buying them the year after they were added to the DOW. Again, we are limited to looking at the dates and stocks where we have full stock information, including the effect of reinvested dividends and splits. The results are compared to the total S&P 500 data, which also includes the effect of reinvested dividends.

The Formula buy dates are 1974, 1978, 1979, 1980, 1981, and 1982. The Formula sell date for all these stocks, also from Figure 9-4, is 1986.

Recent Dow Stocks vs. S&P 500 Using Formula Buy-days

Buy Year	Sell Year	Company	S&P 500 Total Gain	Company Total Gain
1974	1986	Alcoa	528%	3600%
1978	1986	3M	272%	4070%
1979	1986	3M	212%	3471%
1980	1986	IBM	135%	463%
1981	1986	IBM	147%	424%
1982	1986	IBM	104%	254%

Start	End	S&P 500 Annual Yield	Company	Company Annual Yield
1974	1986	16.5%	Alcoa	36%
1978	1986	17.8%	3M	60%
1979	1986	17.7%	3M	67%
1980	1986	15.3%	IBM	36%
1981	1986	19.8%	IBM	43%
1982	1986	19.4%	IBM	41%

The average weighted annual yield difference between the S&P 500 and the above company stocks that were bought and sold per the Formula dates was 29.6% - the recent additions to the Dow bought per the Formula low price trigger-dates beat the S&P 500 by almost 30% per year! This is versus the 16% difference when the stocks were bought the year after getting in the Dow and then held for 10 years. The Formula "buy" trigger, which is the price/dividend being at or below 17.2, makes the "buy the most recent stock in the Dow" method look even more attractive.

There is no magic on why this works. Recent Dow stocks get overpriced when the market is doing well because of the publicity they get. These stocks would have already been well known, and adding them to the Dow just gives them even more visibility. When the market tanks, these overpriced stocks get hit extra hard in the drop, because they were overpriced. Then, once the stock market again gets favorable, the recent Dow stocks are the ones the public and the mutual fund managers like, and the stocks to which they return. So, it is strictly market timing that makes this work. Incidentally, there is something called *beta* that is a measure of a stock's relative movement versus the total market. The recent Dow additions will generally have high betas.

Although six pieces of data are usually enough to determine if averages are statistically significantly different, since only three companies are involved in the previous analysis, and the data are overlapping, the data are not truly independent. So statistical significance tests can not be run. However, the results look so impressive that we want to test them in the actual full Formula method (Figure 9-14 below), where we are buying TIPS when the market price/dividend ratio is too high. If you recall, in the Formula we:

Buy stocks (in this case, the most recent additions to the Dow) anytime the price/dividend ratio of the S&P 500 is at or below 17.2. We will not only be putting new investment money into buying these stocks, but we will also sell all the TIPS we have accumulated, and use those funds to buy stocks. When the price/dividend of the S&P 500 again goes above 17.2, we will stop buying stocks with new investment money and start buying TIPS. If the price/dividend of the S&P 500 then goes above 28, we will sell any stocks we have accumulated and use the funds from the sale to buy TIPS.

We will start in 1955 since we have no total individual stock information (including the effect of dividends and splits) before that year. As in the prior model, $100 per year in 2003 dollars is invested as a way of keeping score. The costs of trades are not included because the cost of buying individual stocks per the Formula method and the cost of buying an S&P 500 index fund would be similar, so the comparisons are valid with or without these trade costs. This comparisons are shown in Figure 10-14 below. The numbers within the table represent dollars (in 2003 dollar equivalents).

Most Recent Dow Stocks Bought and Sold per the Formula
The numbers within the table, except the year, are dollars
(in 2003 dollar equivalents)

Accum Alcoa	Accum 3M	Accum IBM	Accum Formula Stock	Accum TIPS	Year (Bold When Buy Stocks)	Accum Formula TIPS&Stks	Accum S&P
			0	15	1955	15	15
			0	30	1956	30	31
			0	47	1957	47	43
			0	65	1958	65	77
			0	84	1959	84	102
			0	104	1960	104	119
			0	125	1961	125	167
			0	147	1962	147	169
			0	170	1963	170	224
			0	194	1964	194	278
			0	221	1965	221	330
			0	253	1966	253	314
			0	286	1967	286	407
			0	327	1968	327	471
			0	376	1969	376	451
			0	430	1970	430	490
			0	478	1971	478	582
			0	532	1972	532	715
			0	617	1973	617	633
738	0	0	738	0	**1974**	738	491
754			754	29	1975	783	703
770			770	62	1976	832	901
787			787	100	1977	886	869
803	146		949	0	**1978**	949	960
820	208		1027	0	**1979**	1027	1176
2459	356	42	2857	0	**1980**	2857	1601
3278	504	93	3876	0	**1981**	3876	1570
5737	830	190	6757	0	**1982**	6757	1960
13934	1809	464	16207	54	1983	16261	2456
15573	2432	542	18547	114	1984	18661	2666
22949	3677	799	27426	179	1985	27605	3570
			0	39013	1986	39013	4297
			0	41974	1987	41974	4583

				0	45152	1988	45152	5408
				0	48672	1989	48672	7188
				0	53173	1990	53173	7035
				0	56472	1991	56472	9252
				0	59880	1992	59880	10033
				0	63401	1993	63401	11123
				0	67079	1994	67079	11350
				0	70877	1995	70877	15698
				0	75443	1996	75443	15819
				0	79078	1997	79078	25968
				0	82814	1998	82814	33478
				0	87612	1999	87612	40613
				0	93301	2000	93301	37008
				0	97965	2001	97965	32705
				0	102551	2002	102551	25560
				0	107951	2003	107951	32943

Figure 10-14

You can see that the TIPS/stock Formula buys are currently worth three times what the straight S&P 500 investment is worth. And if the stock market takes a dive and loses over half its value as predicted, that will make the Formula method of buying the most recent additions to the Dow even more attractive vs. the S&P 500. Let's look at these results on a logarithmic graph, Figure 10-15.

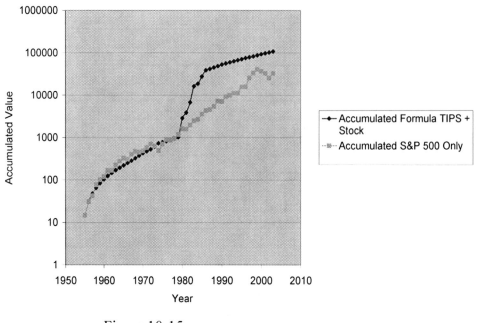

Figure 10-15

You can see that the two methods tracked each other for the first nineteen years, and then the Formula method sold all the TIPS and began buying the most recent stock additions to the Dow. All these stocks were sold in 1986, and since then all the purchases have been TIPS.

The Formula method, which uses the price/dividend ratio to determine when to buy and sell stocks, is far less risky than buying the S&P 500 on a regular basis. This is because in the above example, stocks were owned only twelve of the 48 years of the example. This means that we were in the market only 25% of the time, with the other 75% of the time owning only TIPS, a very low-risk investment.

Since only three stocks were included in the above example that used the Dow additions in conjunction with the Formula, this is too small of a sample to be certain that these results will repeat. But since we were able to do statistical tests on the earlier sample of nine stocks that were just admitted to the Dow (without including the Formula timing), this gives us some sense that this investment method is at least worth considering, especially given the outstanding results.

In the above example, only three stocks are shown even though there were six "buy" years. The reason only three stocks are shown is that the complete returns data (including the effects of dividends) on the three other recent additions to the Dow was not available. This may have been due to companies being bought by other companies, mergers, or some limitations in the references I was using for this data. In following the Formula in a real-world scenario, six different stocks would have been purchased from the recent additions to the Dow list, to give diversity to the portfolio of stocks.

This method of investing in the most recent additions to the Dow is presented only as an example of how buying individual stocks may be better than an index fund. The number of stocks and incidences referenced above are not enough to be sure this approach is statistically valid. However, it seems that the worst someone is likely to do with this approach is to match the market, without the negatives inherent in index funds. As stated earlier, the mutual fund managers are the primary determinant of stock prices, and they are basing their decisions on which stocks have the best short-term potential. By definition, looking for longer-term returns should offer a type of arbitrage opportunity for investors, since stocks priced by mutual fund managers may *not* be ideally priced for long-term.

Referenced Books

Some of the reference books listed in this book's Appendix show how the overall performance of the stock market can be exceeded by following that book's own specific investment strategy. If the improved market performance as shown in these books was truly valid, it could be incorporated into any savings assumptions, and the resultant higher yields would greatly reduce any retirement savings requirements. However, when these books' theories for "beating the market" are analyzed closely, they seem to have some issues.

First, some general comments on some of the analyses done in the referenced books, especially related to each author's own theories of "beating the market". The authors didn't seem to make statistical errors when they were discussing the stock market in general, but they did when they were trying to prove their own theories.

The reference books chosen were generally limited to those that showed or described the data they used in forming their conclusions. People, even scientists, often slant data that supports their preconceived notions. The test goal in this book was be able to independently validate the conclusions of the authors of the reference books and to check any statistical methods used, since this is often another source of error. It was necessary to make sure that the authors weren't just mining data (looking at reams of data) until some sort of correlation was found that supported their theories but had no real logic basis. After all, most statistical tests are to a 95% confidence level, so if you look at 20 random events, one is likely to test as being statistically significant just due to random cause.

Most of the books referenced were published after the year 2000. This requirement was included because the market drop in 2000 gives an additional significant market event that should be included in any analysis.

Books that emphasized the detail of digging into a company's balance sheets were not referenced. This is because this type of analysis is already being done by countless experts working at the major brokerage firms. They have powerful computers, vast data bases, and complex programs with which no individual (or writer) can hope to compete. Everyone doing that type of analyses tends to reach the same general conclusions, and any effect is usually already included in the stock price.

The stock market has been studied by countless people. Any new way of "beating the market" should be suspect, if for no other reason than why haven't other intelligent people already discovered this finding? Perhaps the observations made in reviewing the reference books will give you pause when you find *any* book, including this one, making a point on the market and seemingly to be "proving it with data". The reader must apply his or her own logic tests.

A book called *Winning with the Dow's Losers*, by Charles Carlson, tests the theory that the Dow Jones Industrial Average's poorest performers for a given year will to do better the following year. This is not a new idea, which Mr. Carlson acknowledges. He just gives a different spin to the concept, which he backs up with many years of data. This back-up data is what he believes makes his book unique and valid. In some of his examples, he uses a 73-year investment time period to "prove" his theory, which, as we previously discussed, may be of statistical interest but has little real-world application. Generally, no one's investment window is 73 years.

Mr. Carlson also compares five year and ten year outputs against the overall Dow and concludes that the *variation* with his plan is less than the variation of the Dow. Five or ten pieces of annual data are enough to compare averages, but not enough to make a valid statistical comparison of *variation* with any degree of confidence, so his conclusion is not statistically defensible.

In other analyses, Mr. Carlson includes six months of 2003 as an equivalent full year because six months is all the data he had in 2003 before publishing. Without including 2003, many of his conclusions weren't quite as impressive! Using six months of data that is a primary support of a theory, even if the intent is not to mislead, is suspect where everything else is yearly data.

In *Yes, You Can Time the Market*, by Ben Stein and Phil DeMuth, in the Chapter "The Power of Price," the book shows an analysis comparing buying stocks when the S&P 500 price is below its 15-year moving average (the book's plan) versus buying the S&P 500 stocks on a consistent-buy-basis, disregarding the price. They chose a time period of 1977 to 2002.

At the beginning eight years of this period the market price *is* below the 15-year S&P 500 moving average price, so the book "allows" the book's plan to *double* the investment (versus the consistent-buy-basis plan) during this favorable time period. At the end of the total 25 year example period, the authors show that the book's plan did 89% better than buying the market for the example time period.

The comparison, however, is not valid because they had different investment amounts invested at different time periods. This is comparing apples to oranges. Also, the actual difference between the two methods, as far as comparing the *total* gains, was only 4%. Nowhere in the book's analysis did they account for the fact that the book's "plan" was allowed to invest almost $10,000 extra (doubling) at the beginning of the time period, with no consideration for discounting whatever loss occurred from taking the funds from another investment. This is also a problem several other places in the book.

The time period chosen for the above example is fortuitous for the authors. Had the example stopped one year earlier, the result would have favored the consistent investment plan, not the book's investment method.

Early in the book, the authors of *Yes, You Can Time the Market* seem to demonstrate some misunderstanding of Dollar Cost Averaging. They *negatively state* that, in Dollar Cost Averaging, when the stock market goes up in price you buy fewer shares of stock with the same dollars.

This is *not* a negative. That is the whole *essence* of dollar averaging: that you buy more shares when the price is low and buy fewer shares when the stock price is high. In this way, with the up and down variations of the market over time, the average price *paid per share* of stock would be less than the average price of the stock during the same time period. This is because the normal mathematical way to calculate an "average" would be to assume that you bought the same *number of shares* each time you purchased shares, whereas in

Dollar Averaging the constant is the *number of dollars* each time you purchase shares. Since investment plans through payroll deduction are based on number of dollars, not number of shares, many investors practice dollar averaging without even realizing it.

In *The Four Pillars of Investing*, by William Bernstein, generally an excellent book, there is confusing advice in the Chapter "Measuring the Beast". After many pages of careful analysis, the author concludes that, in the future, real stock returns will be close to 3.5%. He then goes on to say that an aggressive investor should have no more than 80% invested in stocks. If the author really believes his own conclusion about future returns on stocks being only 3.5%, not much more than risk-free TIPS (Treasury Inflation Protected Securities), investing 80% in stocks wouldn't be "aggressive", it would be 'foolhardy'!

The portfolios William Bernstein pushes at the end of the book, which seemingly include every domestic and overseas investment instrument currently available, would take a full-time investment advisor to manage. Of course, since he *is* a professional investment advisor, there could be some self-serving view of investment-needs here!

Andrew Smithers and Stephen Wright's *Valuing Wall Street* is a book about something called the q ratio, which is the ratio of "Stock Price" divided by "Corporate Net Worth per Share". The book shows that there is an almost 100% correlation between the percent change in the q ratio and the percent change in the stock price. So why not just use stock price change directly and get away from the acknowledged problem of the accuracy of the included Corporate Net Worth per Share measurement?

In fact, in the above mentioned book, *Yes, You Can Time the Market*, the authors show that price alone is somewhat superior to the q ratio when tested on historical results. It should be noted, however, that the Corporate Net Worth per Share value is obtained in a somewhat different manner in one book versus the other.

Winning the Loser's Game, by Charles D. Ellis, presents a somewhat confusing statistic. Without going through all the preliminary data of the example in the book's chapter "Time", the author concludes that an annualized rate of return is between a profit of 405% and a loss of 372%. Besides giving a range of outcomes that is so wide as to be meaningless, how can you lose more than 100% without selling shares short, which is not part of the book's methodology?

PART III
Surviving and Saving During the Coming Depression

Chapter 11: How should one Survive the coming Depression?
Keep a job, limit debts, and stay away from the stock market until it tanks.

Chapter 12: Managing to Save Before and During the Depression
You have to be realistic about how much savings it takes to reach a financial goal with available interest rates. Use the charts in this chapter to determine required savings.

Chapter 13: I Want To Retire Soon? How Much Money Will I Need?
Anyone retiring soon should be sure that they have sufficient funds, especially given the fact that someone retiring within the next few years may spend their whole retirement in an economic depression. Use the charts in this chapter to determine how much money is required.

CHAPTER 11
So How Should One Survive the Coming Depression?

Obviously, having a job during the depression is critical, unless someone is already very comfortably retired or is extremely wealthy. During most recessions and depressions the majority of people *do* stay employed, and those are the people I am addressing in this chapter. Anyone thinking of leaving his or her job at this time may want to review that decision, given the likelihood of a depression in 2007 or so. This is probably not the time to initiate a war with your boss or to tell him exactly what you think about him or your job! Also, it probably is not a good time to start a business that is relying on growth in the general economy.

In the coming depression, versus in the 2000 stock market drop, or even the 1929 depression, more of the middle class and upper-middle class are going to be dramatically affected. Some people in these "comfortable" classes will have their homes foreclosed because they are so extended in their mortgages and other debts. Not only are they at risk of losing their jobs, but also their homes and cars. Many families have payments that rely on two incomes, so even the loss of one of the family jobs will put their whole economic existence at risk.

Those who are overburdened with a mortgage payment, a situation that was encouraged by the recent very low mortgage rates that encouraged refinancing, or buying with little or no down payment, should take this opportunity before the depression to downsize, even if that means taking a small loss on their existing home. Once the depression starts, home prices may stay fairly stable for a year or so before the full weight of the depression causes them to drop in price. If a family has two incomes, strive to make the mortgage payment low enough such that one of you could lose their job without jeopardizing the ability to make the house payment. You can lose your expensive car or they can cancel your credit cards. Not good, but not the end of the world, either. Losing these is nothing compared to losing your job or your home.

This doesn't mean that those who have homes that are paid for, or whose mortgage payments are not overwhelming, should sell and downsize. When all the dust settles and the recovery is in full swing, real assets like a home will still have value that will then start to appreciate. And you will be able to live in relative comfort during the depression, while many others are not doing so well. This is nothing that should generate guilt. Most people have the opportunity to control their expenses versus their income, and you should get the rewards that come from frugality. Those who use their seed corn to fill their stomachs now can not be surprised, or whine, when they have no crops the following year.

Having many people from the middle or upper-middle class in economic straits is extremely dangerous for the government itself. This group has experienced power and can mobilize itself to action, and not always in a positive vein. They *will* find someone else to blame for their woes. The victims of their ire will not only be the normal groups that are persecuted, who are the minorities and immigrants, but also those who are extremely wealthy or powerful. Of special risk will be CEOs and government leaders who are still drawing obscene salaries during the depression. It is very likely that, for this elite group, the fear of outside terrorists will be replaced by a fear of internal groups or individuals looking to avenge their own devastating situation. During the 1929 depression, communism became popular to many in the United States, and Hitler and the Nazis came to power during economic hard times in Germany. People will be attracted to any group that gives them a simplistic cause of the depression and that holds some promise for a quick recovery, even if this solution involves hurting other innocent groups.

Not being overly in debt is critical, so that any rise in living costs and interest rates doesn't drive you into bankruptcy. You want enough of a cushion such that a reduction in wages or work does not push you over some economic cliff. You want to be able to quietly stand aside from the turmoil that will dominate society, until the depression bottoms out and the slow recovery begins. This turmoil will last many years, because it will not be easy to mollify all the forces coming together to cause this depression. But the turmoil will eventually end!

Having savings in inflation protected government securities (TIPS) and being out of the stock market until the depression bottoms are critical. At the depression bottom, there will be great opportunities for depression survivors. Relative bargains will be available on homes and other high dollar items. One of these relative bargains will be stocks, because either no one will want to buy them or other potential investors will have already lost all their money. How funds should be saved until you are able to capitalize on these bottom-of-depression opportunities is the subject of future chapters.

We have seen in the earlier chapters that current stock prices are historically very high, and there is likely to be another severe drop in the stock market in the near future. Even if the stock market were to stay at its current level for several years before this drop occurs, the only real benefit in owning stocks would be the current 1.5% dividend. This is lower than the 3% we assumed for Treasury Inflation Protected Securities (TIPS).

CHAPTER 12
Managing to Save Before and During the Depression

The coming depression will be very long and hard. The 1929 depression really didn't end until the fifties, at least as far as the stock market goes, and it is difficult to determine if World War II shortened or lengthened that depression. Fifteen or twenty years would be a reasonable estimate for how long the coming depression will last. So for many people, a third of their working career may be spent living through the coming depression. Because of this, we must talk about how you can save for the future while you are trying to survive a depression.

Even in a severe depression, people will still have goals, such as saving for a child's college education or for their own comfortable retirement. Life will go on during and after the depression, and so will planning for the future, especially for those fortunate enough to still be employed. However, blindly putting money into a mutual fund, in the hope that the savings will skyrocket in value, probably never was a very effective plan, and it certainly isn't going to work during the depression. Buy-and-Hold as a stock investment plan will become Buy-and-Weep! Savings before and during the initial stages of the depression will have to be very conservative and out of the stock market.

We have to get realistic about how much savings it takes to reach a financial goal with available interest rates. *Money never has liked to work very hard. The end of the last century temporarily hid this fact, but only the very wealthy have ever been able to live solely on the earnings from their money.* You must satisfy yourself that real gains of 10% per year on your savings are not going to be obtainable. They generally weren't available in the past and certainly are not going to be in the immediate future.

Simple Savings to get a Known Lump Dollar Sum

Before we review required annual savings, it helps to understand how to calculate these savings requirements. Those who truly hate data can just skim through the following detail, but having an understanding of calculating even simple savings requirements will give some insight on how savings calculations are complicated by the inclusion of inflation considerations. However, understanding this is not required to use the savings tables and formulas in this book.

Let's look at the simplest type of savings calculation, where we already know how much we want to have saved (in a lump sum) in a specific number of years, like wanting $10,000 saved in ten years. We will assume we are saving the money in TIPS at 3% interest, and for our example, we will initially assume zero inflation. Below, in Figure 12-1, is a table showing how much you would have to save annually to have various amounts from $10,000 to $1,000,000 after a number of years, at 3% interest.

3% interest on money, even after inflation, will seem strikingly low to many of you. But think how great this 3% per year looks compared to those who bought stock in 2000, and whose stock value is now down 25% (at the end of 2003). And think how good that 3% per year will look several years from now, compared to those same stock holders whose stock values will drop an additional 70% from their end-of-2003 value!

The numbers within the table below, Figure 12-1, are the annual savings required. The numbers across the top of the table are the final lump sum savings goals.

Annual Savings Required to Reach Various Goals at 3% Interest

Various Lump Sum Savings Goals

Years	$10,000	$25,000	$50,000	$100,000	$250,000	$500,000	$1,000,000
2	$4,858	$12,144	$24,289	$48,577	$121,443	$242,886	$485,772
4	$2,356	$5,890	$11,780	$23,561	$58,902	$117,804	$235,608
6	$1,523	$3,808	$7,616	$15,233	$38,082	$76,164	$152,328
8	$1,108	$2,769	$5,538	$11,076	$27,690	$55,380	$110,760
10	$859	$2,147	$4,294	$8,587	$21,468	$42,936	$85,872
12	$693	$1,733	$3,467	$6,934	$17,334	$34,668	$69,336
14	$576	$1,439	$2,878	$5,756	$14,391	$28,782	$57,564
16	$488	$1,219	$2,438	$4,877	$12,192	$24,384	$48,768
18	$420	$1,049	$2,098	$4,196	$10,491	$20,982	$41,964
20	$366	$914	$1,828	$3,655	$9,138	$18,276	$36,552
22	$321	$804	$1,607	$3,215	$8,037	$16,074	$32,148
24	$285	$713	$1,425	$2,850	$7,125	$14,250	$28,500

26	$254	$636	$1,272	$2,544	$6,360	$12,720	$25,440
28	$228	$571	$1,142	$2,284	$5,709	$11,418	$22,836
30	$206	$515	$1,030	$2,059	$5,148	$10,296	$20,592
32	$186	$466	$932	$1,865	$4,662	$9,324	$18,648
34	$170	$424	$848	$1,696	$4,239	$8,478	$16,956
36	$155	$386	$773	$1,546	$3,864	$7,728	$15,456
38	$141	$353	$707	$1,414	$3,534	$7,068	$14,136
40	$130	$324	$648	$1,296	$3,240	$6,480	$12,960

Figure 12-1

If you want to save other than the specific amounts shown in Figure 12-1, just proportion your annual savings accordingly. For example, if you wanted to save $20,000 in ten years, you would multiply the $859 shown in the table for $10,000 by two, to get a required annual savings of $1718.

As noted, our above example assumed zero inflation. However, that's not very realistic. Someone ignoring inflation will probably end up with too little savings at the end of their savings period. TIPS will adjust for any inflation on existing savings, so if the savings are in TIPS, and the yearly amount being saved is *also* adjusted annually for inflation, the eventual saved amount after the given number of years will be in current dollar purchasing power. For example, if you wanted to save $10,000 in ten years, per Figure 12-1, your initial annual savings would be $859. However, if after one year, the government announces that inflation in the previous year was 5%, then your annual savings should be increased 5%, to $902. If in the following year inflation really takes off, and goes up another 10%, then the $902 annual savings will have to be increased 10%, to $992 per year.

So, table 12-1 *is* valid during inflationary periods, if the annual savings are adjusted every year for inflation and the savings are in TIPS.

Let's test if this really works. We want a $10,000 savings goal to have current purchasing power in ten years. If there is any inflation at all, the actual dollar savings in ten years will have to be greater than $10,000. Since historical inflation has been 3.5% per year, let's see what final savings amount will be required assuming 3.5% inflation. To get the actual total dollars we will need in ten years, we multiply $10,000 times 1.035 and continue doing this nine more times. This is $10,000 * 1.035^10 = $14,106. Note that if someone *didn't* save in a manner that adjusted for inflation, their $10,000 after ten years would only have $10,000/$14,106 = 0.71, or 71% of their desired real purchasing power.

Let's see if using the above table, Figure 12-1, and an initial annual savings amount of $859, gets us to our goal of $14,106 in actual saved dollars in ten years, if we increase our annual savings amount every year with inflation. To test this, here is a table, Figure 12-2, showing each year's savings with 3.5% inflation added and the accumulated savings increasing each year by 3% interest plus 3.5% inflation. This is what will happen when the savings are in TIPS, at the assumed 3% interest, and we index our annual savings up 3.5% every year to account for inflation.

Ten Year Savings at 3.5% Inflation and 3% Interest

Year	Annual Savings	Accumulated savings
1	$859	$859
2	$889	$1,862
3	$920	$2,963
4	$952	$4,170
5	$986	$5,490
6	$1,020	$6,934
7	$1,056	$8,509
8	$1,093	$10,226
9	$1,131	$12,095
10	$1,171	$14,128

Figure 12-2

The accumulative savings shown can vary somewhat based on the timing of when the interest is assumed applied to the savings, which is why the final number doesn't exactly match $14,106. But the example shows that this approach generally allows the saver to meet the goal of having $10,000 worth of *real* purchasing power after ten years. Although the last savings year will require $1,171 in savings, versus the first year's $859 savings amount, the higher savings requirement in the last year should "feel" about the same as the first year's savings because the higher amount is in inflated future dollars. It is assumed that the saver's income will generally increase with inflation.

The savings determination shown above would be valid for things like saving for a college education for your child. You would estimate the cost of the planned-for education in today's dollars and assume that the cost of the education in future years will increase with inflation. Recently, education costs have been rising *faster* than inflation. But since it is impossible to predict exact future cost increases, assuming a rise in college cost matching inflation is probably the best you can do, and it will get you much closer to your goal than if no inflation allowance were made.

The above calculations for determining monthly savings would also be valid for calculating retirement savings *if* you knew exactly what lump sum, in current dollars, you needed at retirement. However, that is usually *not* known and we have to estimate it. This is covered later in this chapter.

Social Security in the Future

We noted above that, for many readers, one third of their earning years will be during the coming depression. Because of that, besides just surviving the depression, they will have to be looking forward to a time of retirement and planning to have sufficient funds. Before we get into specifics on calculating retirement savings amounts, we need to decide what will be the future of social security benefits.

One of the biggest advantages of social security retirement benefits is that they are indexed up with inflation once a person retires, just like the TIPS savings we are advocating, versus company pensions and annuities which are normally "fixed" at the time withdrawal is begun. This indexing of social security benefits with inflation can make a huge difference for the retiree as he or she progresses years into retirement. Social security retirement benefits often start out with a value less than a company pension, but after years of inflation, social security can become the largest contributor to retirement income. Social security is currently the major income source for many retirees. We therefore have to predict what social security retirement benefits will be available in the future, especially given the fact that we are going into a depression where *all* government programs will be at risk.

Most people are aware of the coming funding crises with social security. The dominant issue in the coming years is the forecasted increase in retirees (due to aging baby-boomers and people living longer), while the number of people in the support worker base will be declining. When social security was first implemented in 1935, the average life expectancy was less than 70. According to the Social Security Administration, life expectancy will be 80 by 2050. In 2003 there were 3.3 workers per retiree receiving social security. Projections show that, by 2030, there will only be 2 workers supporting each retiree, if the social security retirement plan stays the way it is. This will cause the Social Security Retirement System to eventually run out of funds, unless some changes are made in benefits, the retirement age, or the social security taxes of workers.

Technically, the social security plan was supposed to have been accumulating funds in an account built from the excess contributions paid in previous years, when the pension payments received from workers was more than the money paid out in social security benefits. However, the government spent this money on other things, just leaving IOUs in the social security fund. Since the government is already borrowing at an outrageous rate, and they haven't got the money to honor their IOU's, these IOUs may not satisfy the need for ready funds to pay retirees in future years.

In 1983, the full retirement age was raised from 65 to 67, to be implemented slowly until 2027. This was the first step in trying to address the issue of social security future funding. Delaying the retirement age not only reduces the resultant benefits (because people are on social security fewer years before they die), but also keeps people in the workforce longer. This helps address the problem of the proportion of workers to retirees. However, the delay in retirement age must be taken to age 70 to fully address the current funding crisis.

By delaying retirement to age 70, the net effect of both the reduced number of people getting retirement benefits, and the resultant larger workforce, will be to increase the ratio of the number of contributing workers versus the number of retirees receiving social security in 2030 to 3.1, close to what it was in 2003! A delay of retirement age to 70 is the minimum delay given the coming depression. With a higher unemployment number expected during the depression, the number of supporting workers may actually be less than what is assumed above, and retirement age may have to be changed to 72. However, for our calculations we will use age 70, knowing that some adjustment in planned retirement age may have to be made as the realities of the depression unfold.

Since so many people are questioning whether Social Security will even survive, an increase in retirement age will be accepted as a necessary evil. Also, the government has already shown its willingness to adjust retirement age in its earlier delay of retirement to age 67. There will be years of congressional meetings and pulling of hair by Congress and the President, but a further delay in retirement age is what they will eventually implement. There will still be a reduced retirement option at 65 years old, but with *greatly* reduced benefits. This early-retirement option will pacify those still wanting an early out, at least until they see just how very reduced the benefits are!

Given the above analysis, we will assume that someone will be able to get full social security retirement funds (equivalent to the amount someone recently got at age 65), but not until they are 70 years old. For our example, we will assume that these benefits will be $2400 per month for a couple (in 2003 dollars), similar to what the maximum is now. In the calculations used later in the chapter, $25,920 per year is used, which is slightly less than $2200 per month to allow for some taxes on the social security benefits.

Other social security retirement funding solutions all have unacceptable ramifications. For example, President Bush's proposed private savings plan, that would put some portion of current social security withholdings into a stock market private savings plan, would not only put future social security savings at stock market risk, but it would also devastate the current Social Security system. The current retirement system is pay-as-you-go, and current payroll withholdings are used to pay the benefits of those already retired. If you reduce the withholdings going to current retirees by removing some of the funds for stock purchases, the current system will not have enough money remaining to make payments to current retirees. Some have suggested that the government borrow the needed trillions of dollars to enable the overlap of both plans. Even Congress, that has shown no fiscal restraint in the past four years, is not going to fall for that! They don't want any more borrowing! The financial burden the government is going to face, starting in 2006 or 2007, will put *all* new spending off-limits, since the government will be hard-put to sustain current programs with the declining tax income which will occur during the depression.

Increasing taxes on current workers, to keep the current retirement age for future retirees, would require a doubling of social security withholdings. This would cause a worker revolt and an even deeper downturn of the economy, since workers would have less ready funds to spend.

There is also some consideration of changing the formula on how base social security benefits are calculated, which would make for a generally lower benefit. Given that approximately 10% of our current retirees are living below the poverty line, I don't think Congress will go along with any reduced benefit program that will put even *more* of the elderly into dire straits.

Roth IRA's

For our analysis, we will assume that retirement funds are saved in a Roth IRA (described below) and as already stated, the investment mode is TIPS (Treasury Inflation Protected Securities). The Roth IRA is a way to control taxes on savings and their related gains. TIPS are one of the many ways that money can be invested *within* a Roth IRA.

When funds are saved in a regular IRA (Individual Retirement Account), the money is saved "pre-tax," and you pay all taxes at a later date when the funds are withdrawn, generally after age 59 1/2. Taxes are then paid not only on the initial deposited funds, but also on any gains those funds generated. In a *Roth IRA,* the funds are saved *after taxes*, so taxes are paid up-front on the funds as they are being saved. There are no additional taxes on those funds, *nor on any of the related gains,* when the funds are withdrawn, again generally after age 59 ½.

The savings and withdrawal restrictions are less stringent on a Roth IRA than on a traditional IRA. But the biggest advantage for the retiree is that when savings are in a Roth IRA, it is *known* how much will be available at retirement. Net savings will not be at the whim of whatever income tax rate happens to be in effect at fund withdrawal. Nor will the retiree have to worry about other income that would affect their tax rate.

Here are the income and contribution limits on a Roth IRA at the time of this writing. Any person or couple whose wages exceed the partial contribution wage limits shown below are not eligible for a Roth IRA.

	Full Contribution Wage Limit	Partial Contribution Wage Limit
Single/Head of Household	$95,000	$110,000
Married Filing Jointly	$150,000	$160,000

Contribution Limits (per person):

	Under Age 50	Age 50 or Older
2005	$4,000	$4,500
2006 through 2007	$4,000	$5,000
2008	$5,000	$6,000
2009+	$5,000 + Inflation	$6,000 + Inflation

Since all of the retirement savings are assumed to be in a Roth IRA and in TIPS, concerns about taxes and inflation are reduced. Also, Social Security is indexed up with inflation, which keeps its purchasing power constant.

Company Pensions

The next element of retirement savings we must discuss is company pensions. The pension payout amount is fixed at the time of retirement and stays constant throughout the retirement years. In any period with inflation, the real purchasing power of the company pension is essentially reduced. This is especially an issue when inflation is high, which is likely to occur during the coming depression. In our calculations, we assume an annual inflation of 3.5%, which will cut the real purchasing power of any pension in half in 21 years. However, in times of high inflation, for example 10% per year, the pension purchasing power is reduced by 50% in only seven years. That is why we want all elements of our savings, other than the company pension, to be inflation-protected. This is why we specified TIPS as a savings mode. In the retirement savings tables that are shown later in the chapter, the diminishing effect of the pension, with 3.5% inflation, is already factored into the table's required savings values.

Companies generally quote any pension in the actual dollars the employee will receive at the time of retirement at age 65, assuming employment until then. Of course, companies estimate the pension this way because it makes the pension look more impressive because it takes place many years from now, hence with probable inflated dollars. The effect of inflation on diminishing the pension purchasing power is generally not discussed by the company. For example, let's look at a nominal company pension estimated at $20,000 per year (after taxes) at age 65. The person with the example pension is currently 35 years old, so he or she has another 30 years to work until age 65.

Let's see what $20,000 per year is worth 30 years from now in 2003 dollars, assuming 3.5% annual inflation, which is the historical average inflation. To calculate this value divide $20,000 by $1.035^{30} = \$7,125$. This means that the future pension is worth $7,125 per year in 2003 dollars. This is not a trivial amount, but the pension certainly looks less impressive when expressed in current dollars, which gives a more truly representative value of its purchasing power. Since pensions are normally estimated for age 65, where the tables in this book assume the actual retirement is at age 70, the retirement charts assume an additional 10% value over the nominal pension amount because of the five additional years of work. Also, as we noted, since the pension payment amount is fixed, its effective value continues to decline during retirement as inflation does its thing! All of these adjustments are already included in the following charts for estimating retirement saving needs.

70% to 90% of the prior working income is usually estimated for retirement income needs (the estimated amount you will need per year once you retire). So, when estimating your retirement needs, use an assumption of approximately 80% of current (2003 dollars) income, after taxes.

Company Supported IRAs

Some companies offer IRA's, where the company matches the savings amount, or some percent of the savings amount, of the employee. Obviously, these savings should be counted towards the savings requirements. However, if TIPS, or some other inflation adjusted investment vehicle is not an option in the plan, you will be forced to pick some other investment option. At the current stock market prices you should consider a non-stock-market option, such as money-market or government bonds, until the stock market reaches a more sensible level. You will have to watch inflation levels and know that some portion of your savings is at risk due to its not indexing in value with inflation.

You can either account for a reduced value of these savings being applied to your goal, or recognize that the retirement income on which you are planning, may have to be adjusted due to the inflationary effect. In any case, you will have to use a multiplier in the savings to account for the taxes you will have to pay on any gain realized on your investment. If the prior savings and yields are not tax-free, only assume 75% of existing savings when using the charts.

The retirement savings shown in this chapter assume that savings are drained by age 93. Once savings are drained, the only remaining income will be social security and a diminished real-value pension. But by then drawing on other assets, like home value, retirement life styles can be maintained to age 100, or beyond. At the bottom of each table there is also a correction factor for those who want to assume an extended life beyond the age of 93.

Assuming social security retirement kicks in at age 70, and actual retirement is also at age 70, following are tables, Figures 12-3 through 12-8, showing annual savings requirements for a person with different combinations of years-to-retirement, various income needs, different nominal pensions, and varied existing savings amounts. The actual pension is assumed to be 10% larger than the shown nominal pension due to a delayed retirement beyond the usual age of 65, and this correction is already included in the table calculations. The nominal pension amount is assumed to be after estimated taxes. Savings are in TIPS. Existing savings and resultant yields are assumed to be tax-free because they are saved in TIPS, within a Roth IRA. If the prior savings and yields are not tax-free, only assume 75% of existing savings when using the charts.

Immediately following the charts for retirement at age 70, are charts, Figures 12-9 through 12-13, for those who intend to retire at age 65. In these charts, the extra 10% on the nominal pension is *not* included, since retirement is at the company calculated age for the pension.

Note that no stock market benefits are included in any of the retirement savings charts in this book. If someone is fortunate enough to be able to invest in the stock market after it drops 70%, any gains resulting from that activity will be used to reduce required savings only after those gains are truly realized and you are back out of the stock market.

RETIREMENT SAVINGS CHARTS for those planning on Retiring in 15 to 40 Years. (The next chapter has tables and formulas for those who plan to retire sooner, within a relatively few years. Feel free to jump ahead, if applicable.)

Following are tables to be used for people planning to retire at least 15 years from now. Don't get overwhelmed by the number of tables in this section. Anyone wanting to reference these tables can go directly to the one that applies to them, or they can peruse the whole remaining section to get a better understanding on how these tables were developed. Perusing the whole section and seeing the examples is best.

The tables in this chapter are in two groupings. The first group is for those planning to retire at age 70 (Figures 12-3 through 12-8); the second group of tables is for those planning to retire at age 65 (Figures 12-9 through 12-14). In each grouping there is a table for retiring in 40 years, 35 years, 30 years, 25 years, 20 years, and 15 years.

Both the nominal pension and prior savings are assumed to be after taxes. The "prior savings" are what you currently have saved for retirement. The numbers within the tables are what you have to save every year. These annual savings requirements will have to be adjusted every year for inflation. The desired income is the after-tax retirement income you desire in current dollars.

RETIRING at the Age of 70

ANNUAL SAVINGS FOR RETIRING IN 40 YEARS, AT AGE 70

| Prior Savings: | Zero | $50,000 | $100,000 | $150,000 | $200,000 | $250,000 | $500,000 |
Desired Income	Nominal Pension	Annual Savings	Annual Savings	Annual Savings	Annual Savings	Annual Savings	Annual Savings	Annual Savings
$40,000	$0	$3,198	$2,550	$1,902	$1,254	$606	$0	$0
$40,000	$10,000	$2,737	$2,089	$1,441	$793	$145	$0	$0
$40,000	$20,000	$2,276	$1,628	$980	$332	$0	$0	$0
$40,000	$30,000	$1,816	$1,168	$520	$0	$0	$0	$0
$40,000	$40,000	$1,355	$707	$59	$0	$0	$0	$0
$40,000	$50,000	$895	$247	$0	$0	$0	$0	$0
$40,000	$60,000	$434	$0	$0	$0	$0	$0	$0
$50,000	$0	$5,469	$4,821	$4,173	$3,525	$2,877	$2,229	$0
$50,000	$10,000	$5,008	$4,360	$3,712	$3,064	$2,416	$1,768	$0
$50,000	$20,000	$4,547	$3,899	$3,251	$2,603	$1,955	$1,307	$0
$50,000	$30,000	$4,087	$3,439	$2,791	$2,143	$1,495	$847	$0
$50,000	$40,000	$3,626	$2,978	$2,330	$1,682	$1,034	$386	$0
$50,000	$50,000	$3,166	$2,518	$1,870	$1,222	$574	$0	$0
$50,000	$60,000	$2,705	$2,057	$1,409	$761	$113	$0	$0
$60,000	$0	$7,740	$7,092	$6,444	$5,796	$5,148	$4,500	$1,260
$60,000	$10,000	$7,279	$6,631	$5,983	$5,335	$4,687	$4,039	$799
$60,000	$20,000	$6,818	$6,170	$5,522	$4,874	$4,226	$3,578	$338
$60,000	$30,000	$6,358	$5,710	$5,062	$4,414	$3,766	$3,118	$0
$60,000	$40,000	$5,897	$5,249	$4,601	$3,953	$3,305	$2,657	$0
$60,000	$50,000	$5,437	$4,789	$4,141	$3,493	$2,845	$2,197	$0
$60,000	$60,000	$4,976	$4,328	$3,680	$3,032	$2,384	$1,736	$0
$70,000	$0	$10,239	$9,526	$8,814	$8,101	$7,419	$6,771	$3,531
$70,000	$10,000	$9,732	$9,020	$8,307	$7,623	$6,958	$6,310	$3,070
$70,000	$20,000	$9,226	$8,513	$7,800	$7,146	$6,498	$5,850	$2,610
$70,000	$30,000	$8,719	$8,016	$7,336	$6,685	$6,037	$5,389	$2,130
$70,000	$40,000	$8,212	$7,520	$6,872	$6,224	$5,576	$4,928	$1,651
$70,000	$50,000	$7,729	$7,060	$6,412	$5,764	$5,116	$4,468	$1,202
$70,000	$60,000	$7,247	$6,599	$5,951	$5,303	$4,655	$4,007	$753
$80,000	$0	$12,738	$11,961	$11,183	$10,406	$9,690	$9,042	$5,802

$80,000	$10,000	$12,186	$11,408	$10,631	$9,911	$9,230	$8,582	$5,342
$80,000	$20,000	$11,633	$10,856	$10,078	$9,417	$8,769	$8,121	$4,881
$80,000	$30,000	$11,080	$10,323	$9,611	$8,956	$8,308	$7,660	$4,420
$80,000	$40,000	$10,527	$9,791	$9,143	$8,495	$7,847	$7,199	$3,959
$80,000	$50,000	$10,022	$9,331	$8,683	$8,035	$7,387	$6,739	$3,499
$80,000	$60,000	$9,518	$8,870	$8,222	$7,574	$6,926	$6,278	$3,038

FOR "LIVING FOREVER", ADD 92% TO THE VALUES IN THE TABLE

Figure 12-3

ANNUAL SAVINGS FOR RETIRING IN 35 YEARS, AT AGE 70

Prior Savings:		Zero	$50,000	$100,000	$150,000	$200,000	$250,000	$500,000
Desired Income	Nominal Pension	Annual Savings	Annual Savings	Annual Savings	Annual Savings	Annual Savings	Annual Savings	Annual Savings
$40,000	$0	$3,993	$3,181	$2,372	$1,557	$745	$0	$0
$40,000	$10,000	$3,310	$2,498	$1,689	$874	$59	$0	$0
$40,000	$20,000	$2,627	$1,815	$1,006	$191	$0	$0	$0
$40,000	$30,000	$1,944	$1,132	$323	$0	$0	$0	$0
$40,000	$40,000	$1,260	$448	$0	$0	$0	$0	$0
$40,000	$50,000	$577	$0	$0	$0	$0	$0	$0
$40,000	$60,000	$0	$0	$0	$0	$0	$0	$0
$50,000	$0	$6,829	$6,017	$5,208	$4,393	$3,581	$2,777	$0
$50,000	$10,000	$6,146	$5,334	$4,525	$3,710	$2,897	$2,087	$0
$50,000	$20,000	$5,463	$4,651	$3,842	$3,027	$2,212	$1,397	$0
$50,000	$30,000	$4,780	$3,968	$3,159	$2,344	$1,528	$711	$0
$50,000	$40,000	$4,096	$3,284	$2,476	$1,661	$843	$25	$0
$50,000	$50,000	$3,413	$2,601	$1,793	$978	$163	$0	$0
$50,000	$60,000	$2,729	$1,917	$1,110	$295	$0	$0	$0
$60,000	$0	$9,665	$8,853	$8,044	$7,229	$6,417	$5,613	$1,562
$60,000	$10,000	$8,982	$8,170	$7,361	$6,546	$5,734	$4,930	$879
$60,000	$20,000	$8,299	$7,487	$6,678	$5,863	$5,051	$4,247	$196
$60,000	$30,000	$7,616	$6,804	$5,995	$5,180	$4,368	$3,564	$0
$60,000	$40,000	$6,932	$6,120	$5,311	$4,496	$3,684	$2,880	$0

$60,000	$50,000	$6,249	$5,437	$4,628	$3,813	$3,001	$2,197	$0
$60,000	$60,000	$5,566	$4,754	$3,945	$3,130	$2,318	$1,514	$0
$70,000	$0	$13,035	$12,142	$11,252	$10,355	$9,462	$8,578	$4,398
$70,000	$10,000	$12,283	$11,390	$10,500	$9,604	$8,711	$7,830	$3,715
$70,000	$20,000	$11,532	$10,639	$9,749	$8,853	$7,959	$7,083	$3,032
$70,000	$30,000	$10,780	$9,887	$8,997	$8,101	$7,240	$6,400	$2,349
$70,000	$40,000	$10,028	$9,135	$8,245	$7,349	$6,520	$5,716	$1,666
$70,000	$50,000	$9,277	$8,384	$7,513	$6,657	$5,837	$5,033	$983
$70,000	$60,000	$8,526	$7,633	$6,781	$5,966	$5,154	$4,350	$300
$80,000	$0	$16,404	$15,430	$14,459	$13,481	$12,507	$11,542	$7,234
$80,000	$10,000	$15,585	$14,610	$13,640	$12,662	$11,687	$10,731	$6,551
$80,000	$20,000	$14,765	$13,791	$12,820	$11,842	$10,868	$9,919	$5,868
$80,000	$30,000	$13,945	$12,971	$12,000	$11,022	$10,112	$9,236	$5,185
$80,000	$40,000	$13,125	$12,150	$11,180	$10,202	$9,356	$8,552	$4,501
$80,000	$50,000	$12,305	$11,331	$10,398	$9,502	$8,673	$7,869	$3,818
$80,000	$60,000	$11,486	$10,511	$9,617	$8,802	$7,990	$7,186	$3,135

FOR "LIVING FOREVER", ADD 92% TO THE VALUES IN THE TABLE

Figure 12-4

ANNUAL SAVINGS FOR RETIRING IN 30 YEARS, AT AGE 70

Prior Savings:		Zero	$50,000	$100,000	$150,000	$200,000	$250,000	$500,000
Desired Income	Nominal Pension	Annual Savings	Annual Savings	Annual Savings	Annual Savings	Annual Savings	Annual Savings	Annual Savings
$40,000	$0	$5,081	$4,051	$3,022	$1,991	$961	$0	$0
$40,000	$10,000	$4,049	$3,019	$1,990	$961	$0	$0	$0
$40,000	$20,000	$3,016	$1,986	$957	$0	$0	$0	$0
$40,000	$30,000	$1,984	$954	$0	$0	$0	$0	$0
$40,000	$40,000	$951	$0	$0	$0	$0	$0	$0
$40,000	$50,000	$0	$0	$0	$0	$0	$0	$0
$40,000	$60,000	$0	$0	$0	$0	$0	$0	$0
$50,000	$0	$8,920	$7,787	$6,655	$5,600	$4,570	$3,540	$0
$50,000	$10,000	$7,784	$6,691	$5,611	$4,569	$3,539	$2,509	$0

$50,000	$20,000	$6,648	$5,595	$4,566	$3,537	$2,507	$1,477	$0
$50,000	$30,000	$5,604	$4,499	$3,522	$2,506	$1,476	$446	$0
$50,000	$40,000	$4,560	$3,403	$2,477	$1,474	$444	$0	$0
$50,000	$50,000	$3,516	$2,307	$1,433	$443	$0	$0	$0
$50,000	$60,000	$2,472	$1,211	$388	$0	$0	$0	$0
$60,000	$0	$12,759	$11,523	$10,288	$9,209	$8,179	$7,151	$2,003
$60,000	$10,000	$11,520	$10,363	$9,232	$8,177	$7,147	$6,119	$971
$60,000	$20,000	$10,281	$9,204	$8,175	$7,144	$6,114	$5,086	$0
$60,000	$30,000	$9,225	$8,172	$7,143	$6,112	$5,082	$4,054	$0
$60,000	$40,000	$8,169	$7,139	$6,110	$5,079	$4,049	$3,021	$0
$60,000	$50,000	$7,137	$6,107	$5,078	$4,047	$3,017	$1,989	$0
$60,000	$60,000	$6,104	$5,074	$4,045	$3,014	$1,984	$956	$0
$70,000	$0	$17,090	$15,854	$14,619	$13,461	$12,328	$11,197	$5,612
$70,000	$10,000	$15,851	$14,654	$13,471	$12,325	$11,192	$10,061	$4,464
$70,000	$20,000	$14,612	$13,455	$12,323	$11,189	$10,056	$8,925	$3,317
$70,000	$30,000	$13,464	$12,319	$11,188	$10,053	$8,920	$7,790	$2,387
$70,000	$40,000	$12,317	$11,184	$10,052	$8,918	$7,785	$6,654	$1,458
$70,000	$50,000	$11,181	$10,048	$8,916	$7,782	$6,689	$5,609	$529
$70,000	$60,000	$10,045	$8,912	$7,780	$6,646	$5,593	$4,565	$0
$80,000	$0	$21,420	$20,184	$18,950	$17,712	$16,476	$15,243	$9,221
$80,000	$10,000	$20,181	$18,945	$17,711	$16,473	$15,237	$14,004	$8,189
$80,000	$20,000	$18,942	$17,706	$16,472	$15,234	$13,998	$12,765	$7,156
$80,000	$30,000	$17,703	$16,467	$15,233	$13,995	$12,759	$11,526	$6,124
$80,000	$40,000	$16,464	$15,228	$13,994	$12,756	$11,520	$10,287	$5,091
$80,000	$50,000	$15,225	$13,989	$12,755	$11,517	$10,361	$9,230	$4,059
$80,000	$60,000	$13,986	$12,750	$11,516	$10,278	$9,202	$8,174	$3,026

FOR "LIVING FOREVER", ADD 92% TO THE VALUES IN THE TABLE

Figure 12-5

ANNUAL SAVINGS FOR RETIRING IN 25 YEARS, AT AGE 70

Prior Savings:		Zero	$50,000	$100,000	$150,000	$200,000	$250,000	$500,000
Desired Income	Nominal Pension	Annual Saving	Annual Saving	Annual Savings	Annual Savings	Annual Savings	Annual Savings	Annual Savings
$40,000	$0	$6,639	$5,290	$3,942	$2,592	$1,243	$0	$0
$40,000	$10,000	$4,995	$3,646	$2,298	$950	$0	$0	$0
$40,000	$20,000	$3,351	$2,002	$654	$0	$0	$0	$0
$40,000	$30,000	$1,707	$358	$0	$0	$0	$0	$0
$40,000	$40,000	$63	$0	$0	$0	$0	$0	$0
$40,000	$50,000	$0	$0	$0	$0	$0	$0	$0
$40,000	$60,000	$0	$0	$0	$0	$0	$0	$0
$50,000	$0	$11,962	$10,478	$8,995	$7,510	$6,026	$4,542	$0
$50,000	$10,000	$10,153	$8,669	$7,186	$5,703	$4,219	$2,736	$0
$50,000	$20,000	$8,345	$6,861	$5,378	$3,895	$2,412	$930	$0
$50,000	$30,000	$6,536	$5,052	$3,570	$2,087	$606	$0	$0
$50,000	$40,000	$4,728	$3,244	$1,761	$278	$0	$0	$0
$50,000	$50,000	$2,920	$1,436	$0	$0	$0	$0	$0
$50,000	$60,000	$1,111	$0	$0	$0	$0	$0	$0
$60,000	$0	$17,284	$15,665	$14,048	$12,428	$10,809	$9,327	$2,585
$60,000	$10,000	$15,311	$13,692	$12,075	$10,581	$9,097	$7,683	$785
$60,000	$20,000	$13,338	$11,720	$10,102	$8,735	$7,386	$6,039	$0
$60,000	$30,000	$11,416	$9,932	$8,450	$7,091	$5,742	$4,395	$0
$60,000	$40,000	$9,494	$8,145	$6,797	$5,447	$4,098	$2,751	$0
$60,000	$50,000	$7,850	$6,501	$5,153	$3,803	$2,454	$1,105	$0
$60,000	$60,000	$6,206	$4,857	$3,509	$2,159	$810	$0	$0
$70,000	$0	$22,943	$21,324	$19,706	$18,086	$16,467	$14,918	$7,502
$70,000	$10,000	$20,970	$19,351	$17,733	$16,177	$14,625	$13,110	$5,484
$70,000	$20,000	$18,997	$17,378	$15,761	$14,267	$12,783	$11,302	$3,466
$70,000	$30,000	$17,050	$15,498	$13,948	$12,459	$10,975	$9,493	$1,986
$70,000	$40,000	$15,102	$13,618	$12,135	$10,650	$9,166	$7,685	$506
$70,000	$50,000	$13,294	$11,810	$10,327	$8,842	$7,358	$5,875	$0
$70,000	$60,000	$11,485	$10,001	$8,519	$7,034	$5,550	$4,066	$0
$80,000	$0	$28,601	$26,982	$25,365	$23,745	$22,126	$20,510	$12,419
$80,000	$10,000	$26,628	$25,010	$23,392	$21,772	$20,153	$18,537	$10,574
$80,000	$20,000	$24,656	$23,037	$21,419	$19,799	$18,180	$16,564	$8,728

$80,000	$30,000	$22,683	$21,064	$19,446	$17,826	$16,208	$14,591	$7,084
$80,000	$40,000	$20,710	$19,091	$17,474	$15,854	$14,235	$12,618	$5,440
$80,000	$50,000	$18,737	$17,118	$15,501	$13,881	$12,262	$10,756	$3,796
$80,000	$60,000	$16,764	$15,146	$13,528	$11,908	$10,289	$8,894	$2,152

FOR "LIVING FOREVER", ADD 92% TO THE VALUES IN THE TABLE

Figure 12-6

ANNUAL SAVINGS FOR RETIRING IN 20 YEARS, AT AGE 70

Prior Savings:		Zero	$50,000	$100,000	$150,000	$200,000	$250,000	$500,000
Desired Income	Nominal Pension	Annual Saving	Annual Saving	Annual Savings	Annual Savings	Annual Savings	Annual Savings	Annual Savings
$40,000	$0	$9,020	$7,192	$5,365	$3,536	$1,708	$0	$0
$40,000	$10,000	$6,431	$4,603	$2,776	$949	$0	$0	$0
$40,000	$20,000	$3,841	$2,013	$186	$0	$0	$0	$0
$40,000	$30,000	$1,252	$0	$0	$0	$0	$0	$0
$40,000	$40,000	$0	$0	$0	$0	$0	$0	$0
$40,000	$50,000	$0	$0	$0	$0	$0	$0	$0
$40,000	$60,000	$0	$0	$0	$0	$0	$0	$0
$50,000	$0	$16,609	$14,598	$12,589	$10,577	$8,566	$6,555	$0
$50,000	$10,000	$13,761	$11,750	$9,740	$7,729	$5,719	$3,709	$0
$50,000	$20,000	$10,912	$8,902	$6,892	$4,882	$2,872	$863	$0
$50,000	$30,000	$8,064	$6,053	$4,043	$2,035	$26	$0	$0
$50,000	$40,000	$5,215	$3,205	$1,195	$0	$0	$0	$0
$50,000	$50,000	$2,367	$356	$0	$0	$0	$0	$0
$50,000	$60,000	$0	$0	$0	$0	$0	$0	$0
$60,000	$0	$24,198	$22,005	$19,812	$17,618	$15,424	$13,233	$3,556
$60,000	$10,000	$21,091	$18,897	$16,705	$14,510	$12,383	$10,374	$697
$60,000	$20,000	$17,984	$15,790	$13,598	$11,403	$9,341	$7,515	$0
$60,000	$30,000	$14,876	$12,718	$10,708	$8,696	$6,752	$4,926	$0
$60,000	$40,000	$11,769	$9,646	$7,819	$5,990	$4,162	$2,336	$0
$60,000	$50,000	$9,032	$7,057	$5,230	$3,401	$1,573	$0	$0
$60,000	$60,000	$6,296	$4,468	$2,641	$812	$0	$0	$0
$70,000	$0	$31,885	$29,691	$27,499	$25,304	$23,111	$20,919	$10,598

$70,000	$10,000	$28,786	$26,592	$24,400	$22,205	$20,045	$17,945	$7,077
$70,000	$20,000	$25,687	$23,493	$21,301	$19,106	$16,979	$14,970	$3,556
$70,000	$30,000	$22,572	$20,396	$18,295	$16,191	$14,122	$12,113	$35
$70,000	$40,000	$19,456	$17,298	$15,288	$13,276	$11,265	$9,257	$0
$70,000	$50,000	$16,234	$14,150	$12,140	$10,128	$8,117	$6,107	$0
$70,000	$60,000	$13,013	$11,002	$8,992	$6,980	$4,969	$2,957	$0
$80,000	$0	$39,572	$37,378	$35,186	$32,991	$30,797	$28,606	$17,640
$80,000	$10,000	$36,481	$34,287	$32,095	$29,900	$27,707	$25,515	$14,550
$80,000	$20,000	$33,390	$31,197	$29,004	$26,810	$24,616	$22,425	$11,459
$80,000	$30,000	$30,267	$28,073	$25,881	$23,686	$21,492	$19,301	$8,735
$80,000	$40,000	$27,143	$24,950	$22,757	$20,562	$18,369	$16,178	$6,010
$80,000	$50,000	$23,436	$21,243	$19,050	$16,856	$14,662	$12,574	$3,002
$80,000	$60,000	$19,730	$17,536	$15,344	$13,149	$10,955	$8,970	$0

FOR "LIVING FOREVER", ADD 92% TO THE VALUES IN THE TABLE

Figure 12-7

ANNUAL SAVINGS FOR RETIRING IN 15 YEARS, AT AGE 70

Prior Savings:		Zero	$50,000	$100,000	$150,000	$200,000	$250,000	$500,000
Desired Income	Nominal Pension	Annual Saving	Annual Saving	Annual Savings	Annual Savings	Annual Savings	Annual Savings	Annual Savings
$40,000	$0	$13,655	$10,466	$7,264	$5,072	$2,414	$0	$0
$40,000	$10,000	$9,009	$6,085	$3,162	$238	$0	$0	$0
$40,000	$20,000	$4,363	$1,705	$0	$0	$0	$0	$0
$40,000	$30,000	$0	$0	$0	$0	$0	$0	$0
$40,000	$40,000	$0	$0	$0	$0	$0	$0	$0
$40,000	$50,000	$0	$0	$0	$0	$0	$0	$0
$40,000	$60,000	$0	$0	$0	$0	$0	$0	$0
$50,000	$0	$24,774	$21,585	$18,383	$15,698	$12,775	$9,851	$0
$50,000	$10,000	$19,846	$16,790	$13,727	$10,923	$7,999	$5,075	$0
$50,000	$20,000	$14,919	$11,995	$9,071	$6,147	$3,223	$300	$0
$50,000	$30,000	$9,991	$7,200	$4,409	$1,618	$0	$0	$0
$50,000	$40,000	$5,063	$2,405	$0	$0	$0	$0	$0
$50,000	$50,000	$135	$0	$0	$0	$0	$0	$0
$50,000	$60,000	$0	$0	$0	$0	$0	$0	$0
$60,000	$0	$35,894	$32,704	$29,502	$26,325	$23,135	$19,943	$4,995

$60,000	$10,000	$30,684	$27,494	$24,293	$21,115	$17,925	$14,773	$0
$60,000	$20,000	$25,474	$22,284	$19,083	$15,905	$12,716	$9,603	$0
$60,000	$30,000	$20,264	$17,075	$13,984	$11,072	$8,148	$5,262	$0
$60,000	$40,000	$15,054	$11,865	$8,886	$6,238	$3,580	$920	$0
$60,000	$50,000	$10,292	$7,368	$4,545	$1,721	$0	$0	$0
$60,000	$60,000	$5,529	$2,871	$203	$0	$0	$0	$0
$70,000	$0	$47,013	$43,823	$40,622	$37,444	$34,254	$31,062	$15,614
$70,000	$10,000	$41,803	$38,613	$35,412	$32,234	$29,045	$25,872	$10,304
$70,000	$20,000	$36,593	$33,404	$30,202	$27,024	$23,835	$20,683	$4,995
$70,000	$30,000	$31,383	$28,194	$25,048	$22,003	$18,946	$15,907	$0
$70,000	$40,000	$26,174	$22,984	$19,894	$16,981	$14,057	$11,131	$0
$70,000	$50,000	$21,187	$18,131	$15,118	$11,959	$9,168	$6,356	$0
$70,000	$60,000	$16,201	$13,277	$10,343	$6,938	$4,280	$1,580	$0
$80,000	$0	$58,132	$54,942	$51,741	$48,563	$45,374	$42,182	$26,232
$80,000	$10,000	$52,922	$49,733	$46,531	$43,353	$40,164	$36,972	$21,023
$80,000	$20,000	$47,712	$44,523	$41,321	$38,144	$34,954	$31,762	$15,813
$80,000	$30,000	$42,503	$39,313	$36,111	$32,934	$29,744	$26,552	$10,987
$80,000	$40,000	$37,293	$34,103	$30,902	$27,724	$24,534	$21,342	$6,161
$80,000	$50,000	$32,083	$28,893	$25,692	$22,514	$19,325	$16,133	$1,335
$80,000	$60,000	$26,873	$23,684	$20,482	$17,304	$14,115	$10,923	$0

FOR "LIVING FOREVER", ADD 92% TO THE VALUES IN THE TABLE

Figure 12-8

As mentioned earlier, the savings are assumed to be drained by age 93, and the retirement income at that point will be social security and the initial pension amount. However, draining other assets, like home value, will probably allow lifestyle continuance to age 100. If the live-to-age-93 assumption is felt to be risky because you plan to live to be 120, then the above tabled savings must be increased by 92%. This will allow the real desired income to "last forever", which is assumed to be age 120, since the income on the larger resulting TIPS investment will be sufficient for a longer period of time. However, this is an expensive option that few will be able to afford. Note that the detailed derivation of the "live forever" additional savings is covered in the last chapter in the book.

The savings values in the above charts are, by necessity, approximate. However, they will get you close to your goal; certainly closer than if you had no guidelines or were using tables based on fantasy future stock market performance, which most published retirement savings formulas do.

To make sure that you can use these charts, work through these several simple examples.

Example #1:

A couple is 40 years old and plan to retire at age 70. So they have 30 additional years to work. Their current combined income is $75,000 after taxes. Using 80% as the factor to determine their retirement income needs, their required after-tax retirement income will be 0.8 * $75,000 = $60,000 in 2003 dollars.

The combined company pensions that the couple will receive at age 65 are $40,000 per year, after taxes. To adjust the company quoted pension for expected taxes, when in doubt reduce the company quoted pension by 20%. The tables assume that the nominal pension shown is *after* any tax adjustment. The couple currently has no savings for the purpose of retirement.

Using the chart Figure 12-5, which is for people retiring in 30 years, we find $60,000 in the first column, which is desired income. In the next column we find $40,000, which is the couple's combined nominal pension (as estimated by the company at age 65, but after taxes). Since the couple has no retirement savings, we look in the next column to find the $8,169 after-tax annual savings requirement. Below is a replication of the lines from this chart that we used to find these values.

Prior Savings:		Zero	$50,000	$100,000	$150,000	$200,000	$250,000	$500,000
Desired Income	Nominal Pension	Annual Savings	Annual Savings	Annual Savings	Annual Savings	Annual Savings	Annual Savings	Annual Savings
$60,000	$40,000	**$8,169**	$7,139	$6,110	$5,079	$4,049	$3,021	$0

This $8,169 after-tax annual savings will have to be indexed up every year for inflation. For example, if inflation is 5% after the first year of saving, the second year's saving will have to be 1.05 * $8,169 = $8,577. If the following year has 6% inflation, then the amount saved will again have to be increased: 1.06 * $8,577 = $9,092. It is expected that wage increases will largely compensate for these increases.

Example #2:

A single person is 51 years old and plans to retire at age 70. This person has $50,000 saved for retirement. The person's income is $60,000 after taxes, so using 80% as the factor to determine their retirement income, the after-tax retirement income required will be 0.8 * $60,000 = $48,000 in 2003 dollars.

The person expects a company pension that is forecasted to be $19,000 (after taxes), at age 65.

Since the tables don't have numbers that exactly match the above values, we will use the closest numbers. It is possible to extrapolate into closer numbers, but with the degree of unknowns in the future economy, this effort is generally not worth it. We will use 20 years as the years left to work, $50,000 as the desired income, and a nominal pension of $20,000. The individual already has prior savings of $50,000 set aside for retirement.

Below is the data used from Figure 12-7, ANNUAL SAVINGS FOR RETIRING IN 20 YEARS AT AGE 70.

Prior Savings:		Zero	$50,000	$100,000	$150,000	$200,000	$250,000	$500,000
Desired Income	Nominal Pension	Annual Savings	Annual Savings	Annual Savings	Annual Savings	Annual Savings	Annual Savings	Annual Savings
$50,000	$20,000	$10,912	**$8,902**	$6,892	$4,882	$2,872	$863	$0

From this table, we get an annual after-tax savings requirement of $8,902. The annual savings will then be adjusted every year for inflation.

These tables are applicable to both couples and singles. The single person will generally have less social security income than the couple, and more of their annual savings will be above the Roth IRA savings limits and therefore subject to later taxes. However, the single person will generally have a larger pension because it won't have the survivor provision taken by most couples. Also, with a couple there is a higher likelihood that at least one of them will live to be over 93 years of age. Thus, there is a general wash of plusses and minuses when determining retirement savings for singles and couples, so we use the same tables for both. However, the current income, and therefore the projected required retirement income, is often lower for a single person than it would be for a couple with two incomes, so even though the same table is used, the resultant required annual savings will generally be lower for the single person.

Many of you reading this book will be shocked at the size of the annual required savings amounts. Few of the currently retired people have sufficient funds, which is why the bankruptcy rate among the elderly is the highest of any age group and why 10% of retirees are living below the poverty line.

Retirement, as we currently define it, is a true luxury. Not too many years ago, the elderly were taken into their children's homes, and their living costs were generally only food and limited medicines. Now a retiree expects independent living, perhaps first in their own home in the sunny South where they move after retirement, then in an assisted living facility, and finally in a nursing home, at incredible costs. In the future, few retirees will be able to afford this scenario, even though many people will have this as a goal. However, following the savings requirement shown in this book will give someone a realistic shot at truly living their retirement dreams with adequate funds. Someone retiring after saving at the rates shown in this book's tables is unlikely to get into the dire straits of many of those currently retired and of many of those planning to retire before or after the coming depression.

Retiring Early, at Age 65

Even though Social Security benefits will likely not come into play until age 70, there will be those who want to save for retiring before then. Here are the savings charts, Figures 12- 9 through 12-14, for retiring at 65. Even though there will likely be a reduced Social Security benefit option for age 65, the calculations in these tables assume that the retiree waits until age 70 to collect Social Security benefits, therefore getting a non-reduced Social Security benefit.

ANNUAL SAVINGS FOR RETIRING IN 40 YEARS, AT AGE 65

Prior Savings:		Zero	$50,000	$100,000	$150,000	$200,000	$250,000	$500,000
Desired Income	Nominal Pension	Annual Savings	Annual Savings	Annual Savings	Annual Savings	Annual Savings	Annual Savings	Annual Savings
$40,000	$0	$5,150	$4,502	$3,854	$3,206	$2,558	$1,910	$0
$40,000	$10,000	$4,721	$4,073	$3,425	$2,777	$2,129	$1,481	$0
$40,000	$20,000	$4,292	$3,644	$2,996	$2,348	$1,700	$1,052	$0
$40,000	$30,000	$3,863	$3,215	$2,567	$1,919	$1,271	$623	$0
$40,000	$40,000	$3,434	$2,786	$2,138	$1,490	$842	$194	$0
$40,000	$50,000	$3,506	$2,858	$2,210	$1,562	$914	$266	$0
$40,000	$60,000	$2,577	$1,929	$1,281	$633	$0	$0	$0
$50,000	$0	$7,684	$7,036	$6,388	$5,740	$5,092	$4,444	$1,204
$50,000	$10,000	$7,255	$6,607	$5,959	$5,311	$4,663	$4,015	$775
$50,000	$20,000	$6,826	$6,178	$5,530	$4,882	$4,234	$3,586	$346
$50,000	$30,000	$6,397	$5,749	$5,101	$4,453	$3,805	$3,157	$0
$50,000	$40,000	$5,969	$5,321	$4,673	$4,025	$3,377	$2,729	$0
$50,000	$50,000	$5,540	$4,892	$4,244	$3,596	$2,948	$2,300	$0
$50,000	$60,000	$5,111	$4,463	$3,815	$3,167	$2,519	$1,871	$0
$60,000	$0	$10,262	$9,614	$8,966	$8,318	$7,670	$7,022	$3,782
$60,000	$10,000	$9,789	$9,141	$8,493	$7,845	$7,197	$6,549	$3,309
$60,000	$20,000	$9,360	$8,712	$8,064	$7,416	$6,768	$6,120	$2,880
$60,000	$30,000	$8,931	$8,283	$7,635	$6,987	$6,339	$5,691	$2,451
$60,000	$40,000	$8,503	$7,855	$7,207	$6,559	$5,911	$5,263	$2,023
$60,000	$50,000	$8,074	$7,426	$6,778	$6,130	$5,482	$4,834	$1,594
$60,000	$60,000	$7,645	$6,997	$6,349	$5,701	$5,053	$4,405	$1,165
$70,000	$0	$13,302	$12,654	$12,006	$11,358	$10,710	$10,062	$6,822
$70,000	$10,000	$12,788	$12,140	$11,492	$10,844	$10,196	$9,548	$6,308
$70,000	$20,000	$12,273	$11,625	$10,977	$10,329	$9,681	$9,033	$5,793
$70,000	$30,000	$11,758	$11,110	$10,462	$9,814	$9,166	$8,518	$5,278
$70,000	$40,000	$11,244	$10,596	$9,948	$9,300	$8,652	$8,004	$4,764
$70,000	$50,000	$10,730	$10,082	$9,434	$8,786	$8,138	$7,490	$4,250
$70,000	$60,000	$10,215	$9,567	$8,919	$8,271	$7,623	$6,975	$3,735
$80,000	$0	$16,343	$15,627	$14,911	$14,195	$13,479	$12,763	$9,185
$80,000	$10,000	$15,828	$15,112	$14,396	$13,680	$12,964	$12,248	$8,670

$80,000	$20,000	$15,314	$14,598	$13,882	$13,166	$12,450	$11,734	$8,156
$80,000	$30,000	$14,799	$14,083	$13,367	$12,651	$11,935	$11,219	$7,641
$80,000	$40,000	$14,284	$13,568	$12,852	$12,136	$11,420	$10,704	$7,126
$80,000	$50,000	$13,770	$13,054	$12,338	$11,622	$10,906	$10,190	$6,612
$80,000	$60,000	$13,256	$12,540	$11,824	$11,108	$10,392	$9,676	$6,098

FOR "LIVING FOREVER", ADD 55% TO THE VALUES IN THE TABLE
Figure 12-9

ANNUAL SAVINGS FOR RETIRING IN 35 YEARS, AT AGE 65

Prior Savings:		Zero	$50,000	$100,000	$150,000	$200,000	$250,000	$500,000
Desired Income	Nominal Pension	Annual Savings	Annual Savings	Annual Savings	Annual Savings	Annual Savings	Annual Savings	Annual Savings
$40,000	$0	$6,433	$5,621	$4,809	$3,997	$3,185	$2,373	$0
$40,000	$10,000	$5,797	$4,985	$4,173	$3,361	$2,549	$1,737	$0
$40,000	$20,000	$5,161	$4,349	$3,537	$2,725	$1,913	$1,101	$0
$40,000	$30,000	$4,524	$3,712	$2,900	$2,088	$1,276	$464	$0
$40,000	$40,000	$3,888	$3,076	$2,264	$1,452	$640	$0	$0
$40,000	$50,000	$3,252	$2,440	$1,628	$816	$4	$0	$0
$40,000	$60,000	$2,616	$1,804	$992	$180	$0	$0	$0
$50,000	$0	$9,599	$8,784	$7,969	$7,154	$6,339	$5,524	$1,434
$50,000	$10,000	$8,963	$8,148	$7,333	$6,518	$5,703	$4,888	$798
$50,000	$20,000	$8,326	$7,511	$6,696	$5,881	$5,066	$4,251	$161
$50,000	$30,000	$7,690	$6,875	$6,060	$5,245	$4,430	$3,615	$0
$50,000	$40,000	$7,054	$6,239	$5,424	$4,609	$3,794	$2,979	$0
$50,000	$50,000	$6,418	$5,603	$4,788	$3,973	$3,158	$2,343	$0
$50,000	$60,000	$5,781	$4,966	$4,151	$3,336	$2,521	$1,706	$0
$60,000	$0	$13,317	$12,505	$11,693	$10,881	$10,069	$9,257	$5,197
$60,000	$10,000	$12,554	$11,742	$10,930	$10,118	$9,306	$8,494	$4,434
$60,000	$20,000	$11,790	$10,978	$10,166	$9,354	$8,542	$7,730	$3,670
$60,000	$30,000	$11,027	$10,215	$9,403	$8,591	$7,779	$6,967	$2,907
$60,000	$40,000	$10,263	$9,451	$8,639	$7,827	$7,015	$6,203	$2,143
$60,000	$50,000	$9,583	$8,771	$7,959	$7,147	$6,335	$5,523	$1,463

$60,000	$60,000	$8,947	$8,135	$7,323	$6,511	$5,699	$4,887	$827
$70,000	$0	$17,116	$16,223	$15,330	$14,437	$13,544	$12,651	$8,186
$70,000	$10,000	$16,353	$15,460	$14,567	$13,674	$12,781	$11,888	$7,423
$70,000	$20,000	$15,589	$14,696	$13,803	$12,910	$12,017	$11,124	$6,659
$70,000	$30,000	$14,826	$13,933	$13,040	$12,147	$11,254	$10,361	$5,896
$70,000	$40,000	$14,062	$13,169	$12,276	$11,383	$10,490	$9,597	$5,132
$70,000	$50,000	$13,298	$12,405	$11,512	$10,619	$9,726	$8,833	$4,368
$70,000	$60,000	$12,535	$11,642	$10,749	$9,856	$8,963	$8,070	$3,605
$80,000	$0	$20,896	$19,922	$18,948	$17,974	$17,000	$16,026	$11,156
$80,000	$10,000	$20,132	$19,158	$18,184	$17,210	$16,236	$15,262	$10,392
$80,000	$20,000	$19,368	$18,394	$17,420	$16,446	$15,472	$14,498	$9,628
$80,000	$30,000	$18,605	$17,631	$16,657	$15,683	$14,709	$13,735	$8,865
$80,000	$40,000	$17,841	$16,867	$15,893	$14,919	$13,945	$12,971	$8,101
$80,000	$50,000	$17,078	$16,104	$15,130	$14,156	$13,182	$12,208	$7,338
$80,000	$60,000	$16,314	$15,340	$14,366	$13,392	$12,418	$11,444	$6,574

FOR "LIVING FOREVER", ADD 55% TO THE VALUES IN THE TABLE
Figure 12-10

ANNUAL SAVINGS FOR RETIRING IN 30 YEARS, AT AGE 65

Prior Savings:		Zero	$50,000	$100,000	$150,000	$200,000	$250,000	$500,000
Desired Income	Nominal Pension	Annual Savings	Annual Savings	Annual Savings	Annual Savings	Annual Savings	Annual Savings	Annual Savings
$40,000	$0	$8,182	$7,152	$6,122	$5,092	$4,062	$3,032	$0
$40,000	$10,000	$7,221	$6,191	$5,161	$4,131	$3,101	$2,071	$0
$40,000	$20,000	$6,260	$5,230	$4,200	$3,170	$2,140	$1,110	$0
$40,000	$30,000	$5,299	$4,269	$3,239	$2,209	$1,179	$149	$0
$40,000	$40,000	$4,338	$3,308	$2,278	$1,248	$218	$0	$0
$40,000	$50,000	$3,377	$2,347	$1,317	$287	$0	$0	$0
$40,000	$60,000	$2,416	$1,386	$356	$0	$0	$0	$0
$50,000	$0	$12,649	$11,549	$10,449	$9,349	$8,249	$7,149	$1,649
$50,000	$10,000	$11,496	$10,396	$9,296	$8,196	$7,096	$5,996	$496
$50,000	$20,000	$10,343	$9,243	$8,143	$7,043	$5,943	$4,843	$0
$50,000	$30,000	$9,325	$8,225	$7,125	$6,025	$4,925	$3,825	$0
$50,000	$40,000	$8,364	$7,264	$6,164	$5,064	$3,964	$2,864	$0

$50,000	$50,000	$7,403	$6,303	$5,203	$4,103	$3,003	$1,903	$0
$50,000	$60,000	$6,442	$5,342	$4,242	$3,142	$2,042	$942	$0
$60,000	$0	$17,480	$16,330	$15,180	$14,030	$12,880	$11,730	$5,980
$60,000	$10,000	$16,327	$15,177	$14,027	$12,877	$11,727	$10,577	$4,827
$60,000	$20,000	$15,174	$14,024	$12,874	$11,724	$10,574	$9,424	$3,674
$60,000	$30,000	$14,021	$12,871	$11,721	$10,571	$9,421	$8,271	$2,521
$60,000	$40,000	$12,868	$11,718	$10,568	$9,418	$8,268	$7,118	$1,368
$60,000	$50,000	$11,714	$10,564	$9,414	$8,264	$7,114	$5,964	$214
$60,000	$60,000	$10,561	$9,411	$8,261	$7,111	$5,961	$4,811	$0
$70,000	$0	$22,311	$21,111	$19,911	$18,711	$17,511	$16,311	$9,311
$70,000	$10,000	$21,158	$19,958	$18,758	$17,558	$16,358	$15,158	$8,158
$70,000	$20,000	$20,005	$18,805	$17,605	$16,405	$15,205	$14,005	$7,005
$70,000	$30,000	$18,852	$17,652	$16,452	$15,252	$14,052	$12,852	$5,852
$70,000	$40,000	$17,699	$16,499	$15,299	$14,099	$12,899	$11,699	$4,699
$70,000	$50,000	$16,545	$15,345	$14,145	$12,945	$11,745	$10,545	$3,545
$70,000	$60,000	$15,392	$14,192	$12,992	$11,792	$10,592	$9,392	$2,392
$80,000	$0	$27,143	$25,907	$24,671	$23,435	$22,199	$20,963	$14,783
$80,000	$10,000	$25,989	$24,753	$23,517	$22,281	$21,045	$19,809	$13,629
$80,000	$20,000	$24,836	$23,600	$22,364	$21,128	$19,892	$18,656	$12,476
$80,000	$30,000	$23,683	$22,447	$21,211	$19,975	$18,739	$17,503	$11,323
$80,000	$40,000	$22,530	$21,294	$20,058	$18,822	$17,586	$16,350	$10,170
$80,000	$50,000	$21,377	$20,141	$18,905	$17,669	$16,433	$15,197	$9,017
$80,000	$60,000	$20,223	$18,987	$17,751	$16,515	$15,279	$14,043	$7,863

FOR "LIVING FOREVER", ADD 55% TO THE VALUES IN THE TABLE
Figure 12-11

ANNUAL SAVINGS FOR RETIRING IN 25 YEARS, AT AGE 65

Prior Savings:		Zero	$50,000	$100,000	$150,000	$200,000	$250,000	$500,000
Desired Income	Nominal Pension	Annual Savings	Annual Savings	Annual Savings	Annual Savings	Annual Savings	Annual Savings	Annual Savings
$40,000	$0	$10,827	$9,478	$8,129	$6,780	$5,431	$4,082	$0
$40,000	$10,000	$9,198	$7,849	$6,500	$5,151	$3,802	$2,453	$0
$40,000	$20,000	$7,707	$6,358	$5,009	$3,660	$2,311	$962	$0
$40,000	$30,000	$6,216	$4,867	$3,518	$2,169	$820	$0	$0

$40,000	$40,000	$4,725	$3,376	$2,027	$678	$0	$0	$0
$40,000	$50,000	$3,233	$1,884	$535	$0	$0	$0	$0
$40,000	$60,000	$1,742	$393	$0	$0	$0	$0	$0
$50,000	$0	$17,139	$15,655	$14,171	$12,687	$11,203	$9,719	$2,299
$50,000	$10,000	$15,349	$13,865	$12,381	$10,897	$9,413	$7,929	$509
$50,000	$20,000	$13,560	$12,076	$10,592	$9,108	$7,624	$6,140	$0
$50,000	$30,000	$11,770	$10,286	$8,802	$7,318	$5,834	$4,350	$0
$50,000	$40,000	$9,984	$8,500	$7,016	$5,532	$4,048	$2,564	$0
$50,000	$50,000	$8,493	$7,009	$5,525	$4,041	$2,557	$1,073	$0
$50,000	$60,000	$7,002	$5,518	$4,034	$2,550	$1,066	$0	$0
$60,000	$0	$23,450	$21,831	$20,212	$18,593	$16,974	$15,355	$7,260
$60,000	$10,000	$21,661	$20,042	$18,423	$16,804	$15,185	$13,566	$5,471
$60,000	$20,000	$19,872	$18,253	$16,634	$15,015	$13,396	$11,777	$3,682
$60,000	$30,000	$18,082	$16,463	$14,844	$13,225	$11,606	$9,987	$1,892
$60,000	$40,000	$16,293	$14,674	$13,055	$11,436	$9,817	$8,198	$103
$60,000	$50,000	$14,504	$12,885	$11,266	$9,647	$8,028	$6,409	$0
$60,000	$60,000	$12,714	$11,095	$9,476	$7,857	$6,238	$4,619	$0
$70,000	$0	$29,762	$28,143	$26,524	$24,905	$23,286	$21,667	$13,572
$70,000	$10,000	$27,973	$26,354	$24,735	$23,116	$21,497	$19,878	$11,783
$70,000	$20,000	$26,183	$24,564	$22,945	$21,326	$19,707	$18,088	$9,993
$70,000	$30,000	$24,394	$22,775	$21,156	$19,537	$17,918	$16,299	$8,204
$70,000	$40,000	$22,605	$20,986	$19,367	$17,748	$16,129	$14,510	$6,415
$70,000	$50,000	$20,815	$19,196	$17,577	$15,958	$14,339	$12,720	$4,625
$70,000	$60,000	$19,026	$17,407	$15,788	$14,169	$12,550	$10,931	$2,836
$80,000	$0	$36,074	$34,455	$32,836	$31,217	$29,598	$27,979	$19,884
$80,000	$10,000	$34,284	$32,665	$31,046	$29,427	$27,808	$26,189	$18,094
$80,000	$20,000	$32,495	$30,876	$29,257	$27,638	$26,019	$24,400	$16,305
$80,000	$30,000	$30,706	$29,087	$27,468	$25,849	$24,230	$22,611	$14,516
$80,000	$40,000	$28,916	$27,297	$25,678	$24,059	$22,440	$20,821	$12,726
$80,000	$50,000	$27,127	$25,508	$23,889	$22,270	$20,651	$19,032	$10,937
$80,000	$60,000	$25,338	$23,719	$22,100	$20,481	$18,862	$17,243	$9,148

FOR "LIVING FOREVER", ADD 55% TO THE VALUES IN THE TABLE

Figure 12-12

ANNUAL SAVINGS FOR RETIRING IN 20 YEARS, AT AGE 65

Prior Savings:		Zero	$50,000	$100,000	$150,000	$200,000	$250,000	$500,000
Desired Income	Nominal Pension	Annual Savings	Annual Savings	Annual Savings	Annual Savings	Annual Savings	Annual Savings	Annual Savings
$40,000	$0	$15,428	$13,600	$11,772	$9,944	$8,116	$6,288	$0
$40,000	$10,000	$12,541	$10,713	$8,885	$7,057	$5,229	$3,401	$0
$40,000	$20,000	$9,711	$7,883	$6,055	$4,227	$2,399	$571	$0
$40,000	$30,000	$7,305	$5,477	$3,649	$1,821	$0	$0	$0
$40,000	$40,000	$4,898	$3,070	$1,242	$0	$0	$0	$0
$40,000	$50,000	$2,492	$664	$0	$0	$0	$0	$0
$40,000	$60,000	$86	$0	$0	$0	$0	$0	$0
$50,000	$0	$24,004	$21,993	$19,982	$17,971	$15,960	$13,949	$3,894
$50,000	$10,000	$21,117	$19,106	$17,095	$15,084	$13,073	$11,062	$1,007
$50,000	$20,000	$18,229	$16,218	$14,207	$12,196	$10,185	$8,174	$0
$50,000	$30,000	$15,342	$13,331	$11,320	$9,309	$7,298	$5,287	$0
$50,000	$40,000	$12,454	$10,443	$8,432	$6,421	$4,410	$2,399	$0
$50,000	$50,000	$9,639	$7,628	$5,617	$3,606	$1,595	$0	$0
$50,000	$60,000	$7,233	$5,222	$3,211	$1,200	$0	$0	$0
$60,000	$0	$32,580	$30,386	$28,192	$25,998	$23,804	$21,610	$10,640
$60,000	$10,000	$29,693	$27,499	$25,305	$23,111	$20,917	$18,723	$7,753
$60,000	$20,000	$26,805	$24,611	$22,417	$20,223	$18,029	$15,835	$4,865
$60,000	$30,000	$23,918	$21,724	$19,530	$17,336	$15,142	$12,948	$1,978
$60,000	$40,000	$21,030	$18,836	$16,642	$14,448	$12,254	$10,060	$0
$60,000	$50,000	$18,143	$15,949	$13,755	$11,561	$9,367	$7,173	$0
$60,000	$60,000	$15,255	$13,061	$10,867	$8,673	$6,479	$4,285	$0
$70,000	$0	$41,156	$38,962	$36,768	$34,574	$32,380	$30,186	$19,216
$70,000	$10,000	$38,269	$36,075	$33,881	$31,687	$29,493	$27,299	$16,329
$70,000	$20,000	$35,381	$33,187	$30,993	$28,799	$26,605	$24,411	$13,441
$70,000	$30,000	$32,494	$30,300	$28,106	$25,912	$23,718	$21,524	$10,554
$70,000	$40,000	$29,606	$27,412	$25,218	$23,024	$20,830	$18,636	$7,666
$70,000	$50,000	$26,718	$24,524	$22,330	$20,136	$17,942	$15,748	$4,778
$70,000	$60,000	$23,831	$21,637	$19,443	$17,249	$15,055	$12,861	$1,891

$80,000	$0	$49,732	$47,538	$45,344	$43,150	$40,956	$38,762	$27,792
$80,000	$10,000	$46,845	$44,651	$42,457	$40,263	$38,069	$35,875	$24,905
$80,000	$20,000	$43,957	$41,763	$39,569	$37,375	$35,181	$32,987	$22,017
$80,000	$30,000	$41,069	$38,875	$36,681	$34,487	$32,293	$30,099	$19,129
$80,000	$40,000	$38,182	$35,988	$33,794	$31,600	$29,406	$27,212	$16,242
$80,000	$50,000	$35,294	$33,100	$30,906	$28,712	$26,518	$24,324	$13,354
$80,000	$60,000	$32,407	$30,213	$28,019	$25,825	$23,631	$21,437	$10,467

FOR "LIVING FOREVER", ADD 55% TO THE VALUES IN THE TABLE

Figure 12-13

ANNUAL SAVINGS FOR RETIRING IN 15 YEARS, AT AGE 65

Prior Savings:		Zero	$50,000	$100,000	$150,000	$200,000	$250,000	$500,000
Desired Income	Nominal Pension	Annual Savings	Annual Savings	Annual Savings	Annual Savings	Annual Savings	Annual Savings	Annual Savings
$40,000	$0	$23,210	$20,020	$16,830	$13,640	$10,450	$7,260	$0
$40,000	$10,000	$18,249	$15,059	$11,869	$8,679	$5,489	$2,299	$0
$40,000	$20,000	$13,288	$10,098	$6,908	$3,718	$528	$0	$0
$40,000	$30,000	$8,606	$5,416	$2,226	$0	$0	$0	$0
$40,000	$40,000	$4,472	$1,282	$0	$0	$0	$0	$0
$40,000	$50,000	$338	$0	$0	$0	$0	$0	$0
$40,000	$60,000	$0	$0	$0	$0	$0	$0	$0
$50,000	$0	$35,615	$32,425	$29,235	$26,045	$22,855	$19,665	$3,715
$50,000	$10,000	$30,655	$27,465	$24,275	$21,085	$17,895	$14,705	$0
$50,000	$20,000	$25,694	$22,504	$19,314	$16,124	$12,934	$9,744	$0
$50,000	$30,000	$20,733	$17,543	$14,353	$11,163	$7,973	$4,783	$0
$50,000	$40,000	$15,772	$12,582	$9,392	$6,202	$3,012	$0	$0
$50,000	$50,000	$10,811	$7,621	$4,431	$1,241	$0	$0	$0
$50,000	$60,000	$6,542	$3,352	$162	$0	$0	$0	$0
$60,000	$0	$48,021	$44,831	$41,641	$38,451	$35,261	$32,071	$16,121
$60,000	$10,000	$43,060	$39,870	$36,680	$33,490	$30,300	$27,110	$11,160
$60,000	$20,000	$38,099	$34,909	$31,719	$28,529	$25,339	$22,149	$6,199
$60,000	$30,000	$33,138	$29,948	$26,758	$23,568	$20,378	$17,188	$1,238
$60,000	$40,000	$28,177	$24,987	$21,797	$18,607	$15,417	$12,227	$0
$60,000	$50,000	$23,217	$20,027	$16,837	$13,647	$10,457	$7,267	$0
$60,000	$60,000	$18,256	$15,066	$11,876	$8,686	$5,496	$2,306	$0

$70,000	$0	$60,426	$57,236	$54,046	$50,856	$47,666	$44,476	$28,526
$70,000	$10,000	$55,465	$52,275	$49,085	$45,895	$42,705	$39,515	$23,565
$70,000	$20,000	$50,504	$47,314	$44,124	$40,934	$37,744	$34,554	$18,604
$70,000	$30,000	$45,543	$42,353	$39,163	$35,973	$32,783	$29,593	$13,643
$70,000	$40,000	$40,583	$37,393	$34,203	$31,013	$27,823	$24,633	$8,683
$70,000	$50,000	$35,622	$32,432	$29,242	$26,052	$22,862	$19,672	$3,722
$70,000	$60,000	$30,661	$27,471	$24,281	$21,091	$17,901	$14,711	$0
$80,000	$0	$72,831	$69,641	$66,451	$63,261	$60,071	$56,881	$40,931
$80,000	$10,000	$67,870	$64,680	$61,490	$58,300	$55,110	$51,920	$35,970
$80,000	$20,000	$62,909	$59,719	$56,529	$53,339	$50,149	$46,959	$31,009
$80,000	$30,000	$57,949	$54,759	$51,569	$48,379	$45,189	$41,999	$26,049
$80,000	$40,000	$52,988	$49,798	$46,608	$43,418	$40,228	$37,038	$21,088
$80,000	$50,000	$48,027	$44,837	$41,647	$38,457	$35,267	$32,077	$16,127
$80,000	$60,000	$43,066	$39,876	$36,686	$33,496	$30,306	$27,116	$11,166

FOR "LIVING FOREVER", ADD 55% TO THE VALUES IN THE TABLE
Figure 12-14

Both the savings amounts and the withdrawal amounts after retirement are to be indexed annually for inflation.

As in the retire-at-age-70 tables, the savings as calculated assume that funds will run out at age 93, with the exception of social security and the fixed pension. If someone is uncomfortable with this assumption, by adding 55% to the savings values in the tables the retiree can keep a constant lifestyle "forever", which is assumed to be to age 120 in the example. The reason this adjustment is less than the 92% additional needed in the retire-at-age-70 tables, is that the calculations to retire at age 65 already have an adjustment in the savings for living five years longer in retirement, so the 55% additional amount is being added onto a far larger savings base.

Let's do the same two examples we did earlier under the retire-at-age-70 assumption, but now assuming a retirement age of 65. We will then compare the amount of savings required in both cases.

Example #3 (similar to Example #1, but assuming retirement at age 65):

A couple is 40 years old and plan to retire at age 65. So, they have 25 additional years to work. Their current combined income is $75,000 after taxes. Using 80% as the factor to determine their retirement income needs, their required after-tax retirement income will be 0.8 * $75,000 = $60,000 in 2003 dollars.

The combined nominal company pensions that their companies have projected the couple would receive at age 65 is $40,000 per year (after taxes in future dollars). They currently have no savings for the purpose of retirement.

From Figure 12-12:

Prior Savings:		Zero	$50,000	$100,000	$150,000	$200,000	$250,000	$500,000
Desired Income	Nominal Pension	Annual Savings	Annual Savings	Annual Savings	Annual Savings	Annual Savings	Annual Savings	Annual Savings
$60,000	$40,000	**$16,293**	$14,674	$13,055	$11,436	$9,817	$8,198	$103

This $16,293 after-tax annual savings will have to be indexed up every year for inflation. Note that this annual savings requirement is approximately twice the $8,169 annual savings required to retire at age 70. Few will be able to afford to save the annual amounts needed to retire "early" at age 65.

Example #4 (similar to Example #2, but assuming retirement at age 65):

A single person is 51 years old and plans to retire at age 65. This person has $50,000 saved for retirement. The person's income is $60,000 after taxes, so using 80% as the factor to determine his or her retirement income needs, the retirement income required will be 0.8 * $60,000 = $48,000 in 2003 dollars.

The person expects a company pension that is forecasted to be $19,000 after taxes, at age 65.

Since the tables don't have numbers that exactly match the above values, we will use the closest numbers. It is possible to extrapolate into closer numbers, but with the degree of variation in the future economy this effort is probably not worth it. We will use 15 years as the years left to work, $50,000 as the desired income, and a nominal pension of $20,000 after taxes. The individual already has prior savings of $50,000 set aside for retirement.

From Figure 12-14:

Prior Savings:		Zero	$50,000	$100,000	$150,000	$200,000	$250,000	$500,000
Desired Income	Nominal Pension	Annual Savings	Annual Savings	Annual Savings	Annual Savings	Annual Savings	Annual Savings	Annual Savings
$50,000	$20,000	$25,694	**$22,504**	$19,314	$16,124	$12,934	$9,744	$0

From this table we get an annual after-tax savings requirement of $22,504. The annual savings will then be adjusted every year for inflation. Note that the $22,504 annual savings requirement is 153% higher than the $8902 annual savings required for retiring at age 70. Truly, retiring before age 70 will be an expensive luxury!

CHAPTER 13
I Want To Retire Soon?
How Much Money Will I Need?

This chapter pertains to someone planning to retire within a few years. However, this should be a chapter of interest even for those who won't be retiring for many years, because it highlights just how much money is required. These numbers are generally quite sobering.

In the early part of this chapter are charts that can be used to estimate both retirement income and required savings. To get more exact numbers, there are formulas near the end of the chapter into which exact values can be input. It generally is worthwhile to use both. The charts will get you close, and the formulas will allow you to input your exact values. By doing the chart first, you can have some confidence that you did the formula correctly by comparing the two answers.

The earlier chapter did not include the formula option because with all the variables that exist in a retirement-far-in-the-future calculation, the accuracy just was not needed. However, with the retirement date being near, items like how much social security you will receive, or the size of your pension, will be known with more accuracy, and it then becomes advantageous to enter these values into the formulas to get more accurate output.

Anyone retiring soon should be sure that they have sufficient funds, especially given the fact that someone retiring within the next few years may spend their whole retirement in a depression, and we are not talking about the mental kind (that is, unless you ignore the guidelines in this book)! Some former retirees who came to the realization that they had insufficient funds have been able to go back to work, albeit in jobs that paid little, such as a waitress, cashier, or even the greeter at Wal-Mart. In a depression, such jobs will not be available. Also, those looking at retirement in the next few years are likely to have been influenced by the perceived high stock market gains of the nineties and may have unrealistic expectations on what their savings can earn. This chapter will be extremely valuable for putting savings requirements into the proper prospective and bringing those people back to reality.

No one planning on retiring soon should have any needed funds in the stock market. None! In the best of times this would be good advice for anyone nearing retirement; with the coming depression, this is an absolute necessity.

Most people reading this chapter will be shocked on how much savings it takes to retire and to be sufficient for the rest of your life. It is important that you react to this shock in an intelligent way. If you are planning to retire in just a few years, it is probably too late to increase your savings rate, at least not enough to make a big difference. If you have insufficient funds saved you have only two options: delay retirement or reduce your cost of living during retirement. The tables and formulas in this chapter show you different options of retiring at age 60, 65, or 70. As the retirement age is delayed, everything gets easier. You won't have as many years to live during retirement, any pension you get will be larger, you have additional time to save, and your social security benefit will be larger.

The other option is to reduce retirement living costs. Here are just a few examples of the type of savings you can incorporate into your retirement lifestyle, usually with little change in your life's values. If you are a couple owning two automobiles, one a fairly new SUV and the other a small car that gets good gas mileage, sell the SUV and get along with the other automobile. After all, you are retired with a freer schedule that no longer includes going to a workplace, so that you can adapt to one less automobile. The savings on depreciation, insurance, and taxes could easily be over $5,000 per year. As you will see later, reducing costs by $5,300 per year is equivalent to having an additional $100,000 saved in TIPS! If you live in San Francisco, and have $400,000 equity on your $800,000 home, consider selling your home and moving to someplace like Ohio. You can pay cash for an even nicer home, have no house payment, and save more than half on taxes and insurance. This savings could be in excess of $25,000 per year. Again, this is the equivalent of having an additional half-a-million dollars savings in TIPS! Switch from going out to eat at a restaurant every week to eating out once per month and pocket maybe $1500 per year. You'll probably eat healthier, besides saving a lot of money. Give up the Starbucks lattes every day and save $1200 per year. And do you really need all those cable channels and two cell phones with unlimited calling around the world? We have all gotten accustomed to "extras" that are often very costly, and that we can easily do without. The only way you will identify all these items is to itemize all your expenditures, and see which ones you really need. Reducing retirement costs is so much easier than trying to accumulate additional savings, especially if you are close to retirement.

I mentioned above that it is important that you react to the shock of the size of required savings in an intelligent way. I have an acquaintance who responded in a way that I would *not* judge as being very intelligent. This person signed on for the services of a financial manager a few years ago, explaining to the financial manager that he "needed" 8% real annual gain on his money every year (after the financial manager's fees and after inflation), and the financial manager readily agreed to these goals. What did the financial manager have to lose if the goals weren't reached? He was still getting *his* fees.

The value of this acquaintance's investments has *not* kept up with the 8% goal, but the financial manager has assured my friend that the market will "turn around". The financial manager stated that since no one can predict the economy in the short run, therefore no one can predict the stock market in the short run. The secret of successful investing, per the financial manager's sage advice, is to "ride out the lows." Of course, the financial manager still takes *his* 2% fees, even during the "lows", and, since the financial manager takes no responsibility for the "short run," my acquaintance friend will only know that he has a real financial problem in the "long run!"

It doesn't work to first determine your financial "need" then assume that you can find some investment that will satisfy that "need". This is what my acquaintance was doing when he told the financial manager that he "needed" 8% real annual gain on his savings. He had backed-into that number using his existing savings and assumed retirement costs. If it was really that easy, he could have saved even less, then looked for investments that made 12%, or even 15%! How about 20%?

CHARTS SHOWING RETIREMENT INCOME AND RELATED RETIREMENT SAVINGS, for those retiring within a few years

Below are savings charts on determining what retirement income you can expect at different savings and pension amounts; and alternatively, what savings are required to support a given retirement income. It is assumed that the after-tax retirement income is desired to be constant (as to purchasing power), so retirement income will index up every year with inflation. Otherwise, you would become poorer in the later retirement years.

As was true on the previous chapter's charts, no stock market benefits are included in the charts in this chapter. If someone is fortunate enough to be able to invest in the stock market (with extra funds) after it drops 70%, any gains resulting from that activity should be recognized only after those gains are truly realized, and you are back out of the stock market.

In the charts below, social security is assumed to be somewhat less than what was assumed in the last chapter's charts. This is because the earlier chapter's charts assumed social security benefits starting at age 70. Although the benefits were assumed to be on the same base as current social security, just delayed, the additional years of work would have qualified more people to a somewhat higher social security benefit. However, using the formulas that are later in this chapter will allow someone to input his or her exact social security benefits.

Retire at age 65, Live to Age 93

Not only are many people getting ready to retire in a few years with little savings, but many nearing retirement do not know how much they should have saved to be able to live until age 93 with a comfortable lifestyle without running out of money. As we mentioned in earlier chapters, after age 93 the value of other assets, like the home, can often be drained to extend the same lifestyle to age 100 or so.

Below, in Figure 13-1, is a chart showing how much yearly retirement income you can use without running out of money before age 93. This chart assumes retirement at age 65, with Social Security at $20,000 per year after taxes. Chart output options are given for various savings amounts and pension amounts. Retirement income is assumed to be adjusted up every year with inflation, as is social security. Savings are assumed to be in TIPS, or in some other format to be tax-free or after taxes. Pension is fixed and after taxes. The numbers within the chart are annual after-tax retirement income dollars the retiree can use for living expenses.

RETIREMENT INCOME, ASSUMING RETIRE SOON AT AGE 65 & LIVE TO 93

Pension:	$0	$10,000	$20,000	$30,000	$40,000	$50,000	$60,000
Savings							
0	$20,000	$26,800	$33,600	$40,400	$47,200	$54,000	$60,800
$50,000	$22,632	$29,432	$36,232	$43,032	$49,832	$56,632	$63,432
$100,000	$25,263	$32,063	$38,863	$45,663	$52,463	$59,263	$66,063
$150,000	$27,895	$34,695	$41,495	$48,295	$55,095	$61,895	$68,695
$200,000	$30,526	$37,326	$44,126	$50,926	$57,726	$64,526	$71,326
$250,000	$33,158	$39,958	$46,758	$53,558	$60,358	$67,158	$73,958
$300,000	$35,789	$42,589	$49,389	$56,189	$62,989	$69,789	$76,589
$350,000	$38,421	$45,221	$52,021	$58,821	$65,621	$72,421	$79,221
$400,000	$41,053	$47,853	$54,653	$61,453	$68,253	$75,053	$81,853
$450,000	$43,684	$50,484	$57,284	$64,084	$70,884	$77,684	$84,484
$500,000	$46,316	$53,116	$59,916	$66,716	$73,516	$80,316	$87,116
$550,000	$48,947	$55,747	$62,547	$69,347	$76,147	$82,947	$89,747
$600,000	$51,579	$58,379	$65,179	$71,979	$78,779	$85,579	$92,379
$650,000	$54,211	$61,011	$67,811	$74,611	$81,411	$88,211	$95,011
$700,000	$56,842	$63,642	$70,442	$77,242	$84,042	$90,842	$97,642
$750,000	$59,474	$66,274	$73,074	$79,874	$86,674	$93,474	$100,274

Figure 13-1

For example, using the above chart, if a couple have existing savings of $200,000 in TIPS or equivalent after taxes, and are expecting a pension of $30,000 per year after taxes, they can live on an after-tax retirement income of $50,926 per year, which is then indexed up annually with inflation.

Or if they know how much they need for retirement income during retirement and want to make sure they have enough money saved, they can use the chart below, Figure 13-2. This chart assumes retirement at age 65, Social Security at $20,000 per year after taxes, and various saved amounts and pension amounts. Retirement income is assumed to go up every year with inflation, as is social security. Savings are assumed to be in TIPS or in some other format to be tax-free or after taxes. Pension is fixed and after taxes. Funds are to run out at age 93. The numbers within the chart are the savings required at retirement.

REQUIRED SAVINGS, ASSUMING RETIRE SOON AT AGE 65 & LIVE TO 93

Pension:	$0	$10,000	$20,000	$30,000	$40,000	$50,000	$60,000
Income							
$20,000	$0	$0	$0	$0	$0	$0	$0
$25,000	$95,000	$0	$0	$0	$0	$0	$0
$30,000	$190,000	$60,800	$0	$0	$0	$0	$0
$35,000	$285,000	$155,800	$26,600	$0	$0	$0	$0
$40,000	$380,000	$250,800	$121,600	$0	$0	$0	$0
$45,000	$475,000	$345,800	$216,600	$87,400	$0	$0	$0
$50,000	$570,000	$440,800	$311,600	$182,400	$53,200	$0	$0
$55,000	$665,000	$535,800	$406,600	$277,400	$148,200	$19,000	$0
$60,000	$760,000	$630,800	$501,600	$372,400	$243,200	$114,000	$0
$65,000	$855,000	$725,800	$596,600	$467,400	$338,200	$209,000	$79,800
$70,000	$950,000	$820,800	$691,600	$562,400	$433,200	$304,000	$174,800
$75,000	$1,045,000	$915,800	$786,600	$657,400	$528,200	$399,000	$269,800
$80,000	$1,140,000	$1,010,800	$881,600	$752,400	$623,200	$494,000	$364,800
$85,000	$1,235,000	$1,105,800	$976,600	$847,400	$718,200	$589,000	$459,800
$90,000	$1,330,000	$1,200,800	$1,071,600	$942,400	$813,200	$684,000	$554,800
$95,000	$1,425,000	$1,295,800	$1,166,600	$1,037,400	$908,200	$779,000	$649,800
$100,000	$1,520,000	$1,390,800	$1,261,600	$1,132,400	$1,003,200	$874,000	$744,800
$105,000	$1,615,000	$1,485,800	$1,356,600	$1,227,400	$1,098,200	$969,000	$839,800
$110,000	$1,710,000	$1,580,800	$1,451,600	$1,322,400	$1,193,200	$1,064,000	$934,800
$115,000	$1,805,000	$1,675,800	$1,546,600	$1,417,400	$1,288,200	$1,159,000	$1,029,800
$120,000	$1,900,000	$1,770,800	$1,641,600	$1,512,400	$1,383,200	$1,254,000	$1,124,800
$125,000	$1,995,000	$1,865,800	$1,736,600	$1,607,400	$1,478,200	$1,349,000	$1,219,800

Figure 13-2

For example, using the above chart, Figure 13-2, if someone knew they wanted $60,000 to live on during retirement, and they had a pension of $20,000 per year after taxes, the above chart says that they need to have $501,600 saved in TIPS or equivalent. The $60,000 per year after-tax retirement income is assumed to index every year with inflation and won't run out until age 93.

Retire at age 65, Live to Age 120

There will be those retiring soon who will be uncomfortable with the assumption of running out of money at age 93, even with the provision of using other assets to enable the retirement lifestyle to continue to age 100. For those people who want to be sure they have required funds if they live over 100 years, the following tables assume funds do not run out until age 120, and even that can be extended by draining other assets.

Below, in Figure 13-3, is a chart showing how much after-tax yearly retirement income you can use without running out of money before age 120. This chart assumes retirement at age 65, Social Security at $20,000 per year after taxes, and various saved amounts and pension amounts. Retirement income is assumed to go up every year with inflation, as is social security. Savings are assumed to be in TIPS or in some other format to be tax-free or after taxes. Pension is fixed and after taxes.

RETIREMENT INCOME, ASSUMING RETIRE SOON AT AGE 65 & LIVE TO 120

Pension:	$0	$10,000	$20,000	$30,000	$40,000	$50,000	$60,000
Savings							
$0	$20,000	$24,600	$29,200	$33,800	$38,400	$43,000	$47,600
$50,000	$21,786	$26,386	$30,986	$35,586	$40,186	$44,786	$49,386
$100,000	$23,571	$28,171	$32,771	$37,371	$41,971	$46,571	$51,171
$150,000	$25,357	$29,957	$34,557	$39,157	$43,757	$48,357	$52,957
$200,000	$27,143	$31,743	$36,343	$40,943	$45,543	$50,143	$54,743
$250,000	$28,929	$33,529	$38,129	$42,729	$47,329	$51,929	$56,529
$300,000	$30,714	$35,314	$39,914	$44,514	$49,114	$53,714	$58,314
$350,000	$32,500	$37,100	$41,700	$46,300	$50,900	$55,500	$60,100
$400,000	$34,286	$38,886	$43,486	$48,086	$52,686	$57,286	$61,886
$450,000	$36,071	$40,671	$45,271	$49,871	$54,471	$59,071	$63,671
$500,000	$37,857	$42,457	$47,057	$51,657	$56,257	$60,857	$65,457
$550,000	$39,643	$44,243	$48,843	$53,443	$58,043	$62,643	$67,243
$600,000	$41,429	$46,029	$50,629	$55,229	$59,829	$64,429	$69,029
$650,000	$43,214	$47,814	$52,414	$57,014	$61,614	$66,214	$70,814
$700,000	$45,000	$49,600	$54,200	$58,800	$63,400	$68,000	$72,600
$750,000	$46,786	$51,386	$55,986	$60,586	$65,186	$69,786	$74,386

Figure 13-3

For example, using the above chart, if someone has savings of $200,000 in TIPS or equivalent after taxes, and a pension of $30,000 per year after taxes, they can live on $40,943 per year, which is then indexed up annually with inflation. Note that this is substantially less than the $50,926 retirement income of the live-to-age 93 option.

Or if they know how much they need for living during retirement but just want to make sure they have enough money saved, they can use the chart below, Figure 13-4. This chart assumes retirement at age 65, Social Security at $20,000 per year after taxes, and various saved amounts and pension amounts. Retirement income is assumed to be after taxes, and to go up every year with inflation, as is social security. Savings are assumed to be in TIPS or in some other format to be tax-free or after taxes. Pension is fixed and after taxes. Funds are to run out at age 120.

REQUIRED SAVINGS, ASSUMING RETIRE SOON AT AGE 65 & LIVE TO 120

Pension:	$0	$10,000	$20,000	$30,000	$40,000	$50,000	$60,000
Income							
$20,000	$0	$0	$0	$0	$0	$0	$0
$25,000	$140,000	$11,200	$0	$0	$0	$0	$0
$30,000	$280,000	$151,200	$22,400	$0	$0	$0	$0
$35,000	$420,000	$291,200	$162,400	$33,600	$0	$0	$0
$40,000	$560,000	$431,200	$302,400	$173,600	$44,800	$0	$0
$45,000	$700,000	$571,200	$442,400	$313,600	$184,800	$56,000	$0
$50,000	$840,000	$711,200	$582,400	$453,600	$324,800	$196,000	$67,200
$55,000	$980,000	$851,200	$722,400	$593,600	$464,800	$336,000	$207,200
$60,000	$1,120,000	$991,200	$862,400	$733,600	$604,800	$476,000	$347,200
$65,000	$1,260,000	$1,131,200	$1,002,400	$873,600	$744,800	$616,000	$487,200
$70,000	$1,400,000	$1,271,200	$1,142,400	$1,013,600	$884,800	$756,000	$627,200
$75,000	$1,540,000	$1,411,200	$1,282,400	$1,153,600	$1,024,800	$896,000	$767,200
$80,000	$1,680,000	$1,551,200	$1,422,400	$1,293,600	$1,164,800	$1,036,000	$907,200
$85,000	$1,820,000	$1,691,200	$1,562,400	$1,433,600	$1,304,800	$1,176,000	$1,047,200
$90,000	$1,960,000	$1,831,200	$1,702,400	$1,573,600	$1,444,800	$1,316,000	$1,187,200

$95,000	$2,100,000	$1,971,200	$1,842,400	$1,713,600	$1,584,800	$1,456,000	$1,327,200
$100,000	$2,240,000	$2,111,200	$1,982,400	$1,853,600	$1,724,800	$1,596,000	$1,467,200
$105,000	$2,380,000	$2,251,200	$2,122,400	$1,993,600	$1,864,800	$1,736,000	$1,607,200
$110,000	$2,520,000	$2,391,200	$2,262,400	$2,133,600	$2,004,800	$1,876,000	$1,747,200
$115,000	$2,660,000	$2,531,200	$2,402,400	$2,273,600	$2,144,800	$2,016,000	$1,887,200
$120,000	$2,800,000	$2,671,200	$2,542,400	$2,413,600	$2,284,800	$2,156,000	$2,027,200
$125,000	$2,940,000	$2,811,200	$2,682,400	$2,553,600	$2,424,800	$2,296,000	$2,167,200

Figure 13-4

Using the above chart, Figure 13-4, if someone knew they wanted $60,000 after taxes to live on during retirement, and they had a pension of $20,000 per year after taxes, the above chart says that they need to have $862,400 saved in TIPS or equivalent. The $60,000 per year after-tax retirement income is assumed to index every year with inflation and won't run out until age 120. Note that this savings amount is substantially more than the $501,600 savings required in the live to age 93 option.

Retire at Age 60, Live to 93

There will be those who want to retire early, at age 60. Here are similar tables for those wishing to retire within a few years, at age 60. It is assumed that $20,000 per year social security will kick in at age 65 (even though this may be delayed a year or so by the time you read this), as will the pension. The pension assumed within the tables is reduced 15% due to retiring early, but in the chart headings, the pension amount is shown as the nominal pension at age 65. The pension headings are left that way because companies quote pensions with the assumption of retirement at age 65 and employment until that time. The pension amount shown, however, is assumed to be after estimated taxes.

So for the first five years of retirement, only the existing savings will be used to cover retirement income needs. No other income is assumed. See Figure 13-5 below.

RETIREMENT INCOME, ASSUMING RETIRE SOON AT AGE 60 & LIVE TO 93

Pension:	$0	$10,000	$20,000	$30,000	$40,000	$50,000	$60,000
Savings							
$0							
$50,000							
$100,000	$20,000						
$150,000	$22,083	$26,659					
$200,000	$24,167	$28,743	$33,318	$37,894			
$250,000	$26,250	$30,826	$35,402	$39,978	$44,553	$49,129	
$300,000	$28,333	$32,909	$37,485	$42,061	$46,637	$51,213	$55,788
$350,000	$30,417	$34,993	$39,568	$44,144	$48,720	$53,296	$57,872
$400,000	$32,500	$37,076	$41,652	$46,228	$50,803	$55,379	$59,955
$450,000	$34,583	$39,159	$43,735	$48,311	$52,887	$57,463	$62,038
$500,000	$36,667	$41,243	$45,818	$50,394	$54,970	$59,546	$64,122
$550,000	$38,750	$43,326	$47,902	$52,478	$57,053	$61,629	$66,205
$600,000	$40,833	$45,409	$49,985	$54,561	$59,137	$63,713	$68,288
$650,000	$42,917	$47,493	$52,068	$56,644	$61,220	$65,796	$70,372
$700,000	$45,000	$49,576	$54,152	$58,728	$63,303	$67,879	$72,455
$750,000	$47,083	$51,659	$56,235	$60,811	$65,387	$69,963	$74,538

Figure 13-5

The reason some of the top cells are blank in the Figure 13-5 is that there aren't enough initial savings to cover the first five years at a constant retirement income.

For example, using the above chart, if someone has savings of $250,000 in TIPS or equivalent after taxes, and a pension of $30,000 per year after taxes, they can live on an after-tax retirement income of $39,978 per year, which is then indexed up annually with inflation.

Or, if they know how much they need for retirement income during retirement but just want to make sure they have enough money saved, they can use the chart below, Figure 13-6. This chart assumes retirement at age 60, Social

Security at $20,000 per year after taxes, and various savings amounts and pension amounts. Retirement income is assumed to be after taxes and indexed up every year with inflation, as is social security. Savings are assumed to be in TIPS or in some other format to be tax-free or after taxes. Pension is fixed and after taxes. Funds are to run out at age 93.

REQUIRED SAVINGS, ASSUMING RETIRE SOON AT AGE 60 & LIVE TO 93

Pension:	$0	$10,000	$20,000	$30,000	$40,000	$50,000	$60,000
Income							
$20,000	$100,000	$100,000	$100,000	$100,000	$100,000	$100,000	$100,000
$25,000	$220,000	$125,000	$125,000	$125,000	$125,000	$125,000	$125,000
$30,000	$340,000	$230,180	$150,000	$150,000	$150,000	$150,000	$150,000
$35,000	$460,000	$350,180	$240,360	$175,000	$175,000	$175,000	$175,000
$40,000	$580,000	$470,180	$360,360	$250,540	$200,000	$200,000	$200,000
$45,000	$700,000	$590,180	$480,360	$370,540	$260,720	$225,000	$225,000
$50,000	$820,000	$710,180	$600,360	$490,540	$380,720	$270,900	$250,000
$55,000	$940,000	$830,180	$720,360	$610,540	$500,720	$390,900	$281,080
$60,000	$1,060,000	$950,180	$840,360	$730,540	$620,720	$510,900	$401,080
$65,000	$1,180,000	$1,070,180	$960,360	$850,540	$740,720	$630,900	$521,080
$70,000	$1,300,000	$1,190,180	$1,080,360	$970,540	$860,720	$750,900	$641,080
$75,000	$1,420,000	$1,310,180	$1,200,360	$1,090,540	$980,720	$870,900	$761,080
$80,000	$1,540,000	$1,430,180	$1,320,360	$1,210,540	$1,100,720	$990,900	$881,080
$85,000	$1,660,000	$1,550,180	$1,440,360	$1,330,540	$1,220,720	$1,110,900	$1,001,080
$90,000	$1,780,000	$1,670,180	$1,560,360	$1,450,540	$1,340,720	$1,230,900	$1,121,080
$95,000	$1,900,000	$1,790,180	$1,680,360	$1,570,540	$1,460,720	$1,350,900	$1,241,080
$100,000	$2,020,000	$1,910,180	$1,800,360	$1,690,540	$1,580,720	$1,470,900	$1,361,080
$105,000	$2,140,000	$2,030,180	$1,920,360	$1,810,540	$1,700,720	$1,590,900	$1,481,080
$110,000	$2,260,000	$2,150,180	$2,040,360	$1,930,540	$1,820,720	$1,710,900	$1,601,080
$115,000	$2,380,000	$2,270,180	$2,160,360	$2,050,540	$1,940,720	$1,830,900	$1,721,080
$120,000	$2,500,000	$2,390,180	$2,280,360	$2,170,540	$2,060,720	$1,950,900	$1,841,080
$125,000	$2,620,000	$2,510,180	$2,400,360	$2,290,540	$2,180,720	$2,070,900	$1,961,080

Figure 13-6

For example, using the above chart, Figure 13-6, if someone knew they wanted $60,000 after taxes to live on during retirement, and they had a pension of $20,000 per year after taxes, the above chart says that they need to have $840,360 saved in TIPS or equivalent. The $60,000 per year retirement income is assumed to index every year with inflation, and won't run out until age 93.

Retire at Age 60, Live to 120

There will be those retiring soon, at age 60, who will be uncomfortable with the assumption of running out of money at age 93, even with the provision of using other assets to enable the retirement lifestyle to continue to age 100. For those people who want to be sure they have required funds if they live over 100, the following tables assume funds do not run out until age 120, and even that can be extended by draining other assets.

Below, in Figure 13-7, is a chart showing how much yearly retirement you can use without running out of money before age 120. This chart assumes retirement at age 60, Social Security at $20,000 per year after taxes, and various savings amounts and pension amounts. Retirement income is assumed to be after taxes, and to go up every year with inflation, as is social security. Savings are assumed to be in TIPS or in some other format to be tax-free or after taxes. Pension is fixed and after taxes.

RETIREMENT INCOME, ASSUMING RETIRE SOON AT AGE 60 & LIVE TO 120

Pension:	$0	$10,000	$20,000	$30,000	$40,000	$50,000	$60,000
Savings							
$0							
$50,000							
$100,000	$20,000						
$150,000	$21,515	$24,833	$28,150				
$200,000	$23,030	$26,348	$29,665	$32,983	$36,301	$39,618	
$250,000	$24,545	$27,863	$31,181	$34,498	$37,816	$41,133	$44,451
$300,000	$26,061	$29,378	$32,696	$36,013	$39,331	$42,648	$45,966
$350,000	$27,576	$30,893	$34,211	$37,528	$40,846	$44,164	$47,481
$400,000	$29,091	$32,408	$35,726	$39,044	$42,361	$45,679	$48,996

$450,000	$30,606	$33,924	$37,241	$40,559	$43,876	$47,194	$50,512
$500,000	$32,121	$35,439	$38,756	$42,074	$45,392	$48,709	$52,027
$550,000	$33,636	$36,954	$40,272	$43,589	$46,907	$50,224	$53,542
$600,000	$35,152	$38,469	$41,787	$45,104	$48,422	$51,739	$55,057
$650,000	$36,667	$39,984	$43,302	$46,619	$49,937	$53,255	$56,572
$700,000	$38,182	$41,499	$44,817	$48,135	$51,452	$54,770	$58,087
$750,000	$39,697	$43,015	$46,332	$49,650	$52,967	$56,285	$59,602

Figure 13-7

For example, using the above chart, Figure 13-7, if someone has savings of $200,000 in TIPS or after taxes, and a pension of $30,000 per year after taxes, they can live on an after-tax retirement income of $32,983 per year, which is then indexed up annually with inflation. Note that this is substantially less than the $40,943 retire-at-age 65 option.

Or if they know how much they need for retirement income during retirement, but just want to make sure they have enough money saved, they can use the chart below, Figure 13-8. This chart assumes retirement at age 60, Social Security at $20,000 per year after taxes, and various savings amounts and pension amounts. Retirement income is assumed to be after taxes, and to go up every year with inflation, as is social security. Savings are assumed to be in TIPS or in some other format to be tax-free or after taxes. Pension is fixed and after taxes. Funds are to run out at age 120.

REQUIRED SAVINGS, ASSUMING RETIRE SOON AT AGE 60 & LIVE TO 120

Pension:	$0	$10,000	$20,000	$30,000	$40,000	$50,000	$60,000
Income							
$20,000	$100,000	$100,000	$100,000	$100,000	$100,000	$100,000	$100,000
$25,000	$265,000	$155,520	$125,000	$125,000	$125,000	$125,000	$125,000
$30,000	$430,000	$320,520	$211,040	$150,000	$150,000	$150,000	$150,000
$35,000	$595,000	$485,520	$376,040	$266,560	$157,080	$175,000	$175,000
$40,000	$760,000	$650,520	$541,040	$431,560	$322,080	$212,600	$200,000
$45,000	$925,000	$815,520	$706,040	$596,560	$487,080	$377,600	$268,120
$50,000	$1,090,000	$980,520	$871,040	$761,560	$652,080	$542,600	$433,120
$55,000	$1,255,000	$1,145,520	$1,036,040	$926,560	$817,080	$707,600	$598,120
$60,000	$1,420,000	$1,310,520	$1,201,040	$1,091,560	$982,080	$872,600	$763,120
$65,000	$1,585,000	$1,475,520	$1,366,040	$1,256,560	$1,147,080	$1,037,600	$928,120
$70,000	$1,750,000	$1,640,520	$1,531,040	$1,421,560	$1,312,080	$1,202,600	$1,093,120
$75,000	$1,915,000	$1,805,520	$1,696,040	$1,586,560	$1,477,080	$1,367,600	$1,258,120
$80,000	$2,080,000	$1,970,520	$1,861,040	$1,751,560	$1,642,080	$1,532,600	$1,423,120
$85,000	$2,245,000	$2,135,520	$2,026,040	$1,916,560	$1,807,080	$1,697,600	$1,588,120
$90,000	$2,410,000	$2,300,520	$2,191,040	$2,081,560	$1,972,080	$1,862,600	$1,753,120
$95,000	$2,575,000	$2,465,520	$2,356,040	$2,246,560	$2,137,080	$2,027,600	$1,918,120
$100,000	$2,740,000	$2,630,520	$2,521,040	$2,411,560	$2,302,080	$2,192,600	$2,083,120
$105,000	$2,905,000	$2,795,520	$2,686,040	$2,576,560	$2,467,080	$2,357,600	$2,248,120
$110,000	$3,070,000	$2,960,520	$2,851,040	$2,741,560	$2,632,080	$2,522,600	$2,413,120
$115,000	$3,235,000	$3,125,520	$3,016,040	$2,906,560	$2,797,080	$2,687,600	$2,578,120
$120,000	$3,400,000	$3,290,520	$3,181,040	$3,071,560	$2,962,080	$2,852,600	$2,743,120
$125,000	$3,565,000	$3,455,520	$3,346,040	$3,236,560	$3,127,080	$3,017,600	$2,908,120

Figure 13-8

Using the above chart, Figure 13-8, if someone knew they wanted $60,000 after taxes to live on during retirement, and they had a pension of $20,000 per year after taxes, the above chart says that they need to have $1,201,040 saved in TIPS or equivalent. The $60,000 per year retirement income is assumed to index every year with inflation and won't run out until age 120. Note that this savings amount is substantially more than the $862,400 savings required in the retire-at-age 65 option.

Retire at Age 70, Live to 93

As we mentioned in earlier chapters, after age 93 the value of other assets like the home can be drained to extend the same lifestyle to age 100 or so. Below, in Figure 13-9, is a chart showing how much yearly retirement income you can use without running out of money before age 93. This chart assumes retirement at age 70 and Social Security at $26,400 per year after taxes, which is 32% higher due to the delayed retirement. There are various options for initial savings and pension amounts. Retirement income is assumed to be after taxes, and to go up every year with inflation, as is social security. Savings are assumed to be in TIPS or in some other format to be tax-free or after taxes. Pension is fixed and after taxes, but assumed to be 10% higher than the nominal shown in the tables because of the later retirement.

RETIREMENT INCOME, ASSUMING RETIRE SOON AT AGE 70 & LIVE TO 93

Pension:	$0	$10,000	$20,000	$30,000	$40,000	$50,000	$60,000
Savings							
$0	$26,400	$34,650	$42,900	$51,150	$59,400	$67,650	$75,900
$50,000	$29,341	$37,591	$45,841	$54,091	$62,341	$70,591	$78,841
$100,000	$32,282	$40,532	$48,782	$57,032	$65,282	$73,532	$81,782
$150,000	$35,224	$43,474	$51,724	$59,974	$68,224	$76,474	$84,724
$200,000	$38,165	$46,415	$54,665	$62,915	$71,165	$79,415	$87,665
$250,000	$41,106	$49,356	$57,606	$65,856	$74,106	$82,356	$90,606
$300,000	$44,047	$52,297	$60,547	$68,797	$77,047	$85,297	$93,547
$350,000	$46,988	$55,238	$63,488	$71,738	$79,988	$88,238	$96,488
$400,000	$49,929	$58,179	$66,429	$74,679	$82,929	$91,179	$99,429
$450,000	$52,871	$61,121	$69,371	$77,621	$85,871	$94,121	$102,371
$500,000	$55,812	$64,062	$72,312	$80,562	$88,812	$97,062	$105,312
$550,000	$58,753	$67,003	$75,253	$83,503	$91,753	$100,003	$108,253
$600,000	$61,694	$69,944	$78,194	$86,444	$94,694	$102,944	$111,194
$650,000	$64,635	$72,885	$81,135	$89,385	$97,635	$105,885	$114,135
$700,000	$67,576	$75,826	$84,076	$92,326	$100,576	$108,826	$117,076
$750,000	$70,518	$78,768	$87,018	$95,268	$103,518	$111,768	$120,018

Figure 13-9

Using the above chart, if someone has savings of $200,000 in TIPS or equivalent after taxes, and a pension of $30,000 per year after taxes, they can live on a retirement income of $62,915 per year, which is then indexed up annually with inflation. Note that the $62,915 is much higher than the $50,797 they would have had to live on if they retired at 65.

If someone knows how much they need for living during retirement, but just want to make sure they have enough money saved, they can use the chart below, Figure 13-10. This chart assumes retirement at age 70, Social Security at $26,400 per year after taxes, and has various saved amount and pension amount options. Retirement income is assumed to be after taxes, and to go up every year with inflation, as is social security. Savings are assumed to be in TIPS or in some other format to be tax-free or after taxes. Pension is fixed, but is assumed to be 10% higher than the nominal shown because of a delayed retirement. Pension is after taxes. Funds are to run out at age 93.

REQUIRED SAVINGS, ASSUMING RETIRE SOON AT AGE 70 & LIVE TO 93

Pension:	$0	$10,000	$20,000	$30,000	$40,000	$50,000	$60,000
Income							
$20,000	$0	$0	$0	$0	$0	$0	$0
$25,000	$0	$0	$0	$0	$0	$0	$0
$30,000	$61,200	$0	$0	$0	$0	$0	$0
$35,000	$146,200	$5,950	$0	$0	$0	$0	$0
$40,000	$231,200	$90,950	$0	$0	$0	$0	$0
$45,000	$316,200	$175,950	$35,700	$0	$0	$0	$0
$50,000	$401,200	$260,950	$120,700	$0	$0	$0	$0
$55,000	$486,200	$345,950	$205,700	$65,450	$0	$0	$0
$60,000	$571,200	$430,950	$290,700	$150,450	$10,200	$0	$0
$65,000	$656,200	$515,950	$375,700	$235,450	$95,200	$0	$0
$70,000	$741,200	$600,950	$460,700	$320,450	$180,200	$39,950	$0
$75,000	$826,200	$685,950	$545,700	$405,450	$265,200	$124,950	$0
$80,000	$911,200	$770,950	$630,700	$490,450	$350,200	$209,950	$69,700
$85,000	$996,200	$855,950	$715,700	$575,450	$435,200	$294,950	$154,700
$90,000	$1,081,200	$940,950	$800,700	$660,450	$520,200	$379,950	$239,700
$95,000	$1,166,200	$1,025,950	$885,700	$745,450	$605,200	$464,950	$324,700
$100,000	$1,251,200	$1,110,950	$970,700	$830,450	$690,200	$549,950	$409,700
$105,000	$1,336,200	$1,195,950	$1,055,700	$915,450	$775,200	$634,950	$494,700
$110,000	$1,421,200	$1,280,950	$1,140,700	$1,000,450	$860,200	$719,950	$579,700
$115,000	$1,506,200	$1,365,950	$1,225,700	$1,085,450	$945,200	$804,950	$664,700
$120,000	$1,591,200	$1,450,950	$1,310,700	$1,170,450	$1,030,200	$889,950	$749,700
$125,000	$1,676,200	$1,535,950	$1,395,700	$1,255,450	$1,115,200	$974,950	$834,700

Figure 13-10

For example, using the above chart, Figure 13-10, if someone knew they wanted $60,000 after taxes to live on during retirement, and they had a pension of $20,000 per year after taxes, the above chart says that they need to have $290,700 saved in TIPS or equivalent. The $60,000 per year retirement income is assumed to index every year with inflation, and won't run out until age 93. Note that the $290,700 required savings is substantially less than the $501,600 savings required when retirement was at age 65.

Retire at Age 70, Live to 120

There will be those retiring soon who will be uncomfortable with the assumption of running out of money at age 93, even with the provision of using other assets to enable the retirement lifestyle to continue to age 100. For those people who want to be sure they have required funds if they live over 100 years, the following tables assume funds do not run out until age 120, and even that can be extended by draining other assets.

Below, in Figure 13-11, is a chart showing how much yearly retirement you can use without running out of money before age 120. This chart assumes retirement at age 70, Social Security at $26,400 per year after taxes, and has various savings amounts and pension amount options. Retirement income is assumed to be after taxes, and to go up every year with inflation, as is social security. Savings are assumed to be in TIPS or in some other format to be tax-free or after taxes. Pension is fixed and after taxes, but is 10% higher than the nominal shown because of the delayed retirement.

RETIREMENT INCOME, ASSUMING RETIRE SOON AT AGE 70 & LIVE TO 120

Pension:	$0	$10,000	$20,000	$30,000	$40,000	$50,000	$60,000
Savings							
$0	$26,400	$31,790	$37,180	$42,570	$47,960	$53,350	$58,740
$50,000	$28,252	$33,642	$39,032	$44,422	$49,812	$55,202	$60,592
$100,000	$30,104	$35,494	$40,884	$46,274	$51,664	$57,054	$62,444
$150,000	$31,956	$37,346	$42,736	$48,126	$53,516	$58,906	$64,296
$200,000	$33,807	$39,197	$44,587	$49,977	$55,367	$60,757	$66,147
$250,000	$35,659	$41,049	$46,439	$51,829	$57,219	$62,609	$67,999
$300,000	$37,511	$42,901	$48,291	$53,681	$59,071	$64,461	$69,851
$350,000	$39,363	$44,753	$50,143	$55,533	$60,923	$66,313	$71,703
$400,000	$41,215	$46,605	$51,995	$57,385	$62,775	$68,165	$73,555
$450,000	$43,067	$48,457	$53,847	$59,237	$64,627	$70,017	$75,407
$500,000	$44,919	$50,309	$55,699	$61,089	$66,479	$71,869	$77,259
$550,000	$46,770	$52,160	$57,550	$62,940	$68,330	$73,720	$79,110
$600,000	$48,622	$54,012	$59,402	$64,792	$70,182	$75,572	$80,962

$650,000	$50,474	$55,864	$61,254	$66,644	$72,034	$77,424	$82,814
$700,000	$52,326	$57,716	$63,106	$68,496	$73,886	$79,276	$84,666
$750,000	$54,178	$59,568	$64,958	$70,348	$75,738	$81,128	$86,518

Figure 13-11

For example, using the above chart, if someone has savings of $200,000 in TIPS or after taxes, and a pension of $30,000 per year after taxes, they can live on $49,977 per year, which is then indexed up annually with inflation. Note that this is substantially more than the $40,943 in the retire-at-age 65 option.

If they know how much they need for living during retirement, but just want to make sure they have enough money saved, they can use the chart below, Figure 13-12. This chart assumes retirement at age 70, Social Security at $26,400 per year after taxes, and has various savings amount and pension amount options. Retirement income is assumed to be after taxes, and to go up every year with inflation, as is social security. Savings are assumed to be in TIPS or in some other format to be tax-free or after taxes. Pension is fixed and after taxes, but is calculated within the table at 10% more than the nominal shown due to the delayed retirement. Funds are to run out at age 120.

REQUIRED SAVINGS, ASSUMING RETIRE SOON AT AGE 70 & LIVE TO 120

Pension:	$0	$10,000	$20,000	$30,000	$40,000	$50,000	$60,000
Income							
$20,000	$0	$0	$0	$0	$0	$0	$0
$25,000	$0	$0	$0	$0	$0	$0	$0
$30,000	$97,200	$0	$0	$0	$0	$0	$0
$35,000	$232,200	$86,670	$0	$0	$0	$0	$0
$40,000	$367,200	$221,670	$76,140	$0	$0	$0	$0
$45,000	$502,200	$356,670	$211,140	$65,610	$0	$0	$0
$50,000	$637,200	$491,670	$346,140	$200,610	$55,080	$0	$0
$55,000	$772,200	$626,670	$481,140	$335,610	$190,080	$44,550	$0
$60,000	$907,200	$761,670	$616,140	$470,610	$325,080	$179,550	$34,020
$65,000	$1,042,200	$896,670	$751,140	$605,610	$460,080	$314,550	$169,020
$70,000	$1,177,200	$1,031,670	$886,140	$740,610	$595,080	$449,550	$304,020
$75,000	$1,312,200	$1,166,670	$1,021,140	$875,610	$730,080	$584,550	$439,020
$80,000	$1,447,200	$1,301,670	$1,156,140	$1,010,610	$865,080	$719,550	$574,020
$85,000	$1,582,200	$1,436,670	$1,291,140	$1,145,610	$1,000,080	$854,550	$709,020
$90,000	$1,717,200	$1,571,670	$1,426,140	$1,280,610	$1,135,080	$989,550	$844,020
$95,000	$1,852,200	$1,706,670	$1,561,140	$1,415,610	$1,270,080	$1,124,550	$979,020
$100,000	$1,987,200	$1,841,670	$1,696,140	$1,550,610	$1,405,080	$1,259,550	$1,114,020
$105,000	$2,122,200	$1,976,670	$1,831,140	$1,685,610	$1,540,080	$1,394,550	$1,249,020
$110,000	$2,257,200	$2,111,670	$1,966,140	$1,820,610	$1,675,080	$1,529,550	$1,384,020
$115,000	$2,392,200	$2,246,670	$2,101,140	$1,955,610	$1,810,080	$1,664,550	$1,519,020
$120,000	$2,527,200	$2,381,670	$2,236,140	$2,090,610	$1,945,080	$1,799,550	$1,654,020
$125,000	$2,662,200	$2,516,670	$2,371,140	$2,225,610	$2,080,080	$1,934,550	$1,789,020

Figure 13-12

Using the above chart, Figure 13-12, if someone knew they wanted $60,000 after taxes to live on during retirement, and they had a pension of $20,000 per year after taxes, the above chart says that they need to have $616,140 saved in TIPS or equivalent. The $60,000 per year retirement income is assumed to index every year with inflation and won't run out until age 120. Note that this savings amount is substantially less than the $862,400 savings required in the retire at age 65 option.

Just to show how expensive retiring early or "living forever" is, using the prior tables, here is a comparison of the savings requirement for someone wanting $60,000 retirement income with a nominal pension of $20,000.

Retire age 60, live to 120, savings required = $1,201,040.
Retire age 70, live to 93, savings required = $290,700.

FORMULAS SHOWING RETIREMENT INCOME AND RETIREMENT SAVINGS for those retiring within a few years

For anyone who is comfortable using formulas rather than the above charts, they can plug their own specific values into the below formulas to get more exact values for either retirement income or the TIPS savings that are required. Using the formulas allows someone to input numbers other than the ones shown on the prior tables. Those of you who get headaches from math details may want to skip the rest of this chapter.

In the formulas, we will use RI to represent the after-tax "retirement income," SS for the "social security benefit," TS for the required "TIPS savings," and PN for the "pension benefit."

RETIRE at AGE 65 and Live to Age 93. Determine Retirement Income:

RI = TS/19 + SS + 0.68*PN

Let's try this formula and check the results against the table in Figure 13-1. Assume someone has TIPS savings of $450,000 and a pension of $40,000 after taxes. For this example, as we assumed in the table, Figure 13-1, we will use social security being $20,000 per year after taxes.

RI = TS/19 + SS + 0.68*PN
RI = $450,000/19 + $20,000 + 0.68*$40,000
RI = $23,684 + $20,000 + $27,200

RI = $70,884

Let's now go to the table, Figure 13-1, and look up the table value, with a savings of $450,000 and a pension of $40,000. We see it is $70,884, the same as what we calculated. The advantage of using the formula, however, is that if necessary you can input values other than those shown in the table.

The above equation shows that for every dollar of retirement income RI, you need 19 dollars of TIPS savings TS. The luxury of having an extra automobile that costs $5250 per year in depreciation, insurance, taxes, etc., requires an extra $100,000 in TIPS savings! Obviously, reducing living expenses is much easier than trying to save additional funds!

For those who are inquisitive, the details on the derivations of the "19" divisor and "0.68" multiplier in the above formula are covered in the last chapter of the book.

Now let's look at the other formulas. Again, in all the formulas we will use RI to represent the after-tax retirement income, SS for the social security benefit, TS for the required TIPS savings, and PN for the pension benefit.

RETIRE at AGE 65, Live to Age 93, Determine Required TIPS Savings:

$$TS = 19 * (RI - SS - 0.68PN)$$

Let's try this formula and then compare the results with the table in Figure 13-2. Assume an after-tax retirement income RI of $75,000 and a pension PN of $30,000 after taxes. We will use $20,000 for the after-tax social security benefit, like we did in the tables.

$$TS = 19 * (RI - SS - 0.68*PN)$$
$$TS = 19 * (\$75,000 - \$20,000 - 0.68 * \$30,000)$$
$$TS = 19 * (\$75,000 - \$20,000 - \$20,400)$$
$$TS = 19 * \$34,600$$
$$TS = \$657,400$$

Checking this against the equivalent value in Figure 13-2, we can see that they agree. You will also recognize the multipliers 19 and 0.68 in this formula as being identical to those in the prior formula for retirement income.

Again, in the formulas we will use RI to represent the after-tax retirement income, SS for the social security benefit, TS for the required TIPS savings, and PN for the pension benefit.

RETIRE at AGE 65, Live to Age 120, Determine Retirement Income:

$$RI = TS/28 + SS + 0.46*PN$$

Let's try this formula and check the results against the table in Figure 13-3. Assume someone has TIPS savings of $450,000 and a pension of $40,000 after taxes. As we assumed in the table, Figure 13-3, we will use social security being $20,000 per year after taxes.

$$RI = TS/28 + SS + 0.46*PN$$
$$RI = \$450,000/28 + \$20,000 + 0.46*\$40,000$$
$$RI = \$16,071 + \$20,000 + \$18,400$$
$$RI = \$54,471$$

Let's now go to the table, Figure 13-3, and look up the table value with a savings of $450,000 and a pension of $40,000. We see it is $54,471, the same as what we calculated.

The TS/28 and 0.46*PN were determined in the exactly the same manner as we did for the earlier formulas for retire at age 93, except in this case we required the savings to go negative in 55 years, which gets us from age 65 to age 120.

RETIRE at AGE 65, Live to Age 120, Determine Required TIPS Savings:

$$TS = 28 * (RI - SS - 0.46PN)$$

Let's try this formula and then compare the results with the table in Figure 13-4. Assume an after-tax retirement income RI of $75,000 and a pension PN of $30,000 after taxes. We will use $20,000 for the after-tax social security benefit, like we did in the tables.

TS = 28 * (RI - SS - 0.46*PN)
TS = 28 * ($75,000 - $20,000 – 0.46 * $30,000)
TS = 28 * ($75,000 - $20,000 – $13,800)
TS = 28 * $41,200
TS = $1,153,600

This matches the value in Figure 13-4.

RETIRE at AGE 60, Live to Age 93, Determine Retirement Income:

This formula becomes a little more complex because the first five years of retirement do not include either social security benefits or a pension. Also, it is assumed that the pension is reduced 15% because the employee leaves the company five years before the company pension begins, giving him or her less employment years credited towards the pension.

We account for the above issues by adding five times the annual retirement income onto the required savings, since these savings will be the only income for the first five years. This additional amount is included within the formula. We also must verify savings are a minimum of five times the retirement income. Here is the formula:

RI = 0.0417TS + 0.4576PN + 0.7917SS
(TS must be greater than 5RI, or there will not be sufficient funds for the first five years.)

Let's try this and compare the answer with table 13-5. Assume someone has TIPS savings of $450,000 and a pension of $40,000 after taxes. As we assumed in the table, Figure 13-5, we will use social security being $20,000 per year after taxes.

RI = 0.0417TS + 0.4576PN + 0.7917SS
RI = (0.0417 * $450,000) + (0.4576 * $40,000) + (0.7917 * $20,000)
RI = $18,765 + $18,304 + $15,834
RI = $52,903

(Since the TS of $450,000 is greater than 5 times the RI of $52,903, we have enough funds for the first five years.)

Let's check this result against Figure 13-5. The table value is $52,887, equivalent except for a small amount of round-off error.

RETIRE at AGE 60, Live to Age 93, Determine Required TIPS Savings:

The first five years of retirement do not include either social security benefits or a pension. Also, it is assumed that the pension is reduced 15% because the employee leaves the company five years before the company pension begins, giving him or her less years towards the pension.

We account for the above issues within the formula by adding five times the annual retirement income onto the required savings, since these savings will be the only income for the first five years. We also must verify savings are a minimum of five times the retirement income. Here is the formula:

TS = 24RI – 10.98PN – 19SS
(TS must be greater than 5RI, or there will not be sufficient funds for the first five years.)

Let's try this and compare the answer with table 13-6. Assume an after-tax retirement income RI of $65,000 and a pension PN of $10,000 after taxes. We will use $20,000 for the after-tax social security benefit, like we did in the tables.

TS = 24RI – 10.98PN – 19SS
TS = (24 * $65,000) – (10.98 * $10,000) – (19 * $20,000)

219

TS = $1,560,000 - $109,800 - $380,000
TS = $1,070,200

This agrees with Figure 13-6, other than round-off error.
(Since the TS of $1,070,200 is greater than 5 times the RI of $65,000, we have enough funds for the first five years.)

RETIRE at AGE 60, Live to Age 120, Determine Retirement Income:

The first five years of retirement do not include either social security benefits or a pension. Also, it is assumed that the pension is reduced 15% because the employee leaves the company five years before the company pension begins, giving him or her less years towards the pension.

We account for the above issues within the formula by adding five times the annual retirement income onto the required savings, since these savings will be the only income for the first five years. We also must verify savings are a minimum of five times the retirement income. Here is the formula:

RI = 0.0303TS + 0.3318PN + 0.8485SS
(TS must be greater than 5RI, or there will not be sufficient funds for the first five years.)

Let's try this and compare the answer with table 13-7. Assume someone has TIPS savings of $400,000 and a pension of $40,000 after taxes. As we assumed in the table, Figure 13-7, we will use social security being $20,000 per year after taxes.

RI = 0.0303TS + 0.3318PN + 0.8485SS
RI= (0.0303 * $400,000) + (0.3318 * $40,000) + (0.8485 * $20,000)
RI = $12,120 + $13,272 + $ 16,970
RI = $42,362

Looking at Figure 13-7, the results agree.
(Since the TS of $400,000 is greater than 5 times the RI of $42,362, we have enough funds for the first five years.)

RETIRE at AGE 60, Live to Age 120, Determine Required TIPS Savings:

The first five years of retirement do not include either social security benefits or a pension. Also, it is assumed that the pension is reduced 15% because the employee leaves the company five years before the company pension begins, giving him or her less years towards the pension.

We account for the above issues within the formula by adding five times the annual retirement income onto the required savings, since these savings will be the only income for the first five years. We also must verify savings are a minimum of five times the retirement income. Here is the formula:

$TS = 33RI - 10.95PN - 28SS$
(TS must be greater than 5RI, or there will not be sufficient funds for the first five years.)

Let's try this and compare the answer with table 13-8. Assume an after-tax retirement income RI of $85,000 and a pension PN of $10,000 after taxes. We will use $20,000 for the after-tax social security benefit, like in the tables.

$TS = 33RI - 10.95PN - 28SS$
$TS = (33 * \$85,000) - (10.95 * \$10,000) - (28 * \$20,000)$
$TS = \$2,805,000 - \$109,500 - \$560,000$
$TS = \$2,135,500$

Looking at Figure 13-8, the results agree other than round-off error.
(Since the TS of $2,135,500 is greater than 5 times the RI of $85,000, we have enough funds for the first five years.)

RETIRE at AGE 70, Live to Age 93, Determine Retirement Income:

$RI = (TS/17) + SS + (0.825*PN)$

Let's try this formula and check the results against the table in Figure 13-9. Assume someone has TIPS savings of $450,000 and a nominal pension of $40,000 after taxes. In the formula, the pension is increased 10% over the nominal due to the five years extended employment. As we assumed in the table, Figure 13-9, we will use social security being $26,400 per year after taxes.

RI = TS/17 + SS + 0.825*PN
RI = $450,000/17 + $26,400 + 0.825*$40,000
RI = $26,471 + $26,400 + $33,000
RI = $85,871

Let's now go to the table, Figure 13-9, and look up the table value with a savings of $450,000 and a pension of $40,000. We see it is $85,871, the same as what we calculated.

RETIRE at AGE 70, Live to Age 93, Determine Required TIPS Savings:

TS = 17 * (RI-SS -0.825PN)

Let's try this formula and then compare the results with the table in Figure 13-10. Assume an after-tax retirement income RI of $75,000 and a nominal pension PN of $30,000 after taxes (assumed to be 10% bigger in the formula due to five years additional employment). We will use $26,400 for the after-tax social security benefit, like we did in the tables.

TS = 17 * (RI-SS -0.825PN)
TS = 17 * ($75,000 - $26,400 – 0.825 * $30,000)
TS = 17 * ($75,000 - 26,400 - $24,750)
TS = 17 * $23,850
TS = $405,450

Checking this against the equivalent value in Figure 13-10, we can see that they agree.

RETIRE at AGE 70, Live to Age 120, Determine Retirement Income:

$RI = TS/27 + SS + 0.539*PN$

Let's try this formula and check the results against the table in Figure 13-11. Assume someone has TIPS savings of $450,000 and a pension of nominal $40,000 after taxes (increased 10% in the formula because of the additional five years of employment). As we assumed in the table, Figure 13-11, we will use social security being $26,400 per year after taxes.

$RI = TS/27 + SS + 0.539*PN$
$RI = \$450,000/27 + \$26,400 + 0.539*\$40,000$
$RI = \$16,667 + \$26,400 + \$21,560$
$RI = \$64,627$

Let's now go to the table, Figure 13-11, and look up the table value with a savings of $450,000 and a pension of $40,000. We see it is $64,627, the same as what we calculated.

RETIRE at AGE 70, Live to Age 120, Determine Required TIPS Savings:

$TS = 27 * (RI-SS -0.539PN)$

Let's try this formula and then compare the results with the table in Figure 13-12. Assume an after-tax retirement income RI of $75,000 and a nominal pension PN of $30,000 after taxes (which is increased 10% within the formula to account for the additional five years of employment). We will use $26,400 for the after-tax social security benefit, like we did in the tables.

$TS = 27 * (RI - SS - 0.539*PN)$
$TS = 27 * (\$75,000 - \$26,400 – 0.539 * \$30,000)$

TS = 27 * ($75,000 - $26,400 – $16,170)
TS = 27 * $32,430
TS = $875,610

This matches the value in Figure 13-12.

PART IV
History of Bubbles, Derivations, and Tests

CHAPTER: 14 History of Bubbles
The current stock market, debt, and housing bubbles are not unique. There is quite a history of economic bubbles, all of which eventually broke. No exceptions! And several of these current bubbles are getting awfully close to their size limitations. The only thing we are trying to do is estimate when these bubbles will hit their sharply defined limitations and burst!

CHAPTER 15: Derivation of the Living Forever Savings Adjustment; Testing the Retirement Tables with Inflated Funds; and Derivation of the Divisors and Multipliers in the Retirement Formulas.
This chapter shows detail related to some of the calculations used in earlier tables and formulas. This chapter is for the data-analysis inclined.

CHAPTER 14
History of Bubbles

The current stock market, debt, and housing bubbles are not unique. There is quite a history of economic bubbles, *all of which eventually broke. No exceptions*! An economic bubble occurs when investors get so excited about a stock or some other financial instrument, that the price of the asset (or the size of a debt) gets so high that it is no longer rational. It becomes a form of gambling rather than investing, where someone is betting that there will always be a greater fool who will be willing to pay even more than the current price, or that something miraculous will happen to enable debt payoff. With an asset, once awareness sinks in that the now outrageous prices have no real substance and that there are no more buyers, panic selling ensues, because everyone is trying to save at least some of their investment. With debt, if it keeps growing, eventually the debtor gives up and goes into bankruptcy. When these events involve large numbers of people, they eventually get labeled as bubbles.

When listing past bubbles, many books on the economy start out detailing the Tulip-Bulb craze affecting Holland in 1635. Another major bubble was the South Sea Bubble that occurred in the United Kingdom in 1711. These events were so long ago, and the related economies were so different, that few people can equate them with current events. However, we have had our share of bubbles within the last 100 years that are instructive, at least as far as seeing how they are natural happenings that seem to occur periodically, not unlike earthquakes or hurricanes. Nor do we seem any better at preventing them than the other natural disasters. *Mother* Nature creates earthquakes and hurricanes, whereas *human* nature creates economic bubbles. Human greed drives the creation of bubbles.

The Florida Bubble

In the early 1920's, people began to relocate to Florida in droves, causing property values to skyrocket. Property values would sometimes quadruple within a year. This went on for several years, with some people making huge profits. Of course, these profits attracted ever greater numbers of people "investing" in Florida property, causing the price bubble to get bigger and bigger. Finally, in 1926, as the number of buyers willing to pay the now outrageous prices eventually began to shrink, panic selling ensued and prices dropped precipitously. The bubble burst!

The Great Depression

The (first) Great Depression started in 1929, with the stock market drop in October of that year. In that summer, just prior to the October market drop, Professor Lawrence of Princeton University had declared that the judgment of those buying stocks was that stocks were *not* overpriced. After all, most everyone investing in the stock market was getting more affluent every day. Prices just kept going up, and there seemed to be no reason this would ever end. People bought stock on margin so that they could leverage their market gains by buying even more stocks. Why not? The United States was booming, and people were reaping the benefits of industrialization and the new technologies. This was a new era. Things were good!

But as everyone knows, the market crash *did* come. Just as investors so blindly entered the market with no other knowledge than the observation that others seemed to be getting rich, they just as quickly panicked, without having any other specific reason then the market was beginning to falter, which then triggered panic selling. The bubble had burst. The market drop was then followed by the most costly depression in the history of this country.

The Market Drop of October 19th, 1987: Black Monday

On this day, the stock market lost more than 22% of its value, the largest one day percentage loss ever. There is a lot written on the underlying reasons on why this happened. Certainly, some stocks were over priced, and there were shenanigans going on in the market, like insider trading, that spooked investors. But the reason for the *huge* drop was that computer programs, triggered by stop-loss limits, automatically kicked in and started selling. As prices dropped, additional computer programs kicked in, getting panic selling of a new automated nature. Without those computer programs, which are now required to cut-out if the market drops too fast, the huge drop would probably not have occurred. In this case, people had programmed "panic selling" into the computer programs.

The Market Crash of 2000, 2001, and 2002

As was noted earlier in the book, some call this the Dot-Com Crash; but it affected *all* companies, not just the new technology companies. Granted, the dot-com companies were part of the outrageous stock price rise in the nineties; but other stocks, including those of most of the largest corporations in the country, had also climbed to price levels that made no sense.

I think history will decide that this market drop was the first stage of the coming depression. Two things stopped the market from dropping even further and the economy completely going into the dumper in 2002. First, was the continuing influx of 401(k) pension money coming into the stock market. This on-going input of money into the market stopped the panic selling that would have probably ensued if investors were making their own active decisions on whether to invest in the market on a daily basis. If they were making such a decision, they probably would not have invested, and panic selling would have followed.

The other thing that delayed an economic downturn was the lowering of interest rates, which allowed investors to refinance and switch some of their credit card debt to a lower mortgage-based rate. This also contributed to the current housing bubble. However, as noted earlier, since consumer spending continues unabated and interest rates are rising, by 2006 or 2007, the consumer will no longer be able to continue to overspend, and the economy will begin a long and terrible drop.

The Current Debt, Stock Market, and Housing Bubbles

The current bubbles may be more costly than any of the earlier bubbles mentioned in this chapter because they affect a broader span of the population. Most of the earlier bubbles mentioned affected primarily the wealthy, with the exception of the depression which also devastated the poor and unemployed. The middle classes survived with minimal hurt. *All* classes will be hurt in the coming depression. Many of the middle class will be ruined, since they are active in the stock market, in debt, and leveraged in their home mortgages.

CHAPTER 15

Derivation of the Living Forever Savings Adjustment; Testing the Retirement Tables with Inflated Funds; and Derivation of the Divisors and Multipliers in the Retirement Formulas.

Those who have a natural aversion to data analysis and computation may want to skip this chapter.

Derivation of the Living Forever Savings Adjustment

In the savings tables shown in Chapter 12, at the bottom of the tables there is correction factor to be used if someone wanted to be very conservative and have enough funds at retirement to "live forever", or in this case to age 120. We will now show how that correction factor was derived, revisiting two of the examples used in Chapter 12.

Example #1 from Chapter 12 modified to a "live forever" assumption:

A 40 year old couple plan to retire at age 70. So they have 30 additional years to work. Their current combined income is $75,000 after taxes. Using 80% as the factor to determine their retirement income needs, their required retirement income will be 0.8 * $75,000 = $60,000 in 2003 dollars.

The combined nominal company pensions that their companies have projected the couple will receive at age 65 is $40,000 per year (after tax and in future dollars). They currently have no savings for the purpose of retirement. They want to save enough such that when they retire they can keep their desired lifestyle until age 120.

In the calculations shown below, in Figure 15-1, for the live-to-120 option, we had to add 92% to the savings that were already calculated in Chapter 12 for the live-to-age 93 assumption. The savings requirement that was calculated for the live-to-age-93 assumption was $8,169, whereas the first year savings shown in Figure 15-1 below is $15,684, which is 92% higher than the $8,169. Some of the additional is needed because a portion of the savings are outside the Roth IRA limits, so the amount saved has extra added for expected taxes. This is where the total 92% extra savings number came from. We also track desired income and social security so we can use the inflated numbers in Figure 15-2.

Testing the 92% Savings Additional Amount on the Example #1 Savings

Savings Year	Inflated Annual Actual Savings	Accumulated Savings Including Interest and Inflation	Desired Income Including Inflation	Social Security Including Inflation
1	$15,684	$15,684	$60,000	$25,920
2	$16,233	$32,936	$62,100	$26,827
3	$16,801	$51,878	$64,274	$27,766
4	$17,389	$72,640	$66,523	$28,738
5	$17,998	$95,359	$68,851	$29,744
6	$18,628	$120,185	$71,261	$30,785
7	$19,280	$147,277	$73,755	$31,862
8	$19,954	$176,804	$76,337	$32,977
9	$20,653	$208,949	$79,009	$34,132
10	$21,376	$243,906	$81,774	$35,326
11	$22,124	$281,884	$84,636	$36,563
12	$22,898	$323,105	$87,598	$37,842
13	$23,700	$367,806	$90,664	$39,167
14	$24,529	$416,243	$93,837	$40,538
15	$25,388	$468,686	$97,122	$41,957
16	$26,276	$525,427	$100,521	$43,425
17	$27,196	$586,775	$104,039	$44,945
18	$28,148	$653,064	$107,681	$46,518
19	$29,133	$724,646	$111,449	$48,146
20	$30,153	$801,900	$115,350	$49,831
21	$31,208	$885,231	$119,387	$51,575
22	$32,300	$975,072	$123,566	$53,380
23	$33,431	$1,071,882	$127,891	$55,249
24	$34,601	$1,176,155	$132,367	$57,182
25	$35,812	$1,288,417	$137,000	$59,184
26	$37,065	$1,409,229	$141,795	$61,255

27	$38,362	$1,539,191	$146,758	$63,399
28	$39,705	$1,678,944	$151,894	$65,618
29	$41,095	$1,829,170	$157,210	$67,915
30	$42,533	$1,990,599	$162,713	$70,292
	Tax Adjusted =	$1,866,244		

Figure 15-1

As previously noted, extra had to be saved since some of the accumulated savings is taxable because the savings amount exceeded the Roth maximum savings limits. That is why there is a lower tax adjusted amount of $1,866,244, which is the amount that will be used for the retirement initial savings. We now have to see if these accumulative savings of $1,866,244 last for the 50 years required from retirement at age 70 to the goal of age 120.

Looking at Figure 15-2 below, you can see that with the $1,866,244 initial savings, the accumulated savings in the second column doesn't become negative until the fiftieth year (age 70 through ages 120), so we were successful.

Testing the 92% Additional Savings on the Retirement Funds in Example #1

Retire Year	Accumulated Savings Plus Inflation & Interest	Inflated Outgoing Funds (Desired Income)	Inflated Social Security
1	$1,866,244	$168,408	$72,752
2	$1,932,536	$174,302	$75,298
3	$1,999,572	$180,402	$77,934
4	$2,067,276	$186,717	$80,662
5	$2,135,560	$193,252	$83,485
6	$2,204,330	$200,015	$86,407
7	$2,273,478	$207,016	$89,431
8	$2,342,886	$214,262	$92,561
9	$2,412,422	$221,761	$95,801
10	$2,481,942	$229,522	$99,154
11	$2,551,286	$237,556	$102,624
12	$2,620,277	$245,870	$106,216

13	$2,688,723	$254,475	$109,933
14	$2,756,413	$263,382	$113,781
15	$2,823,115	$272,600	$117,763
16	$2,888,576	$282,142	$121,885
17	$2,952,520	$292,016	$126,151
18	$3,014,647	$302,237	$130,566
19	$3,074,630	$312,815	$135,136
20	$3,132,113	$323,764	$139,866
21	$3,186,709	$335,096	$144,761
22	$3,237,999	$346,824	$149,828
23	$3,285,528	$358,963	$155,072
24	$3,328,804	$371,526	$160,499
25	$3,367,292	$384,530	$166,117
26	$3,400,416	$397,988	$171,931
27	$3,427,552	$411,918	$177,949
28	$3,448,026	$426,335	$184,177
29	$3,461,109	$441,257	$190,623
30	$3,466,016	$456,701	$197,295
31	$3,461,899	$472,685	$204,200
32	$3,447,846	$489,229	$211,347
33	$3,422,871	$506,352	$218,744
34	$3,385,915	$524,075	$226,400
35	$3,335,836	$542,417	$234,324
36	$3,271,406	$561,402	$242,526
37	$3,191,304	$581,051	$251,014
38	$3,094,110	$601,388	$259,800
39	$2,978,295	$622,436	$268,893
40	$2,842,220	$644,222	$278,304
41	$2,684,122	$666,770	$288,044
42	$2,502,107	$690,106	$298,126
43	$2,294,145	$714,260	$308,560
44	$2,058,054	$739,259	$319,360
45	$1,791,495	$765,133	$330,538
46	$1,491,958	$791,913	$342,106
47	$1,156,751	$819,630	$354,080
48	$782,990	$848,317	$366,473
49	$367,580	$878,008	$379,300
50	-$92,792	$908,738	$392,575

Figure 15-2

We will now show how the correction factor was derived for Example #3 from Chapter 12, which had an assumed age of 65 for retirement.

Example #3 from Chapter 12 modified to a "live forever" assumption:

A 40 year old couple plan to retire at age 65. So they have 25 additional years to work. Their current combined income is $75,000 after taxes. Using 80% as the factor to determine their retirement income needs, their required retirement income will be 0.8 * $75,000 = $60,000 in 2003 dollars.

The combined nominal company pensions that their companies have projected the couple would receive at age 65 is $40,000 per year after taxes (in future dollars). They currently have no savings for the purpose of retirement. They want to save enough that when they retire at age 65 they can keep their desired lifestyle until age 120.

In the calculations shown below in Figure 15-3, we had to add 55% to the $16,293 savings that were calculated in Chapter 12 for a live-to-age 93 assumption. 1.55 times $16,293 = $25,254, the first year savings we show in the annual savings column in Figure 14-3. The last line in the third column, $1,897,516, is the tax-adjusted accumulated savings value. This number represents the savings available after expected taxes that occur because the savings amount exceeded the Roth IRA maximums. We are tracking desired income and social security so we can use the inflated numbers in Figure 15-4.

Testing the 55% Additional Savings on the Example #3 Savings

Savings Year	Inflated Annual Actual Savings	Accumulated Savings Including Interest and Inflation	Desired Income Including Inflation	Social Security Including Inflation
1	$25,254	$26,896	$60,000	$25,920
2	$26,138	$54,782	$62,100	$26,827
3	$27,053	$85,396	$64,274	$27,766

4	$28,000	$118,946	$66,523	$28,738
5	$28,980	$155,657	$68,851	$29,744
6	$29,994	$195,769	$71,261	$30,785
7	$31,044	$239,538	$73,755	$31,862
8	$32,130	$287,238	$76,337	$32,977
9	$33,255	$339,163	$79,009	$34,132
10	$34,419	$395,628	$81,774	$35,326
11	$35,623	$456,967	$84,636	$36,563
12	$36,870	$523,540	$87,598	$37,842
13	$38,161	$595,731	$90,664	$39,167
14	$39,496	$673,950	$93,837	$40,538
15	$40,879	$758,636	$97,122	$41,957
16	$42,310	$850,256	$100,521	$43,425
17	$43,790	$949,314	$104,039	$44,945
18	$45,323	$1,056,342	$107,681	$46,518
19	$46,909	$1,171,913	$111,449	$48,146
20	$48,551	$1,296,639	$115,350	$49,831
21	$50,250	$1,431,171	$119,387	$51,575
22	$52,009	$1,576,206	$123,566	$53,380
23	$53,830	$1,732,489	$127,891	$55,249
24	$55,714	$1,900,814	$132,367	$57,182
25	$57,664	$2,082,031	$137,000	$59,184
	Tax Adjusted=	$1,897,516		

Figure 15-3

We now have to see if the $1,897,516 tax adjusted savings in Figure 15-3 last for the 55 years required from retirement at age 65 to the goal of age 120. Looking at Figure 15-4 below, you can see that with the 55% additional savings, the second column, which is the accumulated savings, doesn't become negative until the 55th year, so we were successful.

Testing the 55% Additional Savings on the Retirement Funds in Example #3

Retire Year	Accumulated Savings Plus Inflation & Interest	Inflated Outgoing Funds (Desired Income)	Inflated Social Security
1	$1,897,516	$141,795	$61,255
2	$1,912,443	$146,758	$63,399
3	$1,923,055	$151,894	$65,618
4	$1,928,886	$157,210	$67,915
5	$1,929,435	$162,713	$70,292
6	$1,924,159	$168,408	$72,752
7	$1,989,956	$174,302	$75,298
8	$2,056,465	$180,402	$77,934
9	$2,123,606	$186,717	$80,662
10	$2,191,292	$193,252	$83,485
11	$2,259,424	$200,015	$86,407
12	$2,327,893	$207,016	$89,431
13	$2,396,578	$214,262	$92,561
14	$2,465,345	$221,761	$95,801
15	$2,534,045	$229,522	$99,154
16	$2,602,515	$237,556	$102,624
17	$2,670,576	$245,870	$106,216
18	$2,738,032	$254,475	$109,933
19	$2,804,667	$263,382	$113,781
20	$2,870,245	$272,600	$117,763
21	$2,934,510	$282,142	$121,885
22	$2,997,180	$292,016	$126,151
23	$3,057,950	$302,237	$130,566
24	$3,116,487	$312,815	$135,136
25	$3,172,431	$323,764	$139,866
26	$3,225,387	$335,096	$144,761
27	$3,274,932	$346,824	$149,828
28	$3,320,601	$358,963	$155,072
29	$3,361,897	$371,526	$160,499
30	$3,398,276	$384,530	$166,117
31	$3,429,154	$397,988	$171,931
32	$3,453,898	$411,918	$177,949
33	$3,471,824	$426,335	$184,177
34	$3,482,194	$441,257	$190,623

35	$3,484,211	$456,701	$197,295
36	$3,477,018	$472,685	$204,200
37	$3,459,687	$489,229	$211,347
38	$3,431,222	$506,352	$218,744
39	$3,390,549	$524,075	$226,400
40	$3,336,511	$542,417	$234,324
41	$3,267,865	$561,402	$242,526
42	$3,183,273	$581,051	$251,014
43	$3,081,296	$601,388	$259,800
44	$2,960,389	$622,436	$268,893
45	$2,818,890	$644,222	$278,304
46	$2,655,015	$666,770	$288,044
47	$2,466,849	$690,106	$298,126
48	$2,252,335	$714,260	$308,560
49	$2,009,266	$739,259	$319,360
50	$1,735,276	$765,133	$330,538
51	$1,427,824	$791,913	$342,106
52	$1,084,189	$819,630	$354,080
53	$701,451	$848,317	$366,473
54	$276,481	$878,008	$379,300
55	-$194,072	$908,738	$392,575

Figure 15-4

The reason this 55% adjustment is less than the 92% additional savings in the retire-at-age-70 tables, is that the calculations to retire at age 65 already have adjustments in the savings for living five years longer, social security not kicking in for five years, and a smaller pension. So the 55% adjustment is being added onto a far larger savings base.

Testing the Retirement Tables with Inflated Funds

Testing Example #1 with Inflated Dollars

A couple is 40 years old and plan to retire at age 70. So they have 30 additional years to work. Their current combined income is $75,000 after taxes. Using

80% as the factor to determine their retirement income needs, their required retirement income will be 0.8 * $75,000 = $60,000 in 2003 dollars.

The combined nominal company pensions that their companies have projected the couple would receive at age 65 is $40,000 per year (after taxes and in future dollars). The pension is assumed to be an additional 10% due to delayed retirement for five years. They currently have no savings specifically for the purpose of retirement.

In the table below, Figure 15-5, we will walk through each year of savings before retirement, noting the actual inflated savings each year. The Desired Income and Social Security are also indexed for these 30 years, but they are included here only for the purpose of monitoring their inflating values for later use in our next table.

Savings Detail; 30 Years to Work; Initial Savings of $8,169; 3% Interest; 3.5% Inflation

Savings Year	Inflated Annual Actual Savings	Accumulated Savings Including Interest and Inflation	Desired Income Including Inflation	Social Security Including Inflation
1	$8,169	$8,169	$60,000	$25,920
2	$8,455	$17,155	$62,100	$26,827
3	$8,751	$27,021	$64,274	$27,766
4	$9,057	$37,834	$66,523	$28,738
5	$9,374	$49,668	$68,851	$29,744
6	$9,702	$62,598	$71,261	$30,785
7	$10,042	$76,709	$73,755	$31,862
8	$10,393	$92,088	$76,337	$32,977
9	$10,757	$108,831	$79,009	$34,132
10	$11,134	$127,038	$81,774	$35,326
11	$11,523	$146,819	$84,636	$36,563
12	$11,926	$168,289	$87,598	$37,842
13	$12,344	$191,572	$90,664	$39,167
14	$12,776	$216,800	$93,837	$40,538
15	$13,223	$244,115	$97,122	$41,957

16	$13,686	$273,668	$100,521	$43,425
17	$14,165	$305,622	$104,039	$44,945
18	$14,661	$340,148	$107,681	$46,518
19	$15,174	$377,431	$111,449	$48,146
20	$15,705	$417,669	$115,350	$49,831
21	$16,255	$461,072	$119,387	$51,575
22	$16,823	$507,865	$123,566	$53,380
23	$17,412	$558,289	$127,891	$55,249
24	$18,022	$612,599	$132,367	$57,182
25	$18,653	$671,071	$137,000	$59,184
26	$19,305	$733,996	$141,795	$61,255
27	$19,981	$801,687	$146,758	$63,399
28	$20,680	$874,477	$151,894	$65,618
29	$21,404	$952,722	$157,210	$67,915
30	$22,153	$1,036,802	$162,713	$70,292

Figure 15-5

So at the time of retirement the couple will have saved $1,036,802 in inflated funds. This sounds like an outrageous amount of money, but it is actually equivalent to $369,390 in 2003 dollars. The diminished value of fixed funds, even at an assumed 3.5% annual inflation, can cause someone to be radically under funded at the time of their retirement, if the probable diminished future value of their savings isn't taken into account.

Since we saved funds in a Roth IRA, there will be no tax concerns on these savings. Since our initial savings amount was within the Roth limits, and this limit was adjusted up with inflation, all of the savings and related gains are tax free. Social Security benefits *are* subject to taxation, so the actual benefit amount shown in the below table is reduced somewhat. The pension is also taxed, but we already specified that the pension amount assumed should be after estimated taxes.

We will now want to track what happens to our savings during each year of retirement. In Figure 15-6 below, we start out with the $1,036,802 we just calculated. This is shown as the top value in the second column of the table. Each year we will include the inflation-adjusted social security and the $44,000 fixed pension amount, which includes the assumed additional 10% for delaying retirement, and stays constant throughout. The savings are reduced every year by the outgoing funds, which represent the inflation-adjusted desired retirement income being drawn out.

You can see how, for the first five years, the accumulated savings actually increase somewhat, and then they begin to go down. This is because the pension is fixed and becomes a smaller percentage of the total income with continuing years of inflation. You can see from the table, Figure 15-6, that the inflated income needs actually double over the 23 years shown, while the pension contribution remains fixed.

Retirement Detail; Retire at Age 70; 3% Interest; 3.5% Inflation

Retire Year	Accumulated Savings Plus Inflation & Interest	Inflated Outgoing Funds (Desired Income)	Inflated Social Security	Pension
1	$1,036,802	$168,408	$72,752	$44,000
2	$1,049,181	$174,302	$75,298	$44,000
3	$1,058,799	$180,402	$77,934	$44,000
4	$1,065,352	$186,717	$80,662	$44,000
5	$1,068,511	$193,252	$83,485	$44,000
6	$1,067,923	$200,015	$86,407	$44,000
7	$1,063,204	$207,016	$89,431	$44,000
8	$1,053,945	$214,262	$92,561	$44,000
9	$1,039,700	$221,761	$95,801	$44,000
10	$1,019,993	$229,522	$99,154	$44,000
11	$994,310	$237,556	$102,624	$44,000
12	$962,098	$245,870	$106,216	$44,000
13	$922,762	$254,475	$109,933	$44,000
14	$875,665	$263,382	$113,781	$44,000
15	$820,118	$272,600	$117,763	$44,000
16	$755,384	$282,142	$121,885	$44,000
17	$680,671	$292,016	$126,151	$44,000
18	$595,128	$302,237	$130,566	$44,000
19	$497,842	$312,815	$135,136	$44,000
20	$387,833	$323,764	$139,866	$44,000
21	$264,051	$335,096	$144,761	$44,000
22	$125,369	$346,824	$149,828	$44,000

| 23 | -$29,423 | $358,963 | $155,072 | $44,000 |
| 24 | -$201,619 | $371,526 | $160,499 | $44,000 |

Figure 15-6

You can see from Figure 15-6, by noting when the second column becomes negative, that we run out of savings after 23 years, which takes someone to age 93 if they retire at age 70. So the retiree's income at that point in time would only be the $155,072 social security plus the $44,000 pension, which is a total of $199,072. This is a shortfall of $159,891 versus their $358,963 inflated income needs. However, as we discussed earlier, the couple could then start draining values from other assets like their home, which presumably also doubled in value during the 23 years of retirement, just as their income needs doubled with inflation. This use of other assets would presumably allow them to continue in their current retirement lifestyle until they were 100 years of age or so.

For most people, it would not be worth the financial burden to try to save for living longer than this. This is especially true given that even saving the amounts shown in the above tables will prove to be difficult for many people. However, savings anywhere close to what the tables specify will prevent you from being in the predicament in which many seniors now find themselves: getting ready to retire with only $50,000 or so in savings!

Testing Example #3 with Inflated Dollars

A 40 year old couple plan to retire at age 65. So they have 25 additional years to work. Their current combined income is $75,000 after taxes. Using 80% as the factor to determine their retirement income needs, their required retirement income will be 0.8 * $75,000 = $60,000 in 2003 dollars.

The combined nominal company pension that their companies have projected the couple will receive at age 65 is $40,000 per year after taxes (in future dollars). They currently have no savings for the purpose of retirement.

Below, in Figure 15-7, is a test on the above example. Earlier, we had determined that we would have to start out saving $16,293 annually, then index the savings up every year with inflation, until retirement at age 65, which is 25 years of savings. The second column in the chart below shows what the actual savings will be for each year, assuming inflation of 3.5% per year. You can see from the chart that, by the time of retirement, the yearly savings will be an actual $37,202.

The third column, which is accumulated Savings, includes each year's savings plus prior savings, including interest and inflation, which would be applied automatically when funds are saved in TIPS.

The fourth and fifth columns in Figure 15-7 below, which are desired income and Social Security, are only shown for future reference, because at the time of retirement we will use the inflated values for each.

Savings Detail; 25 Years to Work; Initial Savings of $16,293; 3% Interest; 3.5% Inflation

Savings Year	Inflated Annual Actual Savings	Accumulated Savings Including Interest and Inflation	Desired Income Including Inflation	Social Security Including Inflation
1	$16,293	$17,352	$60,000	$25,920
2	$16,863	$35,343	$62,100	$26,827
3	$17,453	$55,094	$64,274	$27,766
4	$18,064	$76,739	$66,523	$28,738
5	$18,697	$100,424	$68,851	$29,744
6	$19,351	$126,303	$71,261	$30,785
7	$20,028	$154,541	$73,755	$31,862
8	$20,729	$185,315	$76,337	$32,977
9	$21,455	$218,815	$79,009	$34,132
10	$22,206	$255,244	$81,774	$35,326
11	$22,983	$294,818	$84,636	$36,563
12	$23,787	$337,768	$87,598	$37,842
13	$24,620	$384,343	$90,664	$39,167
14	$25,482	$434,807	$93,837	$40,538
15	$26,373	$489,442	$97,122	$41,957
16	$27,296	$548,553	$100,521	$43,425
17	$28,252	$612,460	$104,039	$44,945
18	$29,241	$681,511	$107,681	$46,518

19	$30,264	$756,073	$111,449	$48,146
20	$31,323	$836,541	$115,350	$49,831
21	$32,420	$923,336	$119,387	$51,575
22	$33,554	$1,016,907	$123,566	$53,380
23	$34,729	$1,117,735	$127,891	$55,249
24	$35,944	$1,226,332	$132,367	$57,182
25	$37,202	$1,343,246	$137,000	$59,184

Figure 15-7

This shows that the accumulated savings is $1,343,246. However, when we were setting up the savings plan shown in the table, additional funds were withheld because the $16,293 initial savings exceeded the $10,000 Roth IRA limits, so some of the earnings from the savings will be used for taxes upon retirement. We assume that only 85% of the proportion of the funds susceptible to tax can be used for retirement. This gives us a tax-adjusted savings of $1,265,424. These are the after-tax savings we must now use for testing whether funds are sufficient to last until age 93, which will be 28 years into retirement.

In Figure 15-8 below, column two shows the current accumulated savings for each year of retirement. This accumulated savings is the starting savings, plus pension, minus the outgoing funds, which is the inflated-adjusted desired income. Although the social security benefits are shown in the table for the whole 28 years for purposes of monitoring their inflated values, they are not included in the first five years of accumulated savings calculations. This is because we are assuming that social security benefits will not start until age 70. We could have shown a much reduced benefit starting at age 65, but over the course of the 28 years shown this would have resulted in reduced overall savings. After five years, the social security benefits are included in the annual income. The accumulated savings also includes interest and inflation on any unused savings, which is consistent with TIPS savings. Note that the pension stays at a constant $40,000 per year throughout.

As you can see by looking at Figure 15-8 below, the accumulative savings column goes negative in 28 years, which means that savings are drained at age 93, which was the goal. At that point only social security and the $40,000 pension will be available. As previously mentioned, draining other assets, like the value in a home, will probably allow continued life-style until age 100.

Retirement Detail; Retire at Age 65; 3% Interest; 3.5% Inflation

Retire Year	Accumulated Savings Plus Inflation & Interest	Inflated Outgoing Funds (Desired Income)	Inflated Social Security	Pension
1	$1,265,424	$141,795	$61,255	$40,000
2	$1,239,265	$146,758	$63,399	$40,000
3	$1,206,120	$151,894	$65,618	$40,000
4	$1,165,351	$157,210	$67,915	$40,000
5	$1,116,270	$162,713	$70,292	$40,000
6	$1,058,138	$168,408	$72,752	$40,000
7	$1,067,644	$174,302	$75,298	$40,000
8	$1,074,202	$180,402	$77,934	$40,000
9	$1,077,496	$186,717	$80,662	$40,000
10	$1,077,185	$193,252	$83,485	$40,000
11	$1,072,900	$200,015	$86,407	$40,000
12	$1,064,245	$207,016	$89,431	$40,000
13	$1,050,793	$214,262	$92,561	$40,000
14	$1,032,084	$221,761	$95,801	$40,000
15	$1,007,622	$229,522	$99,154	$40,000
16	$976,875	$237,556	$102,624	$40,000
17	$939,269	$245,870	$106,216	$40,000
18	$894,190	$254,475	$109,933	$40,000
19	$840,975	$263,382	$113,781	$40,000
20	$778,913	$272,600	$117,763	$40,000
21	$707,241	$282,142	$121,885	$40,000
22	$625,139	$292,016	$126,151	$40,000
23	$531,726	$302,237	$130,566	$40,000
24	$426,059	$312,815	$135,136	$40,000
25	$307,125	$323,764	$139,866	$40,000
26	$173,837	$335,096	$144,761	$40,000
27	$25,030	$346,824	$149,828	$40,000
28	-$140,544	$358,963	$155,072	$40,000

Figure 15-8

So our tests of looking at actual inflated savings show that the retirement savings tables, although stated in current dollars, work to give desired retirement incomes when the savings amounts are indexed up annually with inflation.

Derivation of the Divisors and Multipliers in the Retirement Formulas of Chapter 13

In Chapter 13, we presented formulas for determining the retirement income.
In the formulas we used RI to represent "retirement income," SS for the "social security benefit," TS for the required "TIPS savings," and PN for the "pension benefit."

Here is one of the formulas from Chapter 13.

RETIRE at AGE 65, Live to Age 93, Determine Retirement Income:

RI = TS/19 + SS + 0.68*PN

Let's see how the above formula values were developed. First, notice that we divided the TIPS savings TS by 19. The reason this was done is we wanted the savings to slowly be reduced every year and to run out in 28 years, which would get us to age 93, if we retire at age 65. We assume that the savings are getting 3% interest, and that inflation is 3.5%, so any remaining savings are indexed up 6.5% every year. Here is the spread sheet where we show that if we start out using 1/19th of the savings for retirement income, then index that value up every year by 3.5% to account for inflation (we want to keep the purchasing power of the retirement income constant), we run out of savings after 28 years (the savings go negative during the 28th year). See Figure 15-9 below. In this spreadsheet example, we used $50,000 as the starting savings, but any starting number would show the same effect. $2,632, the first number in the Income column below, is 1/19th of $50,000.

Spreadsheet Showing Derivation of TS/19

Year	Accumulated Savings	Inflated Retirement Income
1	$50,000	$2,632
2	$50,447	$2,724
3	$50,826	$2,819
4	$51,127	$2,918
5	$51,343	$3,020
6	$51,464	$3,125
7	$51,481	$3,235
8	$51,382	$3,348
9	$51,156	$3,465
10	$50,791	$3,587
11	$50,272	$3,712
12	$49,587	$3,842
13	$48,718	$3,976
14	$47,650	$4,116
15	$46,364	$4,260
16	$44,841	$4,409
17	$43,060	$4,563
18	$40,999	$4,723
19	$38,634	$4,888
20	$35,940	$5,059
21	$32,888	$5,236
22	$29,449	$5,420
23	$25,591	$5,609
24	$21,281	$5,806
25	$16,481	$6,009
26	$11,153	$6,219
27	$5,255	$6,437
28	-$1,259	$6,662
29	-$8,436	$6,895

Figure 15-9

Similarly, in the above formula we multiplied the pension PN by 0.68. This was done because, since the pension is fixed, its purchasing power would go down if we used its initial full value every year. To keep a constant pension value, we assume that we only use 0.68 of the initial pension, indexing up that value every year with an assumed 3.5% inflation. Excess pension money is invested in a TIPS savings fund, getting 3% interest and 3.5% inflation.

Our goal is to have the pension "savings" go negative after 28 years. Here is the spreadsheet in Figure 15-10 below. We assumed a starting pension of $100, using 0.68 of that amount, or $68. Again, any starting pension amount would have shown the same effect.

Spreadsheet Showing Derivation of 0.68PN

Year	Accumulated Savings	Inflated Retirement Income
1	$100.00	$68.00
2	$135.96	$70.38
3	$170.55	$72.84
4	$203.64	$75.39
5	$235.09	$78.03
6	$264.77	$80.76
7	$292.53	$83.59
8	$318.21	$86.51
9	$341.64	$89.54
10	$362.66	$92.68
11	$381.08	$95.92
12	$396.72	$99.28
13	$409.36	$102.75
14	$418.81	$106.35
15	$424.83	$110.07
16	$427.21	$113.92
17	$425.68	$117.91
18	$420.00	$122.04
19	$409.90	$126.31
20	$395.10	$130.73
21	$375.30	$135.31
22	$350.20	$140.04
23	$319.46	$144.94
24	$282.75	$150.02
25	$239.72	$155.27
26	$189.99	$160.70

27	$133.17	$166.33
28	$68.85	$172.15
29	-$3.40	$178.17

Figure 15-10

You can see in the above spreadsheet that the savings column did go negative until after 28 years, which was our goal.

You may have noticed that the social security benefit had no corrective value. This is because it inflates automatically with inflation, so we don't have to worry about it running out or losing its purchasing power.

APPENDIX

Key Numbers used in the Stock Market Calculations

Note on the Key Numbers. There are many sources for the below numbers, and many of these sources may have slightly different values. This is especially true for Dividends and Inflation. This discrepancy is partially caused by when within the year the numbers are assumed to be taken. Some data is from end-of-the-year, other data may compare averages of one year to the next or even use mid-year values. However, these differences average out and are not critical to the analysis done in this book.

Also, since the S&P 500 was not computed before 1926, all numbers related to the S&P 500 or its dividends before that time are based on estimates done in retrospect.

Year	S&P 500 Value (Not Including dividends)	S&P % Dividend	% Inflation
1900	6.87	3.82	1.33
1901	7.95	3.72	2.63
1902	8.05	3.84	2.56
1903	6.57	4.57	0.00
1904	8.25	3.57	1.25
1905	9.54	3.31	2.47
1906	9.84	3.82	4.82
1907	6.57	6.13	3.45
1908	9.03	4.27	0.00
1909	10.30	4.17	5.56
1910	9.05	5.03	0.00
1911	9.11	4.95	2.11
1912	9.38	4.85	3.09
1913	8.04	5.38	2.04
1914	7.35	5.5	1.00
1915	9.48	4.32	1.98
1916	9.80	5.73	12.62
1917	6.80	9.3	18.10
1918	7.92	7.16	20.44
1919	9.02	5.26	14.55

1920	6.81	7.27	2.65
1921	7.32	5.77	-10.82
1922	8.85	5.63	-2.31
1923	8.72	5.93	2.37
1924	10.35	5.08	0.00
1925	12.76	4.83	3.47
1926	13.49	5.19	-1.12
1927	17.66	4.25	-2.26
1928	24.35	3.48	-1.16
1929	21.45	4.35	0.58
1930	15.34	5.62	-6.40
1931	8.12	7.88	-9.32
1932	6.89	5.98	-10.27
1933	10.10	3.65	0.76
1934	9.50	4.12	1.52
1935	13.44	3.5	2.99
1936	17.18	4.19	1.45
1937	10.54	7.58	2.86
1938	13.21	3.86	-2.78
1939	12.49	4.96	0.00
1940	10.58	6.33	0.71
1941	8.69	8.17	9.93
1942	9.77	6.04	9.03
1943	11.67	5.23	2.96
1944	13.28	4.82	2.30
1945	17.36	3.8	2.25
1946	15.30	4.64	18.13
1947	15.30	5.49	8.84
1948	15.20	6.12	2.99
1949	16.76	6.8	-2.07
1950	20.41	7.2	5.93
1951	23.77	5.93	6.00
1952	26.58	5.31	0.75
1953	24.81	5.84	0.75
1954	35.99	4.28	-0.74
1955	45.48	3.61	0.37
1956	46.68	3.73	2.99

1957	39.99	4.48	2.90
1958	55.21	3.17	1.76
1959	59.89	3.06	1.73
1960	58.11	3.36	1.36
1961	71.55	2.82	0.67
1962	63.10	3.38	1.33
1963	75.02	3.04	1.64
1964	84.75	2.95	0.97
1965	92.43	2.94	1.92
1966	80.33	3.57	3.46
1967	96.47	3.03	3.04
1968	103.86	2.96	4.72
1969	92.06	3.43	6.20
1970	92.15	3.41	5.57
1971	102.09	3.01	3.27
1972	118.05	2.67	3.41
1973	97.55	3.46	8.71
1974	68.56	5.25	12.34
1975	90.19	4.08	6.94
1976	107.46	3.77	4.86
1977	95.10	4.91	6.70
1978	96.11	5.28	9.02
1979	107.94	5.23	13.29
1980	135.76	4.54	12.52
1981	122.55	5.41	8.92
1982	140.64	4.88	3.83
1983	164.93	4.3	3.79
1984	167.24	4.5	3.95
1985	211.28	3.74	3.80
1986	242.17	3.42	1.10
1987	247.08	3.57	4.43
1988	277.72	3.5	4.42
1989	353.40	3.13	4.65
1990	330.22	3.66	6.11
1991	417.09	2.93	3.06
1992	435.71	2.84	2.90
1993	466.45	2.7	2.75

1994	459.27	2.87	2.67
1995	615.93	2.24	2.54
1996	740.74	2.01	3.32
1997	970.43	1.6	1.70
1998	1229.23	1.32	1.61
1999	1469.25	1.14	2.68
2000	1320.28	1.19	3.39
2001	1148.08	1.36	1.90
2002	879.82	1.69	1.58
2003	1111.92	1.69	2.17

Web Site References

1) "Issue of the Week: Demographic Shifts", http://speakout.com/activism/opinions/4751-1.html.

2) "Nine Misconceptions About Social Security – 98.07", http://www.theatlantic.com/issues/98jul/socsec.htm.

3) "What are the limits on a Roth IRA", http://www.turbotax.com/articles/WhatAreTheLimitsOnaRothIRA.html.

4) "Compare the Traditional IRA with information provided by American Ex…, http://finance.americanexpress.com/sif/cda/page/0,1641,14984,00.asp

5) '"Treasury Inflation-Indexed Securities (TIPS)", http://www.publicdebt.treas.gov/sec/seciis.htm.

6) "About TIPS: Treasury Inflation Protected Securities", http://www.investinginbonds.com/TIPS.htm.

7) "Job Crisis in America", http://www.aflcio.org/yourjobeconomy/jobs/jobcrises.cfm.

8) "Bankruptcy Statistics", http://bankruptcyaction.com/USbankstats.htm

9) "US consumer debt reaches record levels", http://www.wsws.org/articles/2004/jan2004/debt-j15.shtml

10) "Yahoo Finance", http://finance.yahoo.com/

11) "Inequality by Design", http://civic-values.archive/199801/msg00149.html

12) "Weak Recovery Claims New Victim: Workers' Wages", http://www.epinet.org/content.cfm/issuebriefs_ib196

13) "Corporate Crisis and Bubble Capitalism" – Social and Economic Policy Fo…", http://www.globalpolicy.org/socecon/crisis/index.htm

14) "London Fix Historical Gold – result", http://www.kitco.com/scripts/hist_charts/yearly_graphs.cgi

15) "Commentary", http://www.cross-currents.net/commentary.htm

16) "401 Kafe.com: Planning to Retire at 65? You May Need to Think Again…", http://www.infoplease.com/finance/commentary/feature/feature_plan.html

17) "What Was the GDP Then?", http://www.eh.net/hmit/gdp_answer.php

18) "United States Summary Demographic Information",
http://www.futuresedge.org/World_Population_Issues/United_States_Summary.html

19) "Population Projections",
http://www.census.gov/population/projections/nation/summary/np-t3-a.txt

20) "Global Financial Data – Data Download/Graphing System",
http://www.globalfindata.com/cgi-bin/data_downloader2.cgi?description=UK+Consumer+...

21) "U.S. consumers are hooked on spending – Oct 3, 2003",
http://money.cnn.com/2003/10/02/markets/consumerbubble/

22) "Current State of Debt",
http://www.ihatedebt.com/CurrentStateofDebt.html

23) "S&P Earnings: 1960-Current",
http://pages.stern.nyu.edu/~adamodar/New_Home_Page/datafile/spearn.htm

24) "Inflation-Indexed Bonds: A Primer for Finance Officers",
http://216.239.37.104/search?q=cache:LGPwT7TMmuYJ:www3.prudential.com/pim/pdf/fi/...

25) "Readers seek tips on Treasury Inflation Protected Securities",
http//www.csmonitor.com/2004/0301/p16s02-wmgn.htm

26) "Using Treasury Inflation Protested Securities (TIPS) to increase your safe withdrawal rate",
http//www.retireearlyhomepage.com/safetips.html

27) "Robbing Peter Jr. to Pay Paul Sr.",
http://www.businessweek.com/bwdaily/dnflash/jan2004/nf20044022_1765_db014.htm

28) "The Historical Price to Earnings Ratio for the S&P 500",
http://www.ttheory.com/public/peratios/price_to_earnings_ratios.htm

29) "Economic Justice for All",
http://www.globalpolicy.org/socecon/inequal/2003/0523forall.htm

30) "Wealth Inequality Charts",
http://www.ufenet.org/research/wealth_charts.html

31) "Low rates fail to cool demand for adjustable-rate loans", http://www.homeboundmortgage.com/Mortgage_Info/Mortgage12_26_03/Mortgage6_Ref...

32) "Occam's Razor", http://pespmc1.vub.ac.be/OCCAMRAZ.html

33) "U.S. Productivity is Booming, with No End in Sight", http://www.bernstein.com/Public/story.aspx?cid=1432

34) "The Basics - - The pension-plan time bomb", http://moneycentral.msn.com/articles/retire/basics/9459.asp

35) "Interview: John Bogle", http://216.239.39.104/search?q=cache:vvufjzH40WwJ:www.sunguard.com/magazine/v330...

36) "SAAFTI – Society of Asset Allocators and Fund Timers, Inc"., http://www.saafti.com/bogle.htm

37) "Readers seek tips on Treasury Inflation Protected Securities", http://www.csmonitor.com/2004/0301/p16s02-wmgn.htm

38) General historical data on the S&P 500, www.globalfindata.com

39) Historical data on S&P 500, interest rates, and inflation, www.economy.com

40) Savings Calculator used to calculate annual savings required, http://beginnersinvest.about.com/gi/dynamic/offsite.htm?site=http%3A%2F%2Fmoneycentral.msn.com%2Finvestor%2Fcalcs%2Fn_savapp%2Fmain.asp

41) Miscellaneous historical stock prices, http://finance.yahoo.com/

42) CNN Money Planner, http://cgi.money.cnn.com/tools/retirementplanner/retirementplanner.jsp

43) "The 15-minute retirement plan," http://money.cnn.com/20004/03/10/retirement/investing_15minute_0404/index.htm

44) "Projections of the Total Resident Population by 5-Year Age Groups…," http://www.census.gov/population/projections/nation/summary/np-t3-f.txt

45) "The Consumer, First Source of Dynamism, Piles on Debt to Sustain World Growth – Soci…,"
http://www.globalpolicy.org/socecon/crisis/2003/1020consumerdebt.htm

46) "Grandfather Family Income Report",
http://mwhodges.home.att.net/family_a.htm

47) "America's Total Debt Report – summary pages – by MWHodges",
http://home.att.net/~mwhodges/nat-debt/debt-nat.htm

48) "Interest and Inflation",
http://www.neatideas.com/inflationwatch/interest-and-inflation.htm

49) "Historical Changes to the Dow Jones Industrial Average",
http://biz.yahoo.com/rf/040401/markets_dowjones_changes_1.html

50) "UN warns of increase in heroin deaths",
http://icwales.icnetwork.co.uk/0100news/0700world/tm_objectid=14987897&method=fu...

51) "CNN.com – Health – Heroin deaths rise throughout US, surge in…",
www.cnn.com/2000/HEALTH/07/20/heroin.overdoses/-42k

52) "DSC: Greenspan's Fed and the American Boom",
http://www.financialpolicy.org/dscchallenge.htm

53) "BondKnowledge::The Federal Reserve",
http://www.bondknowledge.com/fed.html

54) "The Biggest Market Crashes in History",
http://www.investopedia.com/features/crashes/crashes1.asp

55) "End the Rate Increases",
http://www.aei.org/news/filter.,newsID.21402/news_detail.asp

56) "The State of the Nation's Housing 2003",
http://www.jchs.harvard.edu/publications/markets/son**2003**.pdf

57) "Recapping 'an unbelievable year' in real estate",
http://mpelembe.mappibiz.com/archives_02/Real_Eastate_2003.html

58) "AOL Personal Finance: Money Today: Doom for Dollar",
http://pf.channel.aol.com/forbes/investing/doomdollar.adp

59) "FRB: Monetary Policy, Open Market Operations",
http://www.federalreserve.gov/fomc/fundsrate.htm

60) "Mortgage (ARM) Indexes: Constant Maturity Treasury Index (CMT)", http://mortgage-x.com/general/indexes/cmt.asp

61) "1-year Treasury constant maturities", http://www.federalreserve.gov/releases/h15/data.htm

62) "United States – U.S. Statistics – Household and Family Statistics", http://www.infoplease.com/ipa/A0005055.html

63) "MSN Money – The truth about credit card debt", http://moneycentral.msn.com/content/Banking/creditcardsmarts/P74808.asp

BIBLIOGRAPHY

Baer, Gregory, and Gensler, Gary, <u>The Great Mutual Fund Trap</u>, Broadway Books, 2002.

Bernstein, William, <u>The Four Pillars of Investing</u>, McGraw-Hill 2000.

Bonner, William, with Wiggen, Addison, <u>Financial Reckoning Day</u>, John Wiley & Sons, 2003.

Brussee, Warren, <u>Statistics for Six Sigma Made Easy</u>, McGraw-Hill, 2004

Carlson, Charles B., <u>Winning with the Dow's Losers</u>, HarperCollins, 2004.

Ellis, Charles D., <u>Winning the Loser's Game</u>, McGraw-Hill, 2002

Kipplinger, <u>Retire Worry-Free</u>, Kiplinger's Washington Editors, Inc., 2003.

Malkiel, Burton G., <u>A Random Walk Down Wall Street</u>, W. W. Norton & Company, 1999.

Malkiel, Burton G., <u>The Random Walk Guide to Investing</u>, W. W. Norton & Company, 2003.

Netti, Frank L., <u>Retire Sooner, Retire Richer</u>, McGraw-Hill, 2003.

Ottenbourg, Robert K., <u>Retire & Thrive</u>, Kiplinger's Washington Editors, Inc., 2003.

Paulos, John P., <u>A Mathematician Plays the Stock Market</u>, Basic Books, 2003.

Shiller, Robert J., <u>Irrational Exuberance</u>, Broadway Books, 2001.

Smithers, Andrew, and Wright, Stephen, <u>Valuing Wall Street</u>, McGraw-Hill, 2000.

Stein, Ben and DeMuth, Phil, <u>Yes, You Can Time the Market</u>, Johm Wiley & Sons, Inc., 2003.

Woodward, Bob, <u>Maestro: Greenspan's Fed and the American Boom</u>, Simon & Schuster, 2000.

Understanding Logarithmic Charts

In several places in this book, data is displayed on a logarithmic chart. This is because uniformly increasing (or decreasing) data displayed in this manner will show as a sloped straight line.

For example, suppose we had something that was increasing 20% every year, and the initial value was 1. Here is what that data would look like for 10 years.

Year	Value
0	1
1	1.2
2	1.44
3	1.728
4	2.0736
5	2.48832
6	2.985984
7	3.583181
8	4.299817
9	5.15978
10	6.191736

Let's plot this data on a regular and a logarithmic graph, Figure A1 & A2 below.

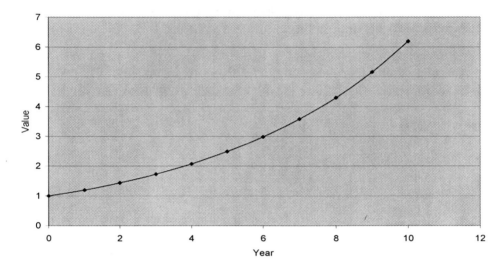

Figure A1

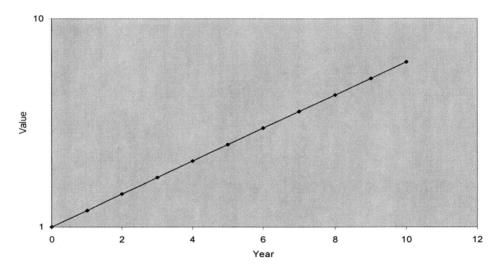

Figure A2

The reason this works is the log is the power to which base "10" must be raised to reach a given number. For example, in the following data:

Base	Power	Number
10	0	1
10	1	10
10	2	100
10	3	1000
10	4	10000
10	5	100000
10	6	1000000

10 to the zero power is 1
10 to the 1st power is 10
10 to the 2nd power is 100
10 to the 3rd power is 1000
Etc.

If you plotted the "numbers" from the above, you will get a curve with a dramatic up-swing. However, if you plot the "power", the graph will be a sloped straight line. On a logarithmic chart (actually semi-log), rather than actually plotting the "power", the vertical axis is spaced equivalent to the power of the number. That is why you see the unusually spaced left-hand axis numbers on the log charts.

A logarithmic chart is useful on data that you suspect is increasing at a steady rate, like dividends increasing at a uniform rate for a number of years. The straight line on the plot tells you that this is happening.

INDEX